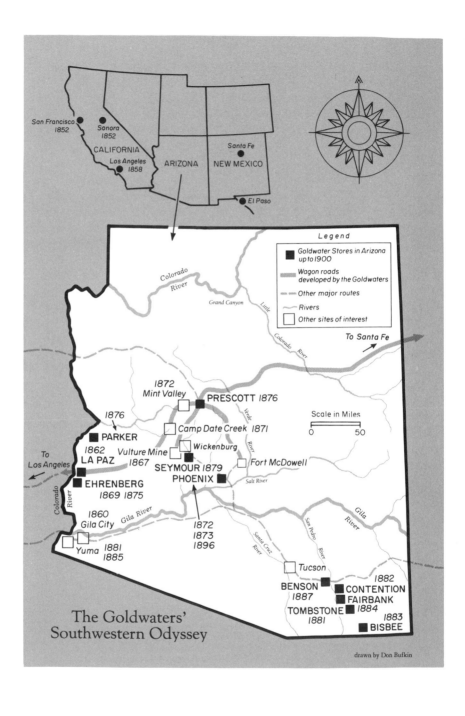

The Goldwaters'
Southwestern Odyssey

Legend

■ Goldwater Stores in Arizona up to 1900
▬ Wagon roads developed by the Goldwaters
▬▬ Other major routes
⌇ Rivers
□ Other sites of interest

San Francisco 1852
Sonora 1852
CALIFORNIA
Los Angeles 1858
ARIZONA
Santa Fe
NEW MEXICO
El Paso

Colorado River
Grand Canyon
Little Colorado River
To Santa Fe

1872 Mint Valley
PRESCOTT 1876
1876
PARKER
Camp Date Creek 1871
Scale in Miles
0   50
To Los Angeles
1862 LA PAZ
Vulture Mine
1867
Wickenburg
SEYMOUR 1879
PHOENIX
Fort McDowell
EHRENBERG 1869 1875
Salt River
Colorado River
1860 Gila City
Gila River
1872 1873 1896
Yuma 1881 1885
San Pedro River
Santa Cruz River
Gila River
Tucson
BENSON 1887
1882 CONTENTION
FAIRBANK
TOMBSTONE 1881
1884
1883 BISBEE

drawn by Don Bufkin

the Goldwaters

of Arizona

Jo Goldwater with children: Bob, Barry (top), and Carolyn

Goldwaters
the
of Arizona

by Dean Smith
Foreword by Barry Goldwater

NORTHLAND PRESS FLAGSTAFF, ARIZONA

Published in cooperation with the Arizona Historical Foundation

To
the memory of Bert Fireman:
historian,
teacher, author and friend.

Most of the photographs included in this book are from the collection
of the Arizona Historical Foundation, which has been most
generous in its assistance; the balance are from
the Goldwater family's personal collection and Mr. and Mrs. Herb McLaughlin.
The map on p. ii is the work of cartographer Don Bufkin.

Contents

Foreword

IT HAS BEEN MORE THAN ONE HUNDRED TWENTY-FIVE YEARS SINCE MY GRAND-
father, Michel Goldwater, first came to what is now Arizona, peddling his
wares from a wagon to the eager gold miners of Gila City. Since that time,
he and his descendants have played important roles in the development of
my native state.

I am justifiably proud of my heritage, and for a half century have been
searching for information about those early Goldwaters. My uncle, Morris
Goldwater, had a fine sense of history, and he kept much of the correspondence, records, photographs, and memorabilia on which this historical
narrative is based. He whetted my appetite for learning more about our
family, and about Arizona history in general. We visited the decaying
building at Ehrenberg that had housed the Goldwater store in the 1870s,
and he showed me many other places where the family's history was
made.

With the help of researchers in California, the East, and in Europe, I was
able to piece together some of the early story of the family. In the late
1950s, historian Bert Fireman did yeoman service in researching the
Goldwater story and in recording the triumphs and defeats of Michel
Goldwater, his brother Joe, and Michel's sons.

Several other researchers have made their contributions. Now Dean
Smith of the Arizona Historical Foundation has done further research,
interviewed family members and others, and written this informative
book.

I am grateful to all those who have worked to bring the Goldwater
history project to this milestone. But the work is still not complete. This
brief volume cannot tell the full stories of prominent members of this
family. We are still at work, researching their lives and their times.

The Goldwater saga is a remarkable one. Michel Goldwasser, as he was
known in his native Poland, escaped Russian persecution there and fled to
Paris in his youth. Later, he migrated to London, where he married Sarah
Nathan in 1850 and settled down to the quiet life of a tailor. When his
younger brother Joe appeared on the scene, urging Michel to come with
him to California, Michel answered the siren call to adventure.

The Goldwater brothers arrived in San Francisco just in time to participate in the boisterous years of the post-Gold Rush era. They launched their first business, a saloon, in the little California mining camp of Sonora in 1854, and later had both successes and failures in business ventures in California and Arizona.

Michel was the principal figure of the early Goldwater story in Arizona. It was he who came to La Paz, across the Colorado River from modern Blythe, California, in the winter of 1862-63 to operate the first Goldwater store in Arizona. It was "Big Mike," as he was known to many Arizona pioneers, who became prominent in freight hauling, government contracting, and the development of wagon roads in that raw, young Territory of Arizona. He and his young son, Morris, opened general stores in the village of Phoenix and in several Arizona boom towns before they made a solid success of their store in Prescott in the late 1870s.

Michel's brother Joe, meanwhile, was a sometime partner in several of the Goldwater ventures, but always seemed to be in the wrong place at the wrong time. When Indians attacked Mike and Joe on a mountain road, it was Joe who was hit by two bullets. When desperadoes sprayed gunfire around Bisbee in the famed "Bisbee Massacre," it was Joe's store they chose to rob. And it was Joe who was stricken with illness in Tombstone and died before his time.

Of Big Mike's five sons, Morris and Baron were by far the most influential in shaping wild Arizona Territory into a modern western state.

Morris, the eldest, was ten times mayor of Prescott, a stalwart of the Arizona Democratic Party, and a renowned leader in Arizona banking and Masonry. His unselfish community service earned him the title "Man of the Century" in Prescott's Centennial year.

Baron, my father, was the youngest of the five brothers. It was he who established the Goldwater store in Phoenix in 1896, and earned a national reputation for inventive merchandising. His labors on behalf of building Phoenix from a frontier village to the threshold of metropolitan stature will long be remembered.

My mother, Josephine Williams Goldwater, was one of the most memorable personalities of early Phoenix. She was unconventional and adventuresome—an outdoors person who didn't know the meaning of fear. A nurse in her youth, she worked for better Phoenix health-care facilities throughout her long life. Her children will always be grateful that she taught them to hunt, fish, and swim, and to enjoy Arizona's wonderful outdoors.

My wife of fifty-one years, Margaret (Peggy) Johnson Goldwater, so successfully avoided the spotlight of publicity that few people knew of her devotion to charitable causes and to the cultural growth of Phoenix. Her death in December 1985 was not only an irreplaceable and tragic loss to her family, but to all the people of Arizona. She was everything good and noble to me, and my life will never again be as rich without her.

My sister, Carolyn Goldwater Erskine, is another lifelong worker for community causes. Her love and support for me through these many years has enriched my life immeasurably. The achievements of my brother Bob have been more widely publicized. Merchant, banker, champion golfer, civic servant, community builder: Bob has been all these and more.

Michel Goldwater's great-grandchildren have already earned prominence in many fields of endeavor, and now their children are coming into their own. The Goldwater story goes on.

My own career has been public knowledge since 1952, when I entered national politics. This is not a book about my life and political career, but rather, an account of the notable members of this family who helped to shape my life and times. I have had much more than my share of public attention during the past thirty-five years. Now it is time that people understand that the Goldwater name had been honored in Arizona for many decades before my arrival on the scene.

I hope this book will shed some light on the lives of those earlier Goldwaters—fascinating people, all of them—and give them some of the credit they so richly deserve.

Barry Goldwater

Preface

BARRY GOLDWATER HAS BECOME A FOLK HERO TO MILLIONS OF AMERICANS during his remarkable career as a United States Senator, author, Air Force major general, "Mr. Conservative," Republican presidential candidate, and leader of a political uprising that paved the way for the election of Ronald Reagan as President of the United States.

Arizona's most famous son, like his late friend John Wayne, is the archtype of the American West and its traditions of adventure, freedom, and self-sufficiency. A unique political figure, Goldwater speaks out boldly, regardless of consequences, and history has proved him right more often than his outraged critics could have imagined.

The end of his thirty-year career in the Senate will not mark the end of Barry Goldwater's influence on American political thought and action. Already he has assumed the mantle of the elder statesman, and he is likely to wear it with distinction for years to come.

Dozens of books by, or about, Barry Goldwater have been selling briskly since 1959, when his *Conscience of a Conservative* dropped like a bombshell on the liberal establishment and eventually sold more than four million copies. But so far, none of these books has examined more than superficially the amazing family that produced this one-of-a-kind American.

This book tells the story of Barry's paternal grandfather, "Big Mike" Goldwater, and his progeny, who did so much to shape and civilize the West. Mike and his younger brother Joe were impoverished Polish Jews who immigrated to California from Europe in 1852 and were drawn to Arizona Territory a decade later.

Joe's sons returned to California to make their fortunes in the early 1890s, but two of Mike's boys put down their roots in Arizona and played major roles in building our forty-eighth state. Morris, the elder of the two, was a respected leader in Arizona politics and business for sixty years. Baron, the younger, was Barry's father. He used his merchandising magic to transform a little Phoenix general store into an institution that has become one of America's best-known department store chains.

It has been said that a man is the sum of all his life experiences. It could be added that the experiences of his forebears also make their vital contributions. Certainly Barry Goldwater has been the product of his remarkable ancestors and the frontier events they did so much to shape.

The saga of the Goldwaters is the saga of Arizona history, ranging as it does from the days before the creation of Arizona Territory, through the decades of hardship and danger, to the civilizing of the wild frontier and the creation of today's progressive western state.

The Goldwater traits of adventuresomeness, self-reliance, leadership—and occasional fun-loving deviltry—made up a part of Barry Goldwater's legacy. Other traits came from the pioneering Robert Royal Williams family of Nebraska, which produced Barry's extraordinary mother, Josephine Williams Goldwater. Her achievements and her courage in overcoming affliction have always been an inspiration to her three children.

Probably Big Mike Goldwater would have been amazed to learn that he had established one of the great families of the American West. When Mike retired from the management of his Prescott, Arizona, store in 1887 and moved to San Francisco, he was neither wealthy nor powerful. But he had planted some vital seeds on the Arizona frontier, and they grew with spectacular results.

The Goldwater family stamp is indelibly imprinted on Arizona's colorful past as well as its present. Many facets of Arizona life owe an eternal debt to the enterprise of one Goldwater or another.

This is their story.

1

The New World
Adventure Begins

The wizened little man with the handlebar mustache pointed the way across the dusty Ehrenberg street to the decaying adobe building. Intrigued, his young nephew followed, shading his eyes against the merciless desert sun.

"Goldwater's store was over here," explained Morris Goldwater, "and the post office was at that end of the room. I spent many a day waiting on customers here in the 1870s. My father moved his business here from La Paz in 1869 and founded this town after the Colorado River changed course and ruined the La Paz steamboat landing, about seven miles upriver from here."

The athletic young man at his side was obviously fascinated by this journey into Arizona's yesteryears. Barry Goldwater was known to be readily infatuated by discoveries. He had already proved himself an outstanding radio ham, a photographer, an all-around athlete, a campus politician—and he was now making a name for himself as a merchandiser in the famed family department store in Phoenix.

Now, in these grim Depression days, it was exhilarating to look back into the proud history of the Goldwater family and the frontier territory they did so much to build. Barry vowed that he must learn much more about his grandfather, Big Mike Goldwater, and Mike's brother Joe, of whom Uncle Morris spoke with such intimate knowledge.

What drew them to this barren little river settlement so long ago? mused Barry. That was before Abraham Lincoln signed the bill creating Arizona Territory in 1863. Why had they stuck it out, defying

*death from Indians and outlaws and bearing those long separations
from their families?*

*Certainly the spartan life of La Paz and Ehrenberg must have made
even the current hard times seem opulent by comparison. This was
bare existence, with little to compensate for the heat, the infuriating
mosquitoes, and the numbing loneliness.*

*"Right here was the wicket where Joe Goldwater operated the
Ehrenberg post office," exclaimed Uncle Morris. "He got himself
appointed the first postmaster of the town, you know."*

*Barry Goldwater inspected the crumbling adobe and the rotting
wooden door frames with increasing excitement. A feeling of gratitude
suffused him as he considered his own good life as one of Phoenix's
moderately wealthy young men-about-town. Since his father's death
in 1929 and his departure from the University of Arizona to take his
father's place in the store, he had enjoyed his new maturity. Already he
had proved himself capable of accepting big responsibilities in the
rugged world of business competition.*

*"Well," he declared, "the Goldwaters started small enough!"
Another look around the tiny room verified that.*

*Again the nagging questions assailed him: What manner of man
was this grandfather of his, this Mike Goldwater? Why had he come
from far-off Poland to risk his life in this dusty wilderness?*

*Barry pumped his Uncle Morris for answers. Before their expedition
to the banks of the Colorado was over, he was determined to find out
much more about his grandfather and the family he had founded in
the Arizona wilderness.*

*This kind of investigation into one's roots could be exhilarating, he
was sure. It made a man all the more determined to match his
ancestors' achievements, and maybe make a name for himself.*

SAN FRANCISCO, 1852

BEWILDERED, APPREHENSIVE, AND WITH STOMACHS STILL QUEASY FROM THEIR
long ocean voyage northward from Nicaragua, the Goldwater brothers
stood on the dock at San Francisco and surveyed the scene in wonderment.

They were a study in contrasts: Michel, the elder at thirty-one, fair-
skinned, muscular, handsome, over six feet tall; Joseph, twenty-two, small,
swarthy, with dark hair and eyes. But they had in common the burning
desire to conquer this new world and to share in the dream of riches that
had lured them across the endless, watery wastes from London to New
York, across Nicaragua, and up the Pacific Coast to the celebrated, sinful

capital of western America. Michel and Joseph could not foresee, of course, that exactly a century in the future—in early November 1952—their ambitious young descendant, Barry Goldwater, would emulate their pioneering adventure.

He left the secure world of the small-town businessman and placed his name before the electorate as a first-time candidate for major public office. His upset victory in that Senate race, achieved by the narrowest of margins over the majority leader of the U.S. Senate, would place him in the national political limelight, change his life for all time to come, and alter the course of American politics for decades.

San Francisco! The name had a magic ring to it, conjuring up visions of sailing vessels unloading the riches of the Orient; prospectors gambling away their gold dust in raucous saloons; painted ladies displaying their charms on gilded stages; and glorious opportunity waiting anyone with daring and a little ambition.

In those last weeks of 1852, after the disastrous Kearny Street fire on November 9, San Francisco was rebuilding once more, and brick and granite were replacing tents and shanties. California had been a state only two years, and the gold rush of 1849 was still luring opportunistic hordes from all over the world, across the deserts and seas, to this amazing conglomeration of wealth and poverty, ambition and sin, glamor and tawdriness.

Hubert Bancroft, the great historian of the West, called the San Francisco of the early 1850s "a straggling city, with dumps and blotches, of hills and hillocks, of bleak spots of vacancy and ugly cuts and raised lines . . . Beyond rude cabins and ungainly superimposed stores, lodging houses in neglected grounds varied with tasteful villas embowered in foliage."

The Ten Commandments were forgotten in this melange of gambling halls, bordellos, saloons, opium dens, and other sinkholes of man's basest desires. Fighting, robbery, murder—it all was here.

But there was an invigorating, raw energy that was unmistakable. Cattle bawled in the livestock markets, sailors and stevedores filled the salty waterfront air with bellowed curses, and hucksters hawked their wares on muddy street corners. Miners in from the hills and farmers bringing their produce to market mingled with well-dressed businessmen and a fascinating collection of women from every social stratum.

When the Goldwater brothers arrived near the end of 1852, the pace of gold mining was already lessening perceptibly. The early birds had snatched the choicest worms, leaving the waves of newcomers little hope for instant wealth. Many a prospector along the American River was averaging only two dollars per long, weary day and paying more than that for a meal. It became obvious to the perceptive man that money was to be made in this new land, not from gold mining but from business.

Mike and Joe Goldwater, carefully protecting their meager savings, checked in at a boarding house and started to look and to listen for signs of opportunity in this strange but fascinating city by the Golden Gate.

For days, they visited the business section of the city, asking questions, assessing needs, examining the merchandise being offered, and doing a bit of careful sampling of the outrageous night life that had made San Francisco famous the world over.

It is possible that neither young man had ever planned to join the gold-seekers along the roaring streams in the wilderness. They were city boys, fitted more for the life of commerce than for the lonely hardships of the prospector or pioneer.

Each evening at the boarding house, they compared notes on the intelligence gathered during the day. It became discouragingly apparent that business prospects for foreign-born newcomers in San Francisco were slim, indeed. One needed large amounts of capital to start almost any kind of store. Even for such a business as a coffee shop or bar, the competition was fierce and the license fees high. Owners of the more than five hundred saloons in the city paid bar license fees of thirty dollars a quarter; restaurant or coffee shop owners, twenty-five dollars; and billiard room operators, twenty-five dollars per table.

Many a Jewish newcomer arriving with thoughts of peddling on the streets was disheartened by the peddler's fee: one hundred dollars per quarter! It seemed that San Francisco did not want a young man, no matter how ambitious, to launch a business here.

So Mike and Joe turned their eyes to the hinterland. Mining had spread from the Mother Lode to many other locations, spawning camps and towns by the hundreds. Mark Twain and Bret Harte immortalized many of their names: Poker Flat, Mad Mule Gulch, Gouge Eye, Cut-Throat Bar, Hangtown. Hangtown changed its name to Placerville, Bed Bug became Ione, and Tuleburg became Stockton. One of the camps in the foothills of the Southern Mines area, settled originally by Mexicans from Sonora, was flourishing, reported some visitors from that sector. It was a new town, called Sonora, and as raw as they came. But miners were coming to town with gold to spend, and business prospects looked good.

Mike and Joe Goldwater decided to book passage on the next stage to Sonora.

Their arrival in San Francisco was the beginning of a new adventure for these youthful Polish Jews, two of twenty-two children born to Hirsch and Elizabeth Goldwasser of Konin, in central Poland.

In that year, 1852, both already had experienced more death-defying adventure than most young men of today will ever encounter. Existing in those days as a Jew in Russian-dominated Poland was hazardous enough. Anti-Semitic prejudice spawned repeated pogroms—killings, burnings, and lootings—and the Czar's military recruiters were always waiting to snatch a boy as soon as he became old enough to carry a gun.

Unfortunately, neither Michel nor Joe recorded their memories of youth in Konin, nor did they spend much time talking about it with their children. Michel told his son Morris, after a fire burned their store in 1880, that a fire had destroyed the family home at Konin when Mike was a boy of twelve. On that occasion, he raced back inside the house and carried his grandmother to safety. He recalled on another occasion that two of the Goldwasser children had been crippled, and that one of them, named Samuel, was such a genius with figures that he was called to Berlin to demonstrate his prowess.

The name "Goldwasser," perhaps earlier known as "Giltwasser," was also the name of a brandy produced in northern Poland, which was mixed with a small quantity of pulverized gold leaf. As a mark of disdain for their true names, Eastern European officials in earlier decades had been known to give Jews the names of locally manufactured products when registering them for a census. So it is very possible that the name came to Hirsch in this manner.

Michel, born in October 1821, was one of the older Goldwasser children. He was apprenticed to a tailor and soon became skilled with needle and thread. Any hopes he had for formal education were extinguished by Russian laws of the period, which denied schooling to Jews and restricted their right to own land or prepare for professions.

When he reached his teens, he apparently became involved with a group of underground Jewish dissidents who conspired against their Russian oppressors. Fearful of police reprisals, and of his approaching conscription into the Czar's army, he bade goodbye to his distraught parents (he was never to see them again) and made his way across Poland, into Germany, and eventually to Paris. There he found employment in a tailor shop and for several years enjoyed the gay nightlife that Paris offered a handsome, unattached young man.

But this period of peace and gaiety was but a brief respite in Michel Goldwasser's adventure-filled life. On February 24, 1848, the French government of King Louis Philippe collapsed and revolution flared in the Paris streets. Rebellion was soon to spread to capitals across Europe in that bloody year. For Michel, the carefree life of a bon vivant became a nightmare of class warfare and hard economic times.

The young man who had so recently escaped the perils of Poland now found his life in daily danger as the streets of Paris ran red with the blood of revolutionaries who eventually deposed Louis Philippe and set up France's Second Republic. Before that goal was achieved, however, Michel Gold-wasser had put together his few belongings and made his way to London, where he hoped fervently for a little calm and quiet in his life.

With each move came the necessity to learn a new language, and Michel applied himself to the task of mastering English while he looked for work as a tailor. He found it, and soon prospered.

He had been in London only a few weeks when he met a young lady who was to be his wife through decades of turmoil and striving. Historian Bert Fireman, whose tireless research on the Goldwater family has revealed much of its nineteenth century history, recorded the 1848 meeting of Michel and his future bride in these words:

> Sarah's daughters recalled their mother often telling the story of how she first met their father. She and Esther Tash, an older sister, were walking in Petticoat Lane in London. Coming toward them, wearing a stunning green coat, was a handsome man, blond and tall. Sarah whispered that they should walk slower to look him over carefully.
>
> Protesting that she knew him, and that "he's only a greener," Esther tried to urge her sister along: "You shameless flirt!" The young girl was headstrong and insistent. Sarah Nathan was introduced to Michel Goldwasser there and then. As Sarah walked on she impulsively said that she would marry that handsome hunk of man, whether or not he was a greenhorn.

Sarah Nathan, daughter of Moses and Hannah Nathan, was a member of a Jewish family of considerable means. Her father was a furrier in the 1830s, and had gone to Hudson Bay in Canada to seek new supplies of furs. There, he contracted tuberculosis and died when Sarah was sixteen. Sarah took over management of the family fur-processing factory, and later learned the dressmaker's trade. Although she had almost no formal schooling, she taught herself to read, but never learned to write.

When she met Michel, she was a pretty young woman of twenty-two— short, olive complexioned, with black hair and matching eyes. An unknown artist who painted a wedding portrait of Michel and Sarah pictured her in a wine-colored velvet gown with a bustle, and a cap adorned with flowers. On her right wrist was a heavy gold bracelet, and on her bust was an enormous brooch. The portrait became the property of Sarah and Mike's eldest daughter, Caroline, after Sarah's death in 1905.

After their first chance meeting, Sarah and Michel did not see each other again for more than a year. She had nearly forgotten the engaging gentle-man from Poland until one evening when her older sister remarked that she had invited a guest for dinner at the Nathans'. Because many other young men had been invited over for inspection as possible husbands for Sarah, she did not think much of it. But the moment she recognized this guest as the stranger from Petticoat Lane, the old romantic desire revived with a rush, and she could see Michel felt the same.

Their feverish courtship culminated in a wedding on March 6, 1850, in the Great Synagogue of London, performed by none other than Chief Rabbi Nathan Adler.

In their marriage contract, or "ketubah"—a formal scroll written in Hebrew characters and composed in the ancient Aramaic language— Michel pledged to "work for you, honor, support, and maintain you in accordance with the custom of Jewish husbands." He promised her one hundred pieces of silver (which was academic, since he had no such sum of money at that time) immediately and another one hundred to be paid later.

Like his sons in later decades, Michel waited much longer than normal to take a wife. He was twenty-nine when he married Sarah, who at twenty-four, was also much older than the typical bride of the mid-nineteenth century.

Michel had become quite Anglicized during his two years in London. He not only had changed his name from "Goldwasser" to "Goldwater," but had learned to speak fluent English and had built up a thriving tailoring business. When he and Sarah set up housekeeping in a cottage at 27 St. Mary Axe and on December 22, 1850, welcomed their first child— Caroline—into the world, it must have seemed that nothing could pry Michel from his satisfying life of peace and family love. The arrival of their second child—Morris—on January 16, 1852, tightened the bond even more securely. If ever a man seemed destined to live out his days in middle-class London domesticity, it was Michel Goldwater.

The course of history is often shaped by seemingly insignificant events. There would have been no Goldwater saga in America had not an emaciated young immigrant from Poland suddenly appeared on the London scene during the summer of 1851 and presented himself to Michel and Sarah Goldwater.

He was Joseph, Michel's twenty-year-old brother, who had followed Michel's footsteps and fled from Poland only a stride ahead of the Russian military conscription officers. His journey westward across Europe had been marked by considerable hardship, and he descended on the Gold-water household like a lost dog who has found his way home. Swarthy, slight, and clean-shaven, he bore only casual resemblance to his tall, moustachioed elder brother.

Joe had been in London for only a few weeks when he started regaling Michel with stories he had heard about the wealth that men were finding in the California gold fields.

"I talked this morning with a landsman from Lodz," he said one day. "In San Francisco he opened a store to sell dry goods and clothing. In a year, so many miners came to buy with gold that he is now going back to Poland to get married. There is room for everybody in California, he told me, and they don't harm Jews there. Doesn't it sound wonderful? Let's go to California!"

Michel, secure in his role as husband and father, at first scoffed at Joseph's wild stories. But under his veneer of domestic contentment was a longing for adventure that he had almost forgotten.

California. Gold. A new land, waiting to be tamed. What an opportunity!

Sarah sensed his restlessness and her alarm turned into resentment toward Joseph, who was threatening to break up her snug nest. "If only this brother hadn't come!" she must have said with bitterness.

Her sister, Esther, was even more resentful. The man she had once called a "greener" she now called a fool for considering this wild idea of emigrating to America. It was all Joseph's doing, she raved; this dreamer who had nothing better to do than to live off his older brother and take him away from his wife and two babies.

"He's going, Sarah, you might as well make the best of it," she declared at last. "We got along without him when he was wallowing with the pigs in Konin and the loose women of Paris, and we'll get along without him again."

Fortunately for Michel, he was enthusiastically backed by Sarah's two brothers, Nathan and Isaac. They pledged to guarantee Sarah's support until Michel had made his fortune and was able to send for his family. It was their enthusiasm that eventually led Sarah to give tearful approval to the California adventure.

Her eyes were still moist on that morning in August 1852, when Michel and Joseph put their single trunk and two handbags into a carriage and started over cobbled streets to the London docks. With them in the carriage were Sarah; the two small Goldwater children, Caroline and Morris; and Esther and her brothers.

To save money, the two adventurers had bought tickets in steerage, that cramped, malodorous, hell-hole in which so many immigrants made their tortuous way across the Atlantic to America.

The discomforts were many, but in fair weather, steerage passengers were sometimes allowed to come up for a breath of fresh air. To save coal for the inefficient steam engines of this period the ship captains often broke out their sails when the wind was favorable. This practice lengthened the voyage's duration, which was normally two to three weeks, but salt beef, herring, and potatoes for the passengers were cheaper than coal for the boilers.

The Goldwater brothers made some friends during their voyage—among them a young Polish Jew named Philip Drachman, who was headed for Philadelphia to pursue his trade as a tailor. California and its mad search for gold did not interest him, he said. Perhaps Michel would change his mind and join him in a tailor shop in Philadelphia. But Michel declined with polite firmness. It was California or nothing.

Little did either man realize that their paths would cross again, in California and in Arizona. Philip was to come west and become a pioneer builder of Tucson, and Michel was to become the godfather of Philip's eldest son, Harry Arizona Drachman.

At last, the heaving ship entered the smooth waters of New York harbor and the Goldwater brothers raced ashore to stand once more on firm land. They found New York anything but a city of streets paved with gold. Its five hundred thousand residents slogged through mud, along ill-lighted and ugly tenement-lined streets. Hoodlums kept the Lower East Side in terror, and newly arrived immigrants were easy prey for thugs and confidence men.

Fortunately, Michel spoke fluent English, and Joseph was trying hard to master the language. After a brief stop in New York to visit a family named Isaacs, friends of the Nathans, they started making inquiries about the fastest and cheapest way to get to California.

They found that there were three commonly used routes: around Cape Horn, in sailing ships requiring one hundred twenty days or more; to the Isthmus of Panama, which was crossed by foot or muleback; or to Nicaragua, a route considerably shorter than the Panama venture, and somewhat cheaper.

The Goldwaters chose to go via Nicaragua—one hundred eighty dollars each from New York to San Francisco. It was a journey fraught with danger—from robbers, jungle animals, and disease—but they climbed aboard the odiferous ship with light hearts.

Upon arrival at Grey Town, on the Nicaraguan east coast, they crossed the two hundred twelve-mile isthmus in a little more than a week, by native yawl, mule, steamboat, and on foot, through wild jungle and oppressive heat to the west coast port of San Juan del Sur.

The brothers found they were expected to pay for their own food during the crossing of the isthmus, which reduced their savings a bit, and for a grubby hotel room while they awaited the arrival of their ship bound for San Francisco, which reduced their money supply even more.

Many of their fellow travelers succumbed to tropical diseases in Nicaragua, and some died while awaiting the ship to the promised land. But luck was with the Goldwaters, as it would be in many another tight spot on the road to the future.

After a shorter wait than most travelers endured in San Juan del Sur, they boarded their ship for San Francisco in good health and with soaring hopes.

Day by day, the distance to their long-sought goal decreased as the ship crept up the west coast of Mexico and California. At last, through the fog that blanketed the Golden Gate, they got their first eagerly awaited look at San Francisco.

They saw the emerging shapes of hills, and of brick and wooden buildings, two and three stories high, crowding against the shoreline where a few old ships' hulls were being used as warehouses. Most of the shacks and tents of 1849 and 1850 had been replaced by wooden buildings, and in turn, most of those had burned in the frequent conflagrations of the next two years. Now the city was building more substantially.

At last the docks—teeming with sweating stevedores, bawling cattle, rumbling drays, and bobbing ships unloading their mysterious cargoes— came into view.

If only Mike and Joe (the shorter, Americanized names seemed much more appropriate here) had been a bit more literate and had kept diaries of their monumental journeys in one of the great historic epochs of American settlement! But they did not, and they were soon too busy surviving in the rugged California of 1852 to record any of the harrowing experiences of their long voyage.

It was more than enough to them that they had arrived, safely and with enough money to make a start, in the promised land of milk and honey. This was a challenge to make a man's life worth the living. Their new adventure in America was about to begin.

2

M. Goldwater of Sonora

Those who know Barry Goldwater will testify that there is nothing of the prude in his makeup. He has drunk his share of whiskey, cussed like a mule-team driver, associated with gamblers, befriended madams, and raised considerable hell along the way. Moreover, he has maintained friendships with those who succumbed to all the common—and some uncommon—vices.

It is a bit easier to understand this side of his character when one recognizes the kind of environment into which his grandfather came in the 1850s. Mike Goldwater and his brother were not Sunday school boys. They were upright enough, and treated their customers honestly, but they were also the products of their rugged time and place in history. They ran a saloon in the California gold rush days, befriended painted ladies of the evening, and spent more time in casinos than in synagogues.

SONORA, 1853

THEY HAD READ WITH WONDER THE TALES OF TRAVEL IN STAGECOACHES THROUGH the American West, and now in early 1853 the Goldwater brothers were aboard one, headed some one hundred miles eastward from San Francisco to the rough-hewn mining town of Sonora. The region known as the Southern Mines was relatively prosperous, and Sonora was one of its business centers. A town of some four thousand, it lay just south of Calaveras County, of jumping frog fame. The stage paused along its bone-rattling way to drop mail at such stops as Chinese Camp and Shaw's Flat, snaking upward over ridges to Wood's Creek, a branch of the Tuolumne River.

Now the air was a bit drier and cooler, and the forested hills presented vistas of beauty that brought gasps of appreciation from the two European immigrants. At an altitude of just over two thousand feet, they came suddenly upon Sonora, overflowing an irregular bowl enclosed by hillsides thick with oak and pine trees.

Many of the shacks and shanties along the road through the outskirts were deserted, which brought pangs of doubt to the brothers, who had expected a boom town. In the center of town were evidences of the 1852 fire which had caused nearly a million dollars in damage to buildings and merchandise. Their hopes were revived by sight of the main street, which looked busy and thriving.

Not many months before, the California legislature had passed a statute commonly known as the "Anti-Greaser Law," which levied a twenty dollar per month tax on foreign miners. It was aimed primarily at miners from Mexico and South America, and was intended to drive them out of their mining claims. The law was soon repealed, but the hard feelings remained. Since Sonora had been founded by Mexican miners, the animosity between Latin and Gringo residents was at a high pitch when the Goldwaters arrived.

But the two new arrivals found friends among the several Jewish merchants of German origin who were already doing business in Sonora. Competitors though they were, the Jewish contingent shared their homes and their food, offered assistance to those in want, and displayed a genuine affection for one another.

One of the first merchants in Sonora had been Mayer Baer, who came in 1852 to set up a family business that was still operating one hundred thirty years later. Irena Narell, in her book *Our City: The Jews of San Francisco,* tells of Baer's unfortunate baptism to the ways of Sonora:

> In 1852, Mayer Baer put in a full line of crockery, and as an after-thought, a supply of whiskey. The miners celebrated the following Saturday by getting drunk. They smashed the crockery and wrecked the store, leaving Mayer to contemplate the inadvisability of mixing china and liquor.

She also tells of the merchants' informal monetary system, using gold dust in the absence of more traditional forms of currency. There were few reliable scales in Sonora, so the merchants used the following measuring system for the gold dust brought in by miners;

Pinch between fingers $10
Teaspoonful (ounce) $16
Wine glass full $100

Sunday was the gamblers' harvest day, many of whom were looking for easy marks among the hung-over miners. Many a prospector was relieved of his hard-won dust in a few hours of euchre, poker, or casino. The saloons raked in the miners' riches all week, as did the several houses of prostitution.

There were some evidences of cultural advancement—a school, churches, stores, even a physician—in Sonora. But it was, for the most part, a free-wheeling community where a man could do pretty much as he damn well pleased.

It took Mike and Joe only a few days in Sonora to conclude that the business most likely to succeed here was a general merchandise store. With only four thousand residents, Sonora did not offer much hope for a specialized retail business. But a store in which one could buy groceries, mining supplies, clothing, tobacco—that had a chance.

There was only one problem: A general merchandise store required an investment of many times the small total of savings they had left from the long trip from London. The only logical alternative was a business that would cater to most of Sonora's citizens, would require a small investment, and could be housed in small and inexpensive quarters.

The answer was obvious: A saloon.

For a few hundred dollars, they were able to rent a room, put up a rough wooden bar, acquire some tables and chairs, and buy enough liquid stock to get started. The business, established under Mike's name, was on the ground floor of a two-story wooden building. In the upper story was a house of prostitution. Although the two businesses were under separate ownership (contrary to rumors circulated in political campaigns a century later, the Goldwaters never ran a whorehouse), they had the same landlord and many of the same customers.

Those whose sense of morality may be shocked by the arrangement should be aware of the special place that bordellos had in the frontier towns of western America. The predominantly male population needed female companionship, which was only too willingly furnished by adventurous young ladies who had not captured husbands in the East and thirsted for excitement and wealth in the booming West. Wherever gold or cattle lured the men, or wherever the army sent its soldiers, the ladies of the evening were never far behind.

In Sonora, as in most boom towns, these girls were accepted—as long as they stayed in their place. They were not permitted to mix in polite society, or to intrude in the affairs of the so-called decent women of the community.

Not long before the Goldwaters arrived in Sonora, according to Edna Buckbee's book, *The Saga of Old Tuolumne,* a prostitute called "Big Anne" insulted one of the town's respectable women. Members of the volunteer fire brigade, in a warning gesture to the prostitutes, "rolled their engine down to Big Anne's shack and hosed her out of bed."

It was not unheard of, however, for a lonely bordello girl to fall in love with a lonely customer and marry him. More than one prominent western family had such matches in its early history.

The girls above the Goldwater saloon often sent down for a bottle or two, and both Mike and Joe were on amiable terms with them. The proximity of the two businesses was good for both, and both evidently prospered.

Mike, the more personable of the brothers, persuaded other Sonora merchants to guarantee him a line of credit for increasing his purchases from Stockton and San Francisco. Miners were still bringing in gold from their diggings, and Sonora prospered. Within only a few months, the Goldwater saloon had paid off its early debts and was doing well.

Their low overhead also helped to swell their bank accounts. Both Mike and Joe slept on cots behind a canvas partition that divided the saloon from the living quarters, and they ate simply and inexpensively. They spent little on personal needs, and virtually none on entertainment.

Early in the spring of 1854, Mike added up his resources and made a momentous decision: It was time to write to Sarah in London and send her the money to come with the two children to California.

San Francisco had made rapid progress since he had left fifteen months earlier, Mike observed with satisfaction as he strolled about the city in late June. Gas lights were appearing on the busier streets. A horsedrawn streetcar line was operating on Market Street. Hawkers in one-horse carts now dispensed drinking water brought in from Sausalito across the bay.

The sidewheel steamer *Sierra Nevada* was due in San Francisco from Nicaragua on July 2, 1854, but Mike had come to the city a few days early to purchase new stock for resale in Sonora. He and Joe had decided that it was time to expand their business, adding some candies, notions, and gifts for sale during the daylight hours when bar business was slow. They also had decided to invest in a billiard table.

Business was better than ever in Sonora since the discovery of large nuggets of gold in Wood's Creek, running through the heart of town. Every householder had been sifting the gravel on his few feet of creekbed, and for a time it appeared that gold-seekers would tunnel along the creek bed in the center of town, threatening to send the whole downtown area tumbling into the excavation.

On Sunday morning, July 2, Mike was waiting impatiently on the dock for the arrival of Sarah and the two children. To make certain that she would leave London for the wilds of the American West, he had asked

Sarah's sister Esther and Esther's young son, Marcus, to come along. The second-class cabin fare was so ridiculously low in that peak year of immigration—seventy-five dollars to New York—that he thought the investment well worth it.

As the six hundred sixteen passengers began to stream down the gangplank of the *Sierra Nevada,* Mike stood on tip-toe to get his first glimpse of the new arrivals. Carrie would be a big girl now, and Morris should be walking. At last he spotted Sarah, standing placidly beside her wildly waving sister. He recalled in later years that he was disappointed to find that the children did not remember him, and he was a little surprised at Sarah's undemonstrative greeting. But Esther's warm kiss and enthusiasm helped cheer him.

Sarah unleashed a torrent of complaints about the hardships of the journey. The last place that had suited her was Philadelphia, where she had enjoyed a feast of Chesapeake oysters. The food aboard the ships was abominable, the quarters crowded, and the Indians of Nicaragua were foul-smelling savages.

Sarah's outlook on life improved with several days rest and better food in San Francisco. But the British women and children alike were amazed at the noisy celebration of their first Fourth of July in America. They assumed that it was an expression of the wild American character, and resolved to take it all in stride.

The crudeness of San Francisco, coupled with the knowledge that Sonora was infinitely less civilized, depressed Sarah as the day of departure for the hinterland approached. But she resolved to be brave and remembered the words Ruth spoke to Naomi: "Whither thou goest, I will go; and where thou lodgest, I will lodge. Thy people shall be my people and thy God my God."

For a London girl, the dryness of the foothills east of San Francisco seemed alien indeed, and the rough mining camps through which the stagecoach passed seemed virtually uninhabitable.

Was Sonora as God-forsaken? she asked herself. She was soon to learn the answer: It was.

The clapboard house Mike had rented for them was sparsely furnished and devoid of niceties. With three adults and three children to be housed there, it was shockingly crowded. Moreover, the town offered few cultural activities, and the rough nature of its inhabitants was a constant source of alarm to the gentle Londoner. But Sarah bit her lip and resolved that she would stick it out in this American wilderness as long as God gave her strength to do so.

She was immediately glad that her sister Esther had come along, because Esther could cook. As a professional seamstress in London, Sarah had spent little time learning kitchen skills.

While Esther prepared the meals and did much of the other housework, Sarah busied herself sewing clothing for the two women and the children. Soon she found a bookstore in the town, and learned that a local theater offered periodic performances by touring companies. A lecture on November 11, 1854, by Miss Sarah Pelley found Sarah among the listeners. But the subject—"Temperance"—caused many a disapproving glance to be shot her way and left her feeling ashamed of her husband's means of livelihood.

She had been appalled when she learned of the proximity of the Goldwater saloon to the upstairs bordello. Her strident protests about the situation saddened Mike, but there was little he could do about it.

Dissatisfied as she was with life in Sonora, Sarah settled down to make the best of it. Within a month after her arrival, she learned that her third child was on the way.

She continued working almost up to the beginning of her confinement, and took up her needle again a scant two weeks after the arrival of her third child, Elizabeth, on April 11, 1855. Again, her sister Esther was a godsend. She added to her household chores the job of helping Sarah with the care of the new baby.

Joe Goldwater could plainly see that the hostility that Sarah and Esther had expressed toward him in London was still much in evidence. He continued to sleep at the rear of the saloon, and took his meals at the Michel Goldwater home, but he was usually made to feel like an outsider.

Not many weeks after the arrival of Sarah and her family, Joe told his brother that he thought the time had come for him to move on to some other mining camp. They dissolved their partnership amicably, and Joe agreed to give Mike as much time as he needed to pay him his share. Before long, word came back to Sonora that Joe was living in Shasta, where a boom was in progress.

Late in 1856, Joe was back in Sonora, looking for work. Probably with Mike's financial assistance, he set up a saloon and general merchandise store down the street. It apparently did not go well. On February 16, 1857, the wholesale liquor house of Trewtt and Jones of Stockton filed a suit alleging that J. Goldwater and Company owed the plaintiff $604.33 for liquor. When Joe did not appear to contest the suit, Trewtt and Jones was awarded judgment in default and took over his fixtures and meager stock in partial settlement of the debt.

This was but the first of several business failures that were to plague the Goldwater family in the early years of their American adventure. Joe, discouraged and embarrassed, left town for a new start in the Southern California village of Los Angeles.

Sarah and Esther undoubtedly said, "I told you so."

In the boom or bust days of the 1850s in California, financial failure was a commonplace occurrence. Well-established stores went under when placer mines went dry, and even banks closed their doors when the local economy hit a down-turn. One of the victims in early 1855 was the Adams and Company banking office of Sonora, which failed to open for business on the morning of February twenty-third.

Sonora citizens, threatened with the loss of their savings and businesses, took matters into their own hands. They formed a mob, stormed the Adams and Company office, brushed aside the protesting sheriff, and doled out the gold and cash in the vault to customers who presented evidence of funds on deposit.

Legal and financial matters were solved a bit more simply and directly in those days.

Mike, who was perhaps among those making the unauthorized withdrawal from the Adams and Company vault, came close to losing his life in another incident of high adventure not long thereafter. The Sonora *Union-Democrat* printed a news item that related that Mike was walking past a saloon in nearby Columbia when an inebriated celebrant inside fired a shotgun blast through the front door. Some of the buckshot struck Mike, but he escaped serious injury.

It was this kind of lawless deviltry that made Sarah Goldwater increasingly unhappy with her life in Sonora. By the end of 1856, aware that another child was on the way, Sarah seized on that excuse to end her weary sojourn in Sonora.

"This is no place to raise children," she declared. "The children and Esther and I are going back to San Francisco, and we won't be coming back."

Mike gloomily concurred, and put his wife, sister-in-law, and the four children on the stage to San Francisco. There, on July 15, 1857, Samuel Goldwater was born—their second son and fourth child.

Sarah's departure marked the beginning of a thirty-year span during which Mike and Sarah were separated for months and even years at a time. Distance did not cool their love for each other, and their reunions were eagerly awaited by both. It was far from an ideal arrangement, but it was inevitable so long as Mike insisted on seeking his fortune in pioneering communities and Sarah could be happy only among the comforts of San Francisco.

Mike made frequent trips to the city by the Golden Gate during the ensuing months, leaving the operation of his struggling business to hired help. Two results were to be expected: The business slid further into debt and Sarah gave birth to still another child—Henry—on July 27, 1858.

Only three weeks before that, Mike had signed a promissory note for two hundred fifty dollars to M. Bach, whom he still owed for the billiard tables in his saloon. He must have done so only after strong urging by Mr. Bach, because he knew he had little chance of repaying it. Other creditors were already closing in on him, and he had overdue bills for liquor, candies, tobacco, fruit, and a variety of other goods.

One night in late 1858, after the saloon had closed, he sat with head in hands in front of a stack of unpaid bills and tried to figure a way out of his lonely and seemingly hopeless dilemma. Despite its roughness, Mike liked Sonora and the many friends he had made there. He had been among the early members of the Hebrew Benevolent Society in Tuolumne County. His daughter Carrie and son Morris had spent their early childhood years among the hardy miners and merchants of Sonora, and Elizabeth had been born there.

But there was no business future for him in stagnating Sonora. Sadly, he made his decision: He would have to turn his business assets over to his creditors to settle a portion of his indebtedness, and plead with them to give him time to pay the rest.

His brother Joseph had written that things were booming in Southern California. Perhaps the golden streets of the promised land of America were to be found in Los Angeles.

Mike closed the door of the saloon for the last time and bade goodbye to his faded dreams in Sonora.

3

The Peddler of Gila City

Senator Everett Dirksen used the memorable title, "The Peddler's Grandson" in nominating Barry Goldwater for President of the United States at the 1964 Republican convention in San Francisco. The reference seemed strange to many, who obviously believed that the Goldwater family had always been wealthy department-store owners.

Sen. Dirksen knew his Goldwater history. He was well aware that the early Goldwater business enterprises had been miserable failures, and that Mike Goldwater had made his first venture into Arizona as an itinerant peddler, hawking general merchandise from his mule-drawn wagon to the miners of Gila City, eighteen miles east of Yuma, Arizona.

Both Mike and Joe were well acquainted with bankruptcy courts, with nagging creditors, and with humiliating financial failure. Barry Goldwater takes pride in the knowledge that his grandfather and great-uncle overcame adversity and worked at the most humble of occupations until they were finally successful.

GILA CITY, 1860

THE BELLA UNION HOTEL WAS NOT ONLY THE OLDEST AND LARGEST HOSTELRY south of San Francisco, but the center of public life in tiny Los Angeles during the 1850s. Virtually every celebrity who visited Southern California stayed there. Laws had been framed within its walls, and indeed, in 1845-46, it had been California's capital and the official governor's residence. Big money deals were regularly consummated on its verandas.

So it was not surprising that the first Butterfield Overland Stage, arriving in a record twenty days from Missouri on October 7, 1858, made its West Coast terminus stop at the Bella Union. Rattling up Main Street, the coach pulled up before the hotel to the cheers of a roaring crowd who welcomed this new link with the East as the dawn of a new era.

Only a few days after that momentous event, the owners started extensive remodeling of the hotel, including the addition of a billiard salon adjoining the barroom. Existing records indicate that Michel Goldwater was the first proprietor of this billiard salon and of the barroom as well, and that he was doing business in the hotel no later than December 10, 1858.

Other records show Joe Goldwater taking over the tobacco shop across the lobby of the Bella Union at about the same time.

How the brothers chanced to move into these rather choice business opportunities at the beginning of a Los Angeles development boom will probably remain a matter of conjecture. It is possible that Captain Thomas Seeley of the steamer "Senator," who regularly stayed at the Bella Union while his ship was being loaded for the return trip to San Francisco, befriended Michel when he came south after leaving Sonora. He could have recommended Michel as an experienced manager of the billiard room and bar.

At any rate, it was a stroke of rare good fortune that brought Michel to this genteel occupation at one of the low points of his life. Not only did it provide him with food, lodging, and money to send Sarah, but it gave him a listening post for all the news about business opportunities in the area.

Los Angeles could hardly be called a "new" town in 1858. It had been settled by Mexican pioneers seventy-seven years before, and was for years a trading center for the vast ranchos that flourished where the maze of concrete freeways now carry their noisy and malodorous traffic. For decades, it had been a sleepy little village of less than two thousand souls, and by 1858, it only had a population of just over four thousand.

But the arrival of the transcontinental stage, the rapid development of Southern California settlements, the increase in military activity, and sporadic gold strikes along and near the Colorado River helped attract a new breed of adventurer and entrepreneur to Los Angeles. The carefree days of the romantic ranchero were gone and would never return.

Michel and Joseph Goldwater hoped they had come to the right place at the time time.

Prosperity might be just around the corner, but Mike had a dark valley to traverse first. He had not been able to make any substantial payments to his creditors from Sonora days, and his indebtedness totaled $3,260—a staggering sum in that era. The list of his creditors (suppliers of fruit, liquors, tobaccos, gift items, candies, and many other items) still exists in the family records and gives a clear picture of the scope of his Sonora business activity.

On December 19, 1859, attorney Kimball H. Dimmick filed a petition on

Mike's behalf pursuant to "An Act for the Relief of Insolvent Debtors and Protecting Creditors," passed by the California legislature in 1852.

Mike sorrowfully signed the document, which reveals how miserably he had failed to strike it rich in his first California years. It stated that Michel Goldwater . . .

> has been resident of Los Angeles during the past year, but previously engaged in business in Sonora (California) in keeping billiard saloon and bar and vending liquors at retail. Sustained losses by bad debts and by friends of his clerks and servants, was broken in said business and unable to pay debts. Man of family during last year found scarcely able to support his family from his labor and unable to pay large liabilities against him, and is insolvent. Prays court to make an assignment of his estate to his creditors and be discharged from his debts . . .

Before Judge Benjamin Hayes, Mike was sworn and said that an inventory of his wealth consisted of one hundred dollars worth of household furniture for the use of his family, and clothing valued at one dollar. The latter figure was, of course, an understatement accepted by the courts unwilling to take the clothing from the backs of a man and his children.

No opposition to the petition was entered by his creditors, so on March 19, 1860, Mike was declared by the district court to be insolvent, and all his property except the personal items listed above was assigned to his creditors. The United States census of 1860 lists Michel Goldwater's total net worth at one hundred dollars. But at least he was free of his crushing burden of debt.

Here he was, thirty-eight years of age, with a wife and five children, almost penniless, and with few prospects for immediate financial gain. One may only speculate at the long odds that existed at that moment against Mike becoming the founder of a merchandising empire.

By this time, Mike had sent for Sarah and the children, apparently being unable to continue supporting them even in the modest style to which they had become accustomed in San Francisco. Their new home in Los Angeles, much to Sarah's distaste, was in a poor neighborhood of predominantly Mexican-American families. The 1860 census lists three Indians at the same address as the Goldwaters—identified only as "Jose, twenty-five; Jose Antonio, nineteen; and Juan, eighteen."

Mike's humble state of poverty had not dampened his procreative ardor, however. Only thirty-six days before the census taker called on June 20, a baby daughter arrived at the Goldwater home. She was listed as "Leonora" on the census report, but she grew up being called "Annie." (A century later, Annie's eldest daughter, Nita Prager Winkler, expressed surprise to learn that her mother's name had originally been Leonora.)

The same census taker only two days earlier had called on Joe Goldwater, with decidedly different results. Joe was still a carefree bachelor, listing his residence as the Bella Union Hotel and his occupation as tobacco merchant. His personal worth was listed at a handsome total of three thousand dollars.

How quickly had the brothers' economic fortunes been reversed!

Although he had made a legal settlement of his debts, the sting of failure still burned in Mike Goldwater's breast. He had come to America to make his fortune, not to spend his life racking up billiard balls and serving drinks over a bar.

So it was that he listened intently to any scrap of news about money-making opportunities. Travelers stopping at the Bella Union occasionally brought with them stories of gold strikes on and near the Colorado River, and sometimes a well-guarded nugget or two. One such strike that seemed to be building in importance had been made eighteen miles east of Fort Yuma, on the Gila River.

Sometime in the summer of 1860, Mike became acquainted with Dr. Wilson W. Jones, a pioneer Los Angeles physician who had gone into partnership with a man named Alonzo Ridley in a general merchandise store at the site of the Gila River strike.

Little did Mike realize that this new acquaintance, Dr. Jones, was to share many years and many events of his life in the wild young Territory of Arizona.

Mike queried Jones about business prospects at the camp, which some were calling Gila City, and found that an enterprising peddler might do very well if he brought in a wagon load of "Yankee notions" and other specialty merchandise not commonly found in the rough stores there.

Joe Goldwater agreed that it was a good idea, so he advanced the money for Mike to buy a spring wagon, four sturdy mules, and a stock of merchandise to sell to the miners on the Gila.

Mike had been warned of the heat and the barren desert between Los Angeles and Fort Yuma, but he was not really prepared for this arid, empty land. Contrasted with the greenery of Poland, England, and northern California, it seemed virtually uninhabitable. Skeletons of cattle and wrecks of immigrant wagons were strewn along the way. But there was a grandeur about its purple peaks, broad valleys, and endless vistas that intrigued him mightily.

After a journey of two hundred seventy-six miles along the rough wagon road, he arrived at last at Fort Yuma, on the California side of the Colorado River. At the fort, he fed and rested his mules and sold some merchandise from his wagon to soldiers and civilian employees.

Then, after a night's sleep, he crossed the river on the Jaeger ferry to the few clustered adobes of Arizona City (now Yuma) and then pushed on eastward to the busy diggings of Gila City.

On this fall day of 1860—we do not know the exact date—the first Goldwater had arrived in Arizona.

Gila City was typical of gold mining camps all across the West: a beehive of frenzied activity motivated by greed. Men were there for one reason only—to make a quick dollar—and the niceties of community living could go hang.

J. Ross Browne's description of Gila City is memorable:

At one time, over a thousand hardy adventurers were prospecting the gulches and canyons in this vicinity. The earth was turned inside out. Rumors of extraordinary discoveries flew on the wings of the wind in every direction. Enterprising men hurried to the spot with barrels of whiskey and billiard tables; Jews came with ready-made clothing and fancy wares; . . . gamblers came with cards and monte tables.

There was everything in Gila City within a few months but a church and a jail, which were accounted barbarisms by the mass of the population.

One of those Jewish peddlers was Mike Goldwater. His stock on the first trip probably ran more to fancy wares, but on later visits he brought a profusion of items, with some emphasis on clothing.

The population living near the business section totaled about one hundred fifty, but it is safe to assume that several times that number were out in the boondocks sifting through the river sands for gold.

Mike went after business with fervent energy, driving his wagon to the farthest shacks and placers. He sold out quickly, exchanging his wares for gold dust, and at a greater profit than he had hoped.

He could hardly wait to get back to Los Angeles and tell Sarah the good news.

The Goldwater brothers moved frequently, from one money-making opportunity to another, but in most instances they held on to one business for months after starting another. Such was the case in the early 1860s, when Mike was peddling in Arizona, Joe was selling tobacco and candy in the Bella Union, and both were keeping the hotel's bar and billiard parlor in operation.

Sarah and the children remained in Los Angeles through all Mike's goings and comings, and school attendance records still in existence show that the children attended the public grade school there.

Sarah longed to return to the big-city amenities of San Francisco, and eventually she did. But at least Los Angeles was much more civilized than Sonora had been. There were books to read, lectures to attend, social events to enjoy, and female friends of more intellectual inclination than those she made in the Sonora hills. It was also good to have Mike home more frequently than he had been when she was in San Francisco. Annie's arrival in 1860 gave her a balanced family of three daughters and three sons. There were two more to come: Ben on March 23, 1862, and finally, Baron on May 8, 1866.

On July 29, 1861, Michel Goldwater became a citizen of the United States. (Joe had taken that step eleven months earlier.) Mike took this solemn oath in the Los Angeles court, before deputy clerk William C. Shore:

> I, Michael [sic] Goldwater, do solemnly swear that I will support the Constitution of the United States, and that I do, absolutely and entirely, renounce and abjure, all allegiance to every foreign Prince, Potentate, State or Sovereignty; and particularly to Alexander II, Emperor of Russia.

Completing his United States citizenship had not come with perfect ease to him, an immigrant to a country torn between the old Union and the new southern Confederacy. Los Angeles residents, in fact, leaned quite heavily to the cause of the South as the bitter arguments of three decades were about to erupt in the Civil War.

Mike considered himself neutral in that controversy. He had long honored the nation of George Washington and Thomas Jefferson, but he could understand the concerns of the South, which was rapidly becoming subject to the richer, faster-growing North. Some of his friends in Los Angeles were rabid enough about southern rights to return to the South in 1861 and fight for the Confederacy.

But Mike cast his lot with the Union, and became a citizen of the United States a few weeks after the electrifying news of Fort Sumter's fall came to Los Angeles.

Mike returned to Gila City with loads of merchandise, each more carefully fine-tuned to the wants and needs of the people of the mining camp and the scattered settlements along the road. As 1861 breathed its last, he was on the road frequently, not only to Gila City but to other scenes of mining activity along the Colorado River.

Joe was very much a part of the planning and financing of the Goldwaters' mobile store, and he made frequent trips to San Francisco to buy merchandise for the peddling ventures, as well as for his store in the Bella Union and a new one half a block away, in the Mascarel Building.

Probably because of Mike's well-publicized bankruptcy, the stores were in the name of J. Goldwater. In 1862, Joe paid city and county taxes on stock in the Bella Union and in the branch store. The merchandise was similar in both, and included "notions, perfumery and cutlery."

In September 1862, Joe made another trip to San Francisco, this time to pay court to pretty Ellen Blackman, whom he had been meeting on earlier visits. He was thirty-one now, experienced in business, and financially able to support a wife. When he asked Miss Blackman to change her name to Goldwater, she did not hesitate in saying yes.

That trip to San Francisco was a fateful one for Joe in still another way. While there, he selected a substantial variety of merchandise from Leon Sylvester's wholesale house and directed that it be shipped to the stores in Los Angeles.

He paid for the goods with an "on demand" note, dated September 12, 1862, in his own handwriting, for the rather staggering sum of four thousand five hundred dollars. A week later he signed another demand note to Sylvester for two thousand dollars more, payable in gold coin. Both notes carried an interest rate considered today to be usurious: two percent per month.

It was not uncommon to finance purchases in this manner in those days, but it was generally understood in the commercial fraternity that "on demand" meant payment within a reasonable time after the note was called.

Mr. Sylvester was not an understanding brother in the fraternity.

Mike Goldwater was a gregarious soul, a lover of good company and the approbation of his fellow citizens. He had been among the first members of the Hebrew Benevolent Society in Tuolumne County, and had joined the Masonic Lodge in Sonora in 1855. He continued his Masonic and temple affiliations in Los Angeles, and was an active participant in informal associations of Los Angeles merchants.

One of his good friends was Bernard Cohn, also spelled "Cohen" on occasion, who had come to Los Angeles in 1855 or 1856 and started a dry goods store and a pawn shop. The first recorded business dealing between Cohn and the Goldwaters was the transfer of a note from Cohn to Joe in late 1860.

Cohn was a live wire, a man highly sensitive to money-making opportunities. So it was not surprising that he was one of the first to seize upon the chance to do some trading in August 1862, at the Colorado River diggings of La Paz, some seventy miles north of Fort Yuma. The Los Angeles *News* of August 20 noted his arrival from La Paz with exciting stories of gold there. The Los Angeles *Herald* a few days later reported that:

Mr. Cohn arrived last Saturday, with about twenty pounds (of gold).

The largest piece he had . . . weighed fifty-six ounces. The day before he started from the mines, there were about $20,000 weighed out in his store. . . . Provisions are still scarce in the mines. Flour and sugar were worth $1.50 per pound.

No doubt Mike and Joe Goldwater were among the excited business associates who gathered around to hear Cohn's breathless tale of riches at La Paz. But they were far from willing to leave Los Angeles and heed Cohn's invitation to join him in business there.

They were not willing, that is, until Leon Sylvester dropped his bomb.

Sylvester, the San Francisco wholesale merchant who held the two notes signed by Joe, demanded payment of them just two weeks after they had been signed. Whether through panic or by conscious design to ruin Joe, Sylvester pressed for immediate payment.

Sheriff Tomas A. Sanchez advertised the stock at a public sale, to be held the day before Christmas, but promptly postponed it until two days after the holiday of good will.

Word of the devastating legal maneuver soon spread to other Goldwater creditors, who clamored to get in line for repayment. Suppliers who had sold to the Goldwaters profitably for years now screamed for their pound of flesh—and got it.

The last assets ordered sold by Sheriff Sanchez brought tears to Mike's eyes: the spring wagon, harness, and four mules that had carried Mike over so many miles of desert on his peddling trips. According to Sanchez, he got four hundred ninety dollars for the whole lot.

Now the Goldwater brothers were stripped and penniless once more, and without means of making a new start. Little wonder that their rage and frustration knew no bounds.

Suddenly Bernard Cohn's offer to Mike to join him at La Paz looked good, indeed.

"Ho, For The Colorado!"

That was the headline the Los Angeles *Star* had put above a May 24, 1862, story about the gold rush to the diggings on the Colorado River, not far from the present site of Blythe, California. The story continued:

This seems to be the rallying cry of our city at the present time, and if the excitement keeps up for a short time longer at the rate of the past two weeks, there will be a great falling of our population. . . . Gold is fast flowing into our city merchants and traders, and the gold fields of the Colorado are now among the richest of the California placers.

By October 1862, the La Paz strike had so excited the West that a new town was taking shape on a lagoon some two miles from the river, surrounded on all sides by a heavy growth of mesquite. The population at that time was about two hundred fifty souls. Four months before, enterprising Bill Bradshaw had advertised in the *Star* that he had established a ferry across the Colorado, "at a place named Providence Point, the terminus of the straight line of travel from Los Angeles City." The wagon road Bradshaw pioneered from Los Angeles to the La Paz diggings was used by travelers for many years. Passengers and freight were coming upriver from Fort Yuma by steamship.

Again, Mike Goldwater heard the siren call and started making plans to leave his family in Los Angeles and join Cohn in La Paz at the end of 1862. Joe, married by this time, went to San Francisco as soon as his tragic bankruptcy action was completed. There, he went to work for a time for Abraham Goldwater, an older brother, who had come from Poland to start a small store in San Francisco.

Mike read the papers avidly for word of progress in the settlement of La Paz. Most of the reports told of huge nuggets being discovered, of prospectors streaming in from all over the West, and amenities such as a bull ring and billiard parlors being built in the settlement.

Now and again a word of caution was sounded, as in this item from the San Francisco *Bulletin:*

THE COLORADO MINES: Mines a failure, heat so great that even the Papagoes and Sonorans can work only a few hours. Place full of most reckless and desperate characters. Five murders already. Water so scarce it is defended with pistols. Most of whites in destitute condition.

Obviously, it was Mike Goldwater's kind of town.

4

New Start at La Paz

Few men in American public life have a sense of history comparable to that of Senator Barry Goldwater. Since the early 1930s, when his Uncle Morris took him to the remains of once-flourishing La Paz and Ehrenberg, across the Colorado River from today's Blythe, California, Barry has been an avid student of Arizona history.

Drawn by a desire to discover his roots, he has spent much of his life collecting correspondence and documents about his family, poking through abandoned courthouse files, interviewing old-timers, and encouraging others to do research on Arizona's early days. He has written several articles for journals of western history, and his photographs of western beauty spots have been widely published.

The Goldwater family had its first Arizona store in La Paz, the ruins of which are now barely visible seven miles north of Ehrenberg. To Barry Goldwater and his family, this is hallowed ground.

LA PAZ, 1863

MICHEL GOLDWATER WASTED LITTLE TIME IN WRITING HIS NAME ON A FOOTNOTE to the history of Arizona Territory-to-be.

The Civil War was approaching its midpoint in the spring of 1863 while Mike was working as a clerk in Bernard Cohn's general merchandise store at La Paz. Only a year before, on April 15, 1862, Lt. James Barrett and two troopers of the California Column had been killed attacking Confederate pickets at Picacho Peak, in a skirmish generally regarded as the "westernmost battle of the Civil War." However, there had been another clash between Blue and Gray, with one casualty, two weeks before that at Stanwix Station, eighty miles east of Fort Yuma.

And at La Paz, still further west on the Colorado River, soldiers were killed and another crippled for life by a Confederate sympathizer in front of the Cohn-Goldwater store. The date was May 20, 1863. As Lt. E. B. Tuttle recalled the bloody incident in a reminiscence published in the July 1928 issue of the *Arizona Historical Review,* the shooting occurred when a detachment of soldiers from Fort Yuma debarked from their river steamer for an evening at La Paz:

> Several of Lieutenant [James] Hale's soldier escort were in need of supplies and were permitted to go to the town, which was some distance from the river, to make purchases.
>
> The night was dark, and not expecting an attack, they left their arms behind. About 10 o'clock they collected in front of Goldwater's store to return, when fire opened on them from ambush, killing Privates Wentworth and Behn and wounding Private Gainor and one other . . .

Their assailant, a trigger-happy Union-hater named "Frog" Edwards, damned the soldiers for being loyal to the Union and fired on them without provocation, according to witnesses. Edwards disappeared into the night and escaped his pursuers, but his punishment was to be swift and agonizing. An army circular printed July 29, 1863, reported that Edwards had been found, dead of heat and dehydration:

> While fleeing from the scene of his murders toward Sonora, Mexico, he was followed by an avenging God, and famished on the desert.

The reference to "Goldwater's store" in the Tuttle report illustrates how rapidly Mike had established himself at La Paz. It was Cohn's store, but Mike evidently spent much more time there than did his employer. As far as La Paz people were concerned, Goldwater was the proprietor.

Goldwater mercantile organization traditions place Mike at La Paz in 1862, and for decades, the company used "Since 1862" as a slogan. It is barely possible that he was on the job at Cohn's store before the end of December 1862. But, considering that the sheriff's sale of the Los Angeles stores' merchandise did not begin until December 26, it is more likely that Mike did not make the dusty journey to La Paz until some time in January 1863.

The earliest solid evidence of his residence in La Paz is a surviving record in the books of the La Paz Mining District, which contains his signature witnessed by others. The date: February 23, 1863.

The number of miners and investors who had come from Los Angeles to seek their fortunes at La Paz was truly astounding. Damien Marchessault, mayor of Los Angeles, was one of the claimants to a mine in the district, filing his claim on March 28, 1863. Business and professional people left Los Angeles in droves to try their luck.

They came to a settlement described by Sylvester Mowry, one of the chief advocates of separate territorial status for Arizona, as "a single street with the usual number of tents, brush and log houses pertaining to a mining population of several hundred." Mowry observed that there were two stores, one of them presumably Cohn's, with prices "reasonably cheap."

The *San Francisco Bulletin* of July 19, 1862, had described La Paz in these words:

> Laguna de la Paz, meaning the Lake of Peace, is the pretty and not unappropriate name given to the collection of bough-houses and tents which constitute the only town in this region. There is not a foot of lumber employed in all the houses in the place . . .
>
> I have as yet witnessed no quarrels, although these were said to be common prior to the arrival of the Americans. . . . The stock of liquor here is small, nor does it seem to be in much demand. The mosquitoes are a terrible nuisance.

Many of the individuals who would become the biggest names in Arizona history seemed to be in La Paz during this period. Herman Ehrenberg, the German-born mining engineer who had come to Arizona in 1854 with Charles D. Poston, later hailed as "The Father of Arizona," was there. Henry Wickenburg, Sylvester Mowry, Paulino Weaver, and many other early Arizona heroes came for varying periods.

There were those who believed La Paz should be made the capital of the new Arizona Territory, and machinations toward that end continued for five years or more.

Although President Lincoln had signed the bill creating Arizona Territory on February 24, 1863, the new territorial governing party took its time preparing to make the trek westward. So much time passed, in fact, that Lincoln's appointee as Arizona governor, John A. Gurley, died before the group departed. He was replaced in August by John N. Goodwin, who served as first governor of the new territory.

The "government on wheels" moved leisurely west during the fall of 1863 and did not cross the border of Arizona Territory until December 27, 1863. Two days later, at Navajo Springs in northeastern Arizona, Governor Goodwin and other state officials were sworn in.

They arrived at the new army post of Fort Whipple in Chino Valley, some twenty miles north of today's Prescott, on January 22, 1864, and operated the territorial government from there until May 1864, when the capital was settled with some degree of permanence in the raw new village on Granite

Creek, which became known as Prescott. Fort Whipple was relocated just north of the settlement.

The choice of Prescott for the first Arizona capital was made partly because of its central location and safe Union views (Tucson was the only town of any size in the territory, but it was considered too much of a hotbed of secessionist fervor), and because of its proximity to the new gold mines that were attracting fortune-hunters by the hundreds to the creeks and canyons of the Bradshaw Mountains.

Mike Goldwater was sticking close to the store at La Paz through all these months of Arizona's birthing, little knowing that the sprawling infant town of Prescott was destined to become the stage on which he and his sons would play starring roles in the drama of Arizona history.

Despite the crudities and discomforts of La Paz—its withering summer heat, its maddening mosquitoes, its shortages of almost all the luxuries of life—Mike Goldwater had soon found a home in the shanty settlement of the Colorado River. And little wonder, judging by Arizona's first Territorial census of 1864. From the spring of 1863, when he was virtually penniless, to the spring of 1864, when he was counted among the three hundred fifty-two official residents of La Paz, his personal wealth had skyrocketed to fifteen thousand dollars.

He was now Bernard Cohn's partner—not an employee—and was recognized by one and all as the proprietor of the Cohn-Goldwater store. His advancement in the business was due to several factors: the fact that he was eighteen years older than Cohn, his demonstrated aptitude as a merchant, and Cohn's restless inability to spend more than a few hours at a time behind a counter.

The 1864 census, amazingly enough, lists Cohn with assets of only five thousand dollars. Apparently, Mike had made some money outside the store. That source of wealth may be attributed to his side deals with Sol Barth and Aaron Barnett, two traders who had wheedled financing from Goldwater and then made a bundle selling supplies to miners in the new central Arizona gold fields. Several accounts of Barth's pioneering life in early Arizona Territory cite Goldwater as Barth's backer and former employer at La Paz, but make no mention of Cohn.

Records show that the third business establishment started at Prescott (early 1864) was operated by Barth and Barnett in an adobe building at the southwest corner of today's Goodwin and Montezuma streets. This store presumably was supplied, entirely or in large part, by Mike Goldwater.

As adventurers and wealth-seekers poured eastward from the Colorado River to the rich mines of the Arizona interior, La Paz grew in importance as a supplier to those hardy souls. Mike Goldwater had the good sense to profit both from the residents of burgeoning La Paz and from those who used the town only as a launching pad for adventure in the Arizona wilderness.

Each new Arizona strike sent adrenaline coursing through the veins of fortune hunters in Southern California. They rolled eastward in a steady stream from San Bernardino, over the wagon road laid out by Bill Bradshaw, to La Paz and beyond.

The trail "beyond" was blazed at the cost of much human suffering and courageous sacrifice. For the first hundred miles eastward toward the Weaver, Wickenburg, and Prescott mining camps, it passed through a hot, often rocky, desert. Then came the foothills—Date Creek, Skull Valley and other settlements—and finally, the mountains, where Prescott nestled in a valley at just over a mile in altitude.

Riding a horse over that route was one thing; driving a loaded freight wagon and a team of horses or mules over it was quite another. Over the first half-dozen years of Arizona Territory history, two men were among the pioneers of that route from La Paz to Prescott: Dr. W. W. Jones and Mike Goldwater. Later, these two were to blaze a wagon road route to Fort McDowell in the Salt River Valley.

Dr. Jones, it will be remembered, was the Los Angeles physician who had befriended Mike in Los Angeles and had steered him toward the life of a peddler at Gila City. Jones gave up the primitive practice of medicine to branch out into many fields: mining, merchandising, and freight hauling, among others.

He and Mike soon became partners in freighting ventures, and their successful efforts in developing wagon roads to the Arizona interior have won them a place of honor in the early history of the territory.

Mike and Joe were to traverse the road from La Paz to Prescott—sixteen days by wagon—scores of times during the years when La Paz was a bustling center of supply for adventurers to central Arizona. As we shall see, they were to risk death more than once in traveling that route.

Joe Goldwater was in San Francisco during these strenuous days. He had married, fathered two children, and was enjoying city life as a clerk in the store owned by his older brother Abraham. It was beginning to look like his pioneering days were over.

But, just as Joe had lured Mike from London domesticity twelve years before, Mike was about to coax his brother into the more adventuresome life in territorial Arizona.

Henry Wickenburg, the German-born prospector who struck it rich at the Vulture lode near the site of the town that now bears his name, was the man who brought the Goldwater brothers together again.

In July 1864, Wickenburg was struggling to protect his discovery from the swarm of poachers who had descended upon it, and was trying to build an arrastra, a circular pit around which a burro dragged a heavy stone over gold-bearing ore to crush it into reducible form. Crude though the method was, it produced one hundred dollars worth of gold from the first ton of ore processed.

Soon Wickenburg found it necessary to build a stamp mill, but this required money and machinery that he did not possess. He turned to Mike Goldwater and his partner, Bernard Cohn, for help. Mike was excited about the prospect of supplying the mine, and eventually selling merchandise to the miners there.

Mike wrote to Joe in San Francisco, asking him to inquire about the availability and cost of a stamp mill and other mining machinery for the Vulture. Joe made such inquiries, but wrote back that Mike had better come to San Francisco and bring someone along who knew mining equipment better than he did.

So Mike came to San Francisco, bringing with him Jim Cusenbary, a knowledgeable Arizona mining man. With financing by Mike and Bernard Cohn, the deal was arranged and the machinery shipped to the mouth of the Colorado River, thence by steamboat to La Paz, and then freighted to the Vulture mine by wagon. Cusenbary became superintendent of the mine.

Over the next two years, Mike sold the Vulture Mining Company several thousand dollars worth of supplies from his La Paz store, but he and Cohn grew increasingly concerned over the Vulture's slow payment and its increasing debt.

So Mike and Cohn saddled up, rode to the Vulture Mine, and had a frank talk with their friend Jim Cusenbary. There was no disagreement about the amount owed to Goldwater and Cohn ($34,967), but how to pay it?

They arrived at a unique solution: The Vulture Mine ownership was "delivered over" to Goldwater and Cohn; they would be in temporary possession of all mine and mill facilities until such time as the debt was repaid. For each ounce of gold recovered above expenses, the partners were to be paid twenty-two dollars and sixty cents.

So rich was the Vulture ore that the Goldwater-Cohn debt was completely repaid in ninety days. An article in the *San Bernardino Guardian* of July 27, 1867, reported that "liabilities have been discharged and the property turned back to the [Vulture] company."

Thus ended Mike's career as a gold mine operator—and a profitable career it was.

During Mike's visits to San Francisco, he and Joe talked for many an hour about the future. Mike revealed that his partnership with Bernard Cohn was likely to be dissolved soon, not because of any major disagreements, but because their interests were growing apart and Cohn was spending even less time in the La Paz store than before.

Would Joe be interested in leaving the bright lights of San Francisco and joining the pioneers in new and lusty Arizona Territory? And, specifically, would he be willing to renew the business partnership he and Mike had once conducted in California?

Joe did not need much urging. He was feeling hemmed in at the Abraham Goldwater clothing store and he longed for a new adventure.

Mike's travels to San Francisco—and to Los Angeles to visit Sarah and the children—were surprisingly well-chronicled by newspapers of the period. On May 1, 1866, the Los Angeles *Tri-Weekly News* printed this note about his arrival in that city:

> TREASURE—We were shown by M. Goldwater, Esq., who arrived in this city a few days ago from Arizona, about 500 ounces of gold dust, taken principally from Linn's [Lynx] Creek and Weaver District placer mines. Also a large quantity of gold from the celebrated Vulture Lode. Many of the nuggets are worth $100 each . . .

Mike was not in Los Angeles at this time merely to show off his Arizona gold. He had been called home by Sarah to be present at the birth of still another child—one destined to be their last—who arrived on May 8, 1866, and was named Baron.

It was this Baron Goldwater (whose inconvenient arrival in Sarah's already-crowded home created new problems for the family) who was to father Senator Barry Goldwater forty-three years later.

This was a far different Mike Goldwater from the defeated man who had left Los Angeles almost penniless just three years before. Now he was well-dressed, confident, and had plenty of money in his pockets. He was nobody's barkeeper or clerk now, but a financier, an entrepreneur, a man starting to move into the freighting and government contracting businesses. Moving to Arizona had been the smartest thing he ever did, he must've thought.

In the late summer of 1866, Mike visited Sarah in Los Angeles again. This time he encountered a thoroughly unexpected development: His eldest son, Morris, now fourteen but small for his age, clamored to be allowed to return to Arizona with his father. Morris had completed all grades of the public elementary school and the local parochial schools. Since Los Angeles did not then have a high school, Morris's schooling had gone as far as it could.

Sarah reluctantly gave her permission, so in early October father and son set off on their journey to La Paz by stage coach. Before they had reached their first night's stopping point—San Bernardino—Mike had filled the boy with fearsome tales of wild Arizona. But he also told him of the good friends he had made at La Paz: Dr. Wilson W. Jones, the physician-turned-businessman; Henry Wickenburg, the daring prospector who struck it rich; Bernard Cohn, his partner; and Herman Ehrenberg, the popular mining engineer who had become one of Mike's closest friends.

Young Morris's eyes opened wide when they resumed their trip next day, viewing the desert for the first time from San Gorgonio Pass. At Agua Caliente (now Palm Springs) he encountered Indians far wilder and more primitive than any he had seen on the streets of Los Angeles.

By midday on October 9, 1866, they reached the stage stop at Dos Palmos. And here both Mike and Morris gasped in horror. On the floor of the stage station, lying in a pool of his own blood, was a man, later determined to have been killed by Indians who took only his mule and left thirty-five hundred dollars in gold coin in a purse on the body.

Father and son rushed to the man's aid, hoping he might still be alive. It was at that moment that Mike received a second shock.

He knew the murdered man all too well. It was Herman Ehrenberg.

The Mohaves who habitually hung around the front of Mike Goldwater's store at La Paz were friendly in good times, but sulky and threatening when the shifting Colorado River destroyed their crops or drought made their lives difficult. Mike said later that he never had any serious trouble with them, and that they respectfully called him "Don Miguel" or "Don Marcus," names they had heard Mexicans use in addressing him.

But other tribes could be as dangerous as rattlesnakes. Both Mike and his young son Morris saw that first-hand when they found Herman Ehrenberg lying dead at Dos Palmos and performed the sorrowful duty of burying him there that day.

Mike was quoted in the *Alta California* not long after the murder:

The party of Chimahuevis Indians which made a raid on Saw Mill Canyon near San Bernardino last month were overtaken by a party of settlers and several killed. Among this party [of Chimahuevis] was the murderer of Herman Ehrenberg at Dos Palmos—a man who also shot old Dr. Smith last Summer in San Gorgonio Pass. The murderer was followed by the friendly Cohuilas, who corralled him near Agua Caliente about the 28th of January and killed him. He was shot 20 times, but even after [he was] down he killed two of them.

Having been close to the angel of death on so many occasions, Mike and his friends found it hard to understand army officials who sometimes accused Arizona settlers of stirring up Indian trouble simply to get more federal troops and appropriations.

One thing was certain in 1868, however—the Indian depradations were making it more dangerous than ever to live in the territory. To be on the safe side, Mike sent sixteen-year-old Morris back to his mother in San Francisco in the summer of 1868. We may assume that Morris, who loved the excitement of the frontier and had been doing an excellent job as clerk and bookkeeper at the La Paz store, protested this decision mightily, but he had no choice.

Young Morris's return to the safety of San Francisco was more than a precautionary move.

Both Mike and Joe, who had joined him in Arizona by that time, were keenly aware that they lacked training in the arts of merchandising and general business. Their disastrous failures in stores at Sonora and Los Angeles were proof enough of that. So they decided to send Morris to San Francisco for an apprenticeship, a practical course in business that would make the youngster better able to make money as a merchant.

A friend of the Goldwaters, Pincus Berwin of P. Berwin and Company, San Francisco, agreed to give Morris a job in his hat and cap business. He was to start as an apprentice clerk and work his way up as soon as he demonstrated the ability to do so.

It was one of Mike and Joe's wiser decisions. Each of the Mike Goldwater sons, in turn, was to follow this same program of apprenticeship training in a related line of merchandising. And each brought back to the company business skills that were shared with the others.

Joe Goldwater's arrival and partnership with his brother at La Paz launched a new era of the Goldwater saga. In reference to the difference in their sizes, Mike became "Big Mike," and he carried the name with him the rest of his days. Joe was not only smaller and of darker complexion, but his droopy left eye gave him an appearance of shiftiness. There is an unverified legend that Joe had one brown eye and one artificial blue one in later years (the result of a barroom brawl). He supposedly ordered a brown glass eye from a San Francisco firm, but a blue eye was shipped in error. Joe didn't seem to mind, and wore the blue eye thereafter.

Those who have studied Joseph Goldwater's life have concluded that here was one of Arizona's most unlucky men. Throughout his checkered career in the American West he was repeatedly cheated, robbed, shot at, falsely charged with crimes, and generally victimized by almost everyone.

Part of the problem was that he lacked Mike's drive and determination to see a job through to the finish. He trusted the wrong people, too.

Such was the case a few months after his arrival at La Paz, when he generously agreed to be a co-signer on a ten thousand dollar surety bond that a new friend, David King, had to post in order to serve as sheriff of Yuma County. King won the election, and Joe had all but forgotten the matter when county auditors discovered that King had collected two thousand, two hundred fifty dollars in license taxes but had only about one thousand, five hundred dollars in the bank to show for it.

King could not come up with the difference, so the county came calling on Joe Goldwater and fellow guarantors Manuel Ravena and Joseph Tuttle. They had to pay eight hundred dollars, including interest and court costs, for this little lesson.

Joe was involved in another court action in 1868. Freighter Charles Craw ran up a bill of eight hundred sixty-eight dollars with Goldwater's and could not pay. So Joe took him to court. A month later, the Goldwaters took possession of three horses, seven mules, fourteen sets of harness and various other pieces of Craw's freighting equipment.

Because Joe was not blessed with Mike's winning personality, he sometimes irritated people, often with disastrous results. One of his former employees at La Paz, Harris Cohn, set out to destroy Joe in 1871 by filing charges in Yuma district court that claimed Joe had misappropriated some eight thousand dollars Cohn had given him to bind a partnership between the two.

When the court, after thorough investigation, dismissed Cohn's charges, the disgruntled former employee vowed to strike back at Joe in any way he could. He immediately brought new charges, this time a claim that Joe had obtained army supplies by fraud and had sold them for his own profit. For more than a year, this new and expensive court battle raged on, with the same result: Joe was exonerated, and the irate Cohn was assessed court costs.

But the long, drawn-out affair took a heavy toll on both Joe and Mike, and it undoubtedly damaged their hard-won reputations for honest dealing.

Joe must have turned his eyes to heaven and asked, "Why me, Lord? Why always me?" Little could he have realized that his most traumatic bad luck still lay ahead.

The *Arizona Miner* carried a lead story on June 13, 1867, that had great portent for the future of the Goldwater brothers:

The Town of Ehrenberg

We were aware some time since that certain parties, interested in founding a town at some more eligible point upon the Colorado, than that occupied by La Paz, had selected the locality known as Mineral City (where the Bradshaw Ferry crosses) some seven miles below La Paz, for the purpose.

We have seen a map of this new town site, which is to be called "Ehrenberg" in honor of our eminent and lamented pioneer, and upon paper it has an admirable appearance . . . The site embraces one quarter section of land, most of it elevated, and having a fine and accessible frontage directly upon the Colorado. Steamboats can discharge their cargoes in the town as in Arizona City and Yuma, and all the expense of hauling, as now required at La Paz, will be avoided.

Mike Goldwater has been credited with choosing the name of this new settlement, honoring the friend he had found murdered just a year before.

It was during the major Colorado River flooding of the winter of 1866-67 that La Paz's fate was sealed. The site had always been inconvenient for discharging steamboat cargo, but this time the river shifted its course enough to require costly and time-consuming transshipment of heavy freight from river to town. La Paz merchants began looking for a better townsite, and they found it seven miles to the south.

For several years, La Paz and Ehrenberg existed side by side, but there was little doubt that La Paz was dying. One of the chief executioners was Mike Goldwater himself, who exhorted his fellow merchants to move to the new townsite, and erected there the biggest store building in the town—seventy-five feet wide and one hundred fifty feet deep, flanked by corral space and a loading area sufficient to accommodate many freighting teams.

It was built of adobe bricks, but framed with timbers hauled from Prescott. It had attic and air space to help soften the effect of the intense sun. (Nearly half a century after Ehrenberg joined the roll of Arizona ghost towns, historian Bert Fireman visited it and reported that the deserted and decaying Goldwater store still had well-fitted door and window frames, solid lintels, and stood as a sentinel to mark the business center of this once-thriving community.)

The spring of 1869 was one of feverish building activity in the new town of Ehrenberg. J. B. Tuttle was working on a new blacksmith shop and Tom Goodman was building a hotel. Jack Stewart already had his pool room in operation, and his saloon was doing good business. All the necessities were in place.

On September 18, 1869, the *Arizona Miner* carried a sizable advertisement that made an historic announcement:

J. GOLDWATER AND BRO.

Wholesale Dealers in Clothing, Dry-Goods, Boots

Shoes, Grain, Groceries, Provisions, etc.

Respectfully call the attention of the public to the fact
that they are now located at the new

Town of Ehrenburg

where they are prepared to receive merchandise for storage or transportation, free of charge. Ehrenburg is situat [sic] on the east bank of the Colorado River seven miles below La Paz, at the best and most convenient landing on the river. It is connected with the principal towns of the interior by good wagon roads. . . .

For further particulars, inquire of

J. Goldwater and Bro.
Commission—forwarding agents
Ehrenburg

Two interesting points emerge from this advertisement: that Mike and Joe had not learned how to spell "Ehrenberg," and that at least the wholesale and forwarding portion of their business was being advertised under the name "J. Goldwater and Bro."

Two days after this announcement of Goldwater's removal from La Paz to Ehrenberg, the U.S. Post Office Department in Washington approved the appointment of Joseph Goldwater as the first postmaster of Ehrenberg. Had postal authorities been more aware of Joe's impatience with detail and his occasional slothfulness, they might have reconsidered this decision. As several irate citizens were to learn during the ensuing months, the Ehrenberg post office delivered mail when and if it was convenient.

When young Barry Goldwater explored the ruins of the Ehrenberg store many decades later, he made an amazing discovery. "I poked around under the post office wicket in one corner of the store," he recalls, "and there, under a thick level of dirt, were dozens of undelivered letters of that period. Uncle Joe apparently tossed the mail on the floor when he felt he couldn't deliver it, and there it stayed."

Joe had more important things on his mind in 1870. One of them was an attempt to use his influence to get his friend J. B. Tuttle, the blacksmith, appointed justice of the peace. Joe apparently considered himself a personal friend of Arizona Governor Anson P. K. Safford, whom he had met some time earlier at Ehrenberg. In a big, bold hand, he wrote the Governor:

May 5, 1870
Governor Safford

My dear Sir

It is quite a age since I heard of you. Should be very sorry if I have displeased or given an offense to you. If I did, why not let me know? Since you last left my place, I have been traveling and of course prevented me from corresponding with you.

This place is wonderfully improving beyond description and the prospects are very good for to continue. I should therefore beg of you, and recommend, J. B. Tuttle to be appointed as Justice of the Peace, as it is almost absolutely needed for our own protection . . . Trust you had a good time at Washington and hoping soon to heare of you.

I remain yours very truly,

J. Goldwater.

He also served as a member of a Yuma County Grand Jury, and he was so confident of his popularity in the county that he ran for the office of Yuma County Treasurer. When the votes were counted, his opponent, Robert Coles, had received one hundred twenty-one votes; Joe Goldwater had garnered only twenty-nine.

It was the first recorded instance of a Goldwater seeking election in Arizona. There would be many more to come, and usually with happier results.

5

Ambush!

Born in Phoenix three years before Arizona Territory became the forty-eighth state, young Barry Goldwater did not have to go far to live the Wild West adventures that were only impossible dreams to other boys his age.

He was already there.

Cowboys, Indians, prospectors, pioneers—they were all around him in a glorious, true-life western adventure. When he was barely able to walk, he toddled down Washington Street, where Indian merchants spread their wares on the ground for all to see. When he was a little older, he listened in awe as ancient cowpokes told yarns to his family and friends about the days when the West was new and untamed.

With his mother, brother and sister he bounced through the Arizona back country in an open touring car, or headed west across the barely passable Mohave Desert toward California. Sleeping under the stars, where coyotes howled and desert creatures scrambled to be first at nearby water holes, was commonplace for him.

And later, he was to risk his life routinely in the roaring rapids of the Colorado River or on the perpendicular cliffs of northern Arizona's high mountain country. Adventure—in a football uniform, a fast car, or an Air Force jet fighter—has always been a way of life for the senior senator from Arizona.

Pioneering, taking chances, flirting with sudden death a hundred miles from the nearest human settlement: all these are in Barry Goldwater's blood.

So is a love of gadgetry and new technology.

Exploring and adventuring in the field of communications has been a lifelong fascination for the man. He helped build a radio station while still a teen-ager, and he has been a pioneer of both military and civilian *communications ever since. The world's best-known radio ham is still working to develop ever-better networks of understanding among the peoples of the world.*

Many of the Goldwaters have been mechanical innovators. Morris was a life-long gadgeteer, and his memorable feat in bringing the first telegraph line to Phoenix is one which Barry never tires of relating.

An insatiable curiosity about the unknown, whether geographical or technological, is an unmistakable Goldwater trait.

EHRENBERG, 1872

IF HEATED WORDS COULD HAVE SET THE TRAILSIDE FOLIAGE AFIRE, THE BLAZE would have spread from Prescott to Skull Valley on that mid-June day of 1872.

Mike Goldwater and Dr. Wilson Jones were returning from Fort Whipple to Ehrenberg after a most disappointing bid session for supplying grain and hay to Arizona Territory army posts. Not only had Goldwater and Jones been virtually shut out in the bidding, but rival C. P. Head and Co. of Prescott had been awarded almost all the army business for a year to come.

Shockingly, Head had come out of the session with a contract to supply the Army with 12,310,900 pounds of corn and barley, the biggest award made up to that time to a single grain supplier. The contract would bring Head an unprecedented $720,000—a sum too huge to contemplate in those days—and leave every other freighter and army supplier in Arizona struggling to stay in business for the next year.

Mike had come to Prescott early to find out how the bidding was likely to go, and to prepare a bid that would assure Goldwater and Jones at least a reasonable share of the business that Uncle Sam would funnel into the Territory. Jones and Joe Goldwater had considered the bidding session so important that they made the trip as well.

All the major freighting concerns in the territory were represented at the meeting, which had been delayed until General George Crook, the top army commander in Arizona, could get back from Camp Grant.

It was an angry trio that set off for Ehrenberg after the contracts had been awarded. Mike and Dr. Jones drove the lead buggy westward from Prescott down the familiar wagon road through Mint Valley toward Date Creek, and Joe held the reins of the buggy just behind them.

The two carriages had traversed fourteen miles of the road, and every-thing seemed so peaceful on that sunny summer day that all three men had all but forgotten to be on the lookout for marauding Indians.

Even the most careful surveillance would not have helped, however.

Suddenly, a howling host of Mohave-Apaches sprang from behind every rock and tree, taking the travelers completely by surprise. Although there were only about thirty Indians in the ambush party, it must have seemed that every Indian in central Arizona threatened the two buggies.

Rifle shots rang out and bullets slammed into wood, leather, and flesh. Horses reared in panic, but within seconds, the drivers had them under control and were racing down the trail in a desperate attempt to outdistance the raiding party. Miraculously, the two buggies broke through the encircling throng as the raiders continued to pour murderous rifle fire into both of them.

Mike and Dr. Jones must have had angels riding on their shoulders. A dozen bullets whizzed through and past the lead buggy. Dr. Jones felt one of them plow through his shirt, and Mike fingered two bullet holes in his hat.

But Joe, in the trailing carriage, was exposed much longer to the Apache fire and took the brunt of the attack. He screamed in agony as one ball slammed into his lower back and then saw another strike one of his horses in the neck.

Reeling from the attack, he grabbed the reins and shouted at his team to race ahead. At that moment another bullet crashed into his upper back and lodged in his shoulder.

Fighting back pain and panic, he managed to urge his horses through the attackers and to stay close behind the lead buggy. On and endlessly on they went, with the attackers pursuing and firing just behind.

The trio had almost abandoned hope of escape after four miles of the chase, when around the bend they came upon the most welcome sight they had ever seen. Three Walnut Grove ranchers were approaching from the west, riding in a wagon. Quickly sensing the situation, they leaped from their wagon and took up positions behind rocks to greet the pursuing Apaches with a hail of rifle fire.

Despite their numerical superiority, the ambushers lost all desire to continue the chase and vanished into the surrounding hills. The six men breathed a sigh of relief and started assessing the damage.

Joe was drenched with blood and fighting to maintain consciousness. Dr. Jones, recalling his earlier life as a physician, bound up the wounds as best he could and the party started for the ranch of E. F. Bowers in Skull Valley. They found some soldiers from the mail escort there and sent them racing toward Fort Whipple for medical instruments and supplies.

When they returned, Dr. Jones started probing for the bullets. He found one almost immediately in Joe's back, but it took a long and painful search to find the other, lodged in the shoulder.

The next morning, Joe endured the twenty mile jolting ride to Camp

Date Creek, where Dr. Ensign, the camp surgeon, gave him additional care. But it was a week before Joe recovered sufficiently to be moved to Ehrenberg by army ambulance. After a brief rest there, he went on to San Francisco, where his wife Ellen nursed him slowly back to health.

Dr. Jones gave Joe the rifle ball extracted from his back, and the recuperating merchant had it made into a charm for his watch chain, one that he wore until his dying day.

The intrepid lawman, the adventuresome prospector, the romantic cowboy—all these have received more than their share of glory for taming and settling the wild West.

It's time some overdue credit was given to the men who delivered the goods: the freighter, wagonmaster, road station master, and forwarding agent. Without their willingness to endure Indian attacks, extremes of heat and cold, vagaries of market prices, and overwhelming loneliness, civilization might never have gained a foothold in Arizona Territory.

Theirs was a highly speculative business. True, they might turn a thousand-dollar profit on a major contract within a few weeks. But often they risked their lives and their sizable capital investments and came out losers.

Mike Goldwater was such a man during the late 1860s and early 1870s. With his friend and partner, Dr. Jones, he hauled freight to every part of the territory, and to New Mexico and California, too. Moreover, the two traced wagon trails through uncharted stretches of desert and mountain country, seeking always to cut travel time and deliver the resources of civilization to towns and mining camps, to ranches and military posts.

Goldwater and Jones would have been surprised to learn that anyone considered their efforts as heroic. They were out to make an honest dollar, to be sure, and they did quite well at it. But they also earned the grateful thanks of succeeding generations.

A trip from Prescott to Santa Fe took some twenty days each way, and the wagonmaster faced long periods of lonely hardship on such a haul. Jones and Company was one of the best-equipped freighting outfits in Arizona Territory, as they demonstrated by bringing eight complete wagon outfits into Phoenix at one time.

A writer in the San Bernardino *Guardian* of May 20, 1871, had high praise for the Goldwater brothers' efforts on behalf of territorial pioneers:

> The Goldwater Bros. are the most energetic merchants in the Territory, and are supplying grain at Camp Hualpai and Camp Verde. Whether they make a cent or not by their contract, they deserve the kind regard of the people of the Territory. By their energy, they have

opened up a new road from Camp Verde to Cobaro [Cubero], New Mexico, a good road . . .

Goldwater lost many a head of stock, not being sufficiently protected by the government [troops] . . . It requires such men as the Goldwater brothers in a country like this for its advancement and success.

It was true—Indians often stole Goldwater and Jones's animals and wagon mules, burned their wagons, and killed their drivers. Such a loss occurred on April 2, 1871, near Camp Date Creek. A large party of Mohave-Apache raiders attacked a train of five wagons, four of which belonged to the Jones-Goldwater partnership. One man was killed and another severely wounded, and the partners lost virtually all their wagons and cargo.

It did not take many such losses to send a firm into bankruptcy.

Despite the fierce competition on the frontier, and the seeming heartlessness of many transactions, there was room for many an act of charitable kindness. The records are full of proof that Mike and Joe Goldwater were among the most generous to those in need.

One of the most heart-warming is the story of an unfortunate missionary, Mrs. Caroline Cedarholm, who sowed her gospel seeds on rocky ground in Arizona Territory. She recounted her experience in a treatise entitled, amazingly, "A Narrative of the Dangerous Journey of Mrs. Caroline Cedarholm, The Norwegian Missionary, Across the Desert to Arizona with the Strange Experiences and Providential Deliverances on the Way."

She arrived in Prescott on September 17, 1870, after a harrowing hike across the desert from California, and set out to solicit funds to build a Congregational Church there. She and a companion received little but ridicule from the inhabitants of Whiskey Row, so they went to nearby Fort Whipple. There they enlisted ten soldiers in a Bible class, and triumphantly got seventeen to sign the temperance pledge.

The *Arizona Miner,* in May of 1871, wrote of their decision to leave Prescott:

After a long and earnest effort on the part of these ladies to raise Prescott away up toward heaven, they became disgusted at their ill success and our want of godliness as a people; and hence departed for the sunny south in quest of more tractable disciples. May your portion be a grand success and a prolonged absence from Prescott, ladies.

Mike Goldwater was in Prescott at the time, and he was about the only person to show the ladies any sympathy. In her narrative, Mrs. Cedarholm says that "Through a Mr. Goldwater I got recommendations to different persons along the road, and also opportunity to go with a team clear through to San Bernardino."

She left the wagons at Wickenburg and tried her fund-raising in the saloons there, with the same lack of success.

"But I was not cast down," she wrote, "for I felt myself in the path of duty. I gave a lecture that evening in a big store and had a good congregation, that no doubt listened with astonishment to the poor missionary woman."

Her next stop was Ehrenberg, where she looked up Mike Goldwater and asked for help to get back to California.

"Mr. Goldwater promised me free fare on the stage, and provided a good bed, going for me to Dr. Jones. I then started my tour of collecting and got ten dollars. The next morning I left on the stage. Mr. Goldwater fulfilled his promise. It is my duty to testify that the Jews have often shown me more liberality in my missionary duties than professing Christians."

Whatever faults the Goldwater brothers might have had, the history of territorial Arizona is sprinkled with stories of their warm-hearted generosity to those in need.

The railroads were on their way to civilize the West, as evidenced by the completion of the first transcontinental railroad in the dramatic 1869 driving of the Golden Spike at Promontory Point, Utah. But it would be more than a decade before they crisscrossed the land to such an extent that the wagon trains would no longer be profitable. Freighting for the army continued to be one of the most profitable businesses in Arizona, and the Goldwaters stayed with it as long as it remained so.

Because much of the money spent by army posts went for food for the troops and their animals, the army tried to encourage farming ventures closer to the forts. As early as 1867, a group of impoverished Wickenburg miners and adventurers, organized by Jack Swilling, a former Confederate soldier, had experimented with irrigation farming in the barren Salt River Valley. They rebuilt and extended the amazing network of canals used by prehistoric Indian farmers in the valley, and found the land fertile beyond their wildest dreams.

Charles T. Hayden came up from Tucson to develop irrigation canals in the Tempe area and to build a flour mill that still prospers at the foot of Hayden Butte on Mill Avenue in Tempe. John Y. T. Smith, whose haying venture to supply feed for mounts at Camp McDowell was Phoenix's first business enterprise, stayed on to become prominent in business and politics. The word spread quickly about the Salt River Valley's potential as the breadbasket of Arizona, and by the mid-1870s, the Phoenix area was one of the fastest-growing in the West.

Here was something relatively new for Arizona Territory—wealth that did not fade as an exhausted gold mine did, supporting a community that did not boom spectacularly and then just as quickly join the ranks of ghost towns.

Mike Goldwater hauled a lot of freight and supplies to the Salt River Valley, and even as he made his long and lonely freighting runs he dreamed of starting a store in Phoenix, where a man could be safe and enjoy the company of other men in a city with a future.

Traveling from the wagon roads of Arizona to the bustling metropolitan life of San Francisco was akin to traveling to another planet. In the City by the Bay, men wore top hats to the opera, and escorted ladies adorned in plumed and bejeweled splendor. Businessmen wore suits and derby hats in San Francisco and children attended school at least six months of each year.

Mike Goldwater always looked forward to his San Francisco trips, not only to visit Sarah and his fast-maturing children, but to live for a time with the pleasant resources of civilization.

His visit in September 1872 was special. He was anxious to see how brother Joe had recuperated from his wounds of three months previous, and he wanted a serious talk with his eldest son, Morris, about his progress with P. Berwin and Co. Mike already had made arrangements to acquire business property in booming Phoenix and there was much planning to do about the entire future of the Goldwater enterprises.

The Goldwater family had been moving up in the world. At Sarah's insistence, they had given up their residence at 942 Mission Street (a section becoming rapidly commercialized) and moved to a much more fashionable neighborhood at 722 Post Street. Such status symbols were important to Sarah, who enjoyed telling her friends about her husband's rising financial position, and about the new business office the brothers had recently opened at 106 Battery Street in San Francisco to expedite the purchase of merchandise for their Arizona operations.

Sarah was proud, too, of the progress her son Morris had made with the P. Berwin wholesale hat firm. Starting from office boy, he had advanced steadily during the past five years and was now a key man in the company's sales force. He had learned the ways of modern business, too, and was bursting with merchandising ideas to spring on his father and uncle.

Mike and Joe reminisced about the autumn of 1852, just twenty years before, when they crossed the Atlantic and Central America to San Francisco to begin their own great adventure. They must have cast an envious look at young Morris, who was about to launch another generation of Goldwater achievement.

Where would Morris fit best in the complex family business? A tentative decision was reached during Mike's San Francisco visit. It was made known to Arizona Territory in an *Arizona Miner* news story published October 12, 1872:

> Morris Goldwater, son of M. Goldwater, is now a partner in the firm and may take charge of the business at Phoenix. He is said to be an exceedingly intelligent young man.

Arizona was about to be introduced to a young man who would make his mark in an amazing number of fields, and who would help write the history of the territory and the state for sixty-seven years to come.

PHOENIX, 1872

C. H. (Lum) Gray was a Florida native who tried his luck, unsuccessfully, in the California gold rush and returned home just in time to put on Confederate gray. In 1865, he married Mary Adeline Norris and brought her, along with her devoted servant Mary Green, to the Salt River Valley of Arizona Territory in 1868.

Mrs. Gray, known affectionately to pioneers as "Aunt Adeline," was often called the first permanent woman resident of Phoenix. This designation, of course, ignores the equal claim of Mary Green.

Gray enters the Goldwater saga because in early 1872 he started construction of a building at the northwest corner of what are now Jefferson and First streets in Phoenix. It was intended as a two-story Masonic Hall, but Mike Goldwater bought it from Gray during construction and decided to limit it to one story for his purpose. The exact amount Mike paid Gray for the uncompleted building and lots has not been established, but in later years Morris told Barry Goldwater they got the property for one hundred twenty dollars.

The Goldwater buildings, one adobe fifty feet by twenty-five feet and another adjoining it measuring fifty by sixteen feet, were completed by Thanksgiving Day, 1872. They were a bit classier than other new structures in the village because they had wooden floors and shingled roofs.

One could not open a new building in the Phoenix of 1872 without a "housewarming" party, so the Goldwaters planned one of the most elaborate yet held. They called on a local impressario, W. H. Pope, to plan a big dance in the new building, and Pope accepted the assignment with great enthusiasm. He learned that the second recorded marriage of Anglo-Americans in the Salt River Valley was soon to take place, so he arranged to have the wedding reception as part of the open house.

The *Miner* of December 7, 1872, tells the story of this gala:

In this [just completed] building a grand ball was given by W. H. Pope, on Wednesday evening last [Nov. 27] largely attended by the ladies and gentlemen of Phoenix and vicinity, by Mrs. Moore, Miss Mary E. Moore, Charles H. Kenyon and lady [the bride and groom], L. W. Carr and Cria Taylor, all from Maricopa Wells; T. W. McIntosh and lady from the Gila, and a number of gentlemen from [Fort] McDowell. The music by the Fifth Cavalry Band was extremely good . . .

Dancing was kept up all night, and the whole passed off very pleasantly. Thanks are due to Mr. Pope for his untiring energy . . . Mr. Kenyon, looking the picture of happiness, was pronounced the luckiest man living.

On December 11, the Goldwater store opened for business. Unfortunately, no records of that Phoenix enterprise have been preserved, but we can determine from records of shipments from Ehrenberg what the stock was like. There were pants and shirts, garters and hair nets, candles and harness, along with shovels, axes, plows, and every other pioneer necessity.

The first J. Goldwater and Bro. advertisement in the Prescott *Miner* (Phoenix had no newspaper as yet) ran for months unchanged:

J. Goldwater & Bro.

Have on hand a large & complete stock of general merchandise, comprising everything required in a farming country, and which they will sell at the lowest possible prices. Highest prices paid for grain.

Goldwater's advertising department in later years prepared more attractive ads, but this one did the job and told the story.

The community of Phoenix had been in official existence only two years when the Goldwaters opened their first branch store there, but it had made rapid strides. According to historian Thomas E. Farish, the town, with fifteen saloons doing business in the summer of 1872, was prepared for raging thirsts. Gambling was flourishing at the Capitol House saloon on Washington Street. There already was a brewery in operation, several livery stables and blacksmith shops, and a Chinese laundry.

Six raw general merchandise stores were operating when the Goldwaters opened their doors. But energetic little Morris Goldwater was confident of his ability to offer a better assortment of merchandise at lower prices than his competition. Joe returned to Ehrenberg soon after the opening of the new store, and Mike was busy with freighting, wholesaling, and selling grain to the army.

One of the main reasons the Goldwaters had opened their Phoenix branch was to be close to the rapidly expanding ranches of the Salt River

Valley. Mike was so sure that he could purchase at least half of the valley's barley crop that he entered a bid for supplying 2.5 million pounds to the army in 1873.

He did not get that contract, but with Morris's help he did win a hefty contract for supplying beans to three army posts. It was a highly satisfying achievement for young Morris, who had done most of the negotiating, because it was the first major transaction he had handled since becoming a junior partner.

The story of the first telegraph office in Phoenix is treasured by the Goldwater family and by Arizona historians as well.

Congress had appropriated $50,311 in the spring of 1873 to construct a military telegraph line from San Diego to Prescott and Tucson, also serving Yuma and Maricopa Wells. Phoenix, it must be noted, was not considered important enough to be included.

To our generation, sated with stories of Pentagon cost over-runs, it may come as a shock that the contractors completed the line on time, added a supplementary line to serve Florence in Pinal County, and still had $5,000 of the appropriated $50,311 left at the finish.

Morris later explained to Arizona historian James McClintock how he had managed to change army orders and get the line run through Phoenix—and, incidentally, right into the new Goldwater store:

> Capt. [George F.] Price and R. R. Raines, who were building the line, stopped overnight with me. I asked them why they did not run the line through Phoenix. I offered to donate a set of instruments, and promised them office room.

Morris made still another offer: He would serve as operator at the Phoenix office with no pay. It was an offer the army could not refuse.

Obviously, Morris had been preparing for this opportunity. He had learned something about telegraphy while he was living in San Francisco, and probably had learned Morse code there as well. He sent to San Francisco for the telegraph instruments he would need, and was then ready to sell the army on adding the unscheduled Phoenix office.

Rapid communication had long been one of Morris's hobbies. He solved the problem of how to run a telegraph office and a store at the same time in this ingenious fashion: He devised a receiving set that would cut dots and dashes into strips of paper—much like modern teletype technology—so that the message would be recorded on paper when it arrived. He would then transcribe it for delivery the next time he had a spare moment.

The telegraph line was completed on December 2, 1873, and Morris sat poised to tap out the first message ever wired from Phoenix to Tucson:

Phoenix, A. T.
Dec. 2, 1873

Chairman, Board of Supervisors
Tucson, A. T.

Maricopa County congratulates Pima County on the connection by
telegraph. Let evil doers tremble.

C. H. Gray, Chairman
Board of Supervisors

Someone down the line apparently was not aware that Phoenix had
been added to the list of stations. Even before Morris had finished sending
that historic telegram, someone broke in with these equally historic words:
"Get the hell off the line!"

Shrewd Morris Goldwater, of course, had recognized that having a
telegraph office in his store could be a great advantage in those days of
spotty communication. All the news of army procurement would come to
him first, in addition to orders of competitors and a wealth of other
business information.

The town of Phoenix was so overjoyed to have telegraph service,
however, that nobody complained, at least at first. Instead there was a
joyous celebration when the line of poles reached the center of town. As
reported in the *Arizona Miner,*

> The advent into Phoenix was duly celebrated on Saturday evening
> last by raising the pole alongside the store of Joseph Goldwater &
> Bro., corner of Montezuma [First St.] and Jefferson, at which the
> telegraph office is to be.
>
> Sheriff Hayes deposited a Mexican coin under the pole, Judge J. A.
> Rush made an appropriate speech, and three cheers were given for
> General Crook and the Army. Mr. Johnson then spilled some gin, not
> on the pole, but in the irrigating canals . . . Messrs. Cotton, Hayes &
> Lovejoy and others invited the boys to drink to the occasion at their
> expense.

Morris operated the Phoenix telegraph office for nine months. Then he
took back his telegraph key and associated equipment, and later presented
them to the Sharlot Hall Museum in Prescott, where they may be seen
today.

Running a store, investing, and contracting with the federal government
did not use up all of Morris Goldwater's boundless energy. He was developing a hunger for public office, too. He already had served as deputy clerk of
the District Court of Maricopa County during 1873. It was a part-time job,

but it gave Morris his first real look at legal procedures and records.

In the fall of 1874, although he was only twenty-two, he was nominated by the county Democratic convention to run for the House of Representatives in the Eighth Territorial Assembly. His running mate for the two seats was the well-known Winchester Miller of Tempe.

When the votes were in, Morris had tied with Republican William Long for the second highest vote count (Judge John Alsap, the House speaker, topped the voting). Miller, surprisingly, was eliminated.

Under the procedures of that time, the Democrats had the option of substituting a candidate in the runoff election. They persuaded Granville Oury, once Arizona's representative to the Confederate Congress, to run, and Morris graciously stepped aside. Oury captured the vote of most Southerners in the county and beat out Long for the other House seat.

So Morris Goldwater avoided defeat in his first election, but he didn't win either. His vote-getting ability had impressed everyone, however, and he was ready to try again.

And again, and again, as Arizona history was to reveal.

The year 1874 was a banner year for Goldwater political candidacies. In Yuma County, Mike Goldwater was reluctantly persuaded to run for the Council (Senate) in the Eighth Territorial Assembly. Only one candidate could be elected in this race, and the favorite was an Arizona City (Yuma) resident named José Maria Redondo. Mike did not bother to campaign, and even refused to place the usual "announcement of candidacy" card in the Yuma *Arizona Sentinel.* So it was little wonder that the voters elected Redondo to the Council with two hundred twelve votes to Goldwater's one hundred seventy-four.

That same fall, Joe Goldwater entered the political wars, running for school trustee in District Two of Yuma County. He led all vote-getters with one hundred fifteen ballots.

Even in nominally non-partisan races, it may be noted that the Goldwaters usually leaned in the Democratic direction. Later, Morris was to be a prime mover in the organization of the Arizona Democratic Party and to hold high office in the territory and the state. (One may wonder why Barry Goldwater, who learned his political theory at Uncle Morris's knee, later embraced the Republican Party and became its nominee for President of the United States. But the cornerstone of Barry's political philosophy—free enterprise, limited government, individual responsibility, a militarily strong America—were Morris's beliefs, too.)

Arizona Territory was heavily Democratic for several reasons: the large number of settlers from Confederate states, who hated Republicans with a passion; increasing impatience with the territorial governors sent by Republican administrations; the free-silver issue; and the perception that

Republicans were alien easterners—big city financiers and business tycoons—who did not understand the problems of a struggling Arizona pioneer.

Mike and Joe Goldwater, who had done their share to start new towns, were assisted in 1875 by youthful Morris Goldwater in doing their bit to help Phoenix take root in the Salt River Valley.

The *Miner* of January 8, 1875, published this optimistic note about the Goldwater store in Phoenix:

> New Year's is over and people in the valley are turning their attention strictly to business again. In town Mr. Goldwater has opened with a splendid assortment of dry goods and hardware . . .

The reference to dry goods at the Goldwater store reflected Morris's attempt to upgrade the store to new levels of sophistication. As his brother Baron would do twenty years later, he introduced some fashionable women's wear to the Goldwater line.

But he was ahead of his time. Phoenix was not yet ready for such a store, and Morris found his efforts to no avail. The Phoenix experiment was not exactly a failure, but it wasn't a great success, either.

Mike came to Phoenix in April 1875, and together they began the sorrowful procedures of selling out. By now, Mike had amicably dissolved his partnership in the freighting business with Dr. W. W. Jones. Jones was pursuing other money-making schemes, and Mike was increasingly teaming with his son Morris in government contracting and hauling.

The Ehrenberg store seemed to be on a plateau, with no real growth in prospect. The restless Goldwaters began looking around for new business worlds to conquer. There were lots of possibilities for young men with ambition and perhaps a little capital to get started. Mining was becoming profitable again, both in the Wickenburg area and in the Bradshaw Mountains. Prescott, growing steadily and battling to get the territorial capital back from Tucson, offered promise for a branch store. Parker, in Yuma County on the Colorado River, needed a good merchandiser.

What was even more intriguing was the chance to get in on the ground floor of a new stage line being organized to transport passengers and merchandise throughout Arizona. So the Phoenix branch store had been a disappointment. Mike, Joe, and Morris were undismayed as they looked over the exciting possibilities on other fronts. Which offered the best hope of money-making success?

To be certain that they didn't miss a good one, the Goldwaters soon involved themselves in all of them.

6

Success at Last

The friendly little city of Prescott, Arizona has often been called "everybody's hometown."

It's a beautiful town, surrounded by pine forests and lofty mountains, and its mile-high altitude gives Prescott a climate that's cool all summer and not too cold in winter. Arizona history is evident all over town, from the reconstructed 1864 Governor's Mansion to the venerable courthouse square and the delightful Victorian homes on Nob Hill and along Mount Vernon Street. The first enduring capital of Arizona Territory is a treasure house for those who want to know more about Arizona's past.

In a very special sense, Prescott is Barry Goldwater's hometown. His grandfather was one of the early settlers here, and the Goldwater store was an institution for eight decades. Barry's Uncle Morris was mayor for twenty years, and his father, Baron, got his start as a merchant in this historic community.

Barry loved the town as a boy, and he later operated the Goldwater store in Prescott for a time. He joined the Smoki People and helped them recreate the Indian tribal dances at an annual festival. He tramped the nearby woods and canyons, and made friends with many of the pioneers who helped build Arizona.

In 1952, when he made his first major political venture, he launched his campaign from the steps of the Yavapai County courthouse in Prescott. And when he ran for President in 1964, he started that campaign from those same courthouse steps.

Prescott is very special to Barry Goldwater, and his family has played vital roles in the city's development for more than a century. For Mike Goldwater, it was the promised land, the town where he finally found success after so many business failures.

PRESCOTT, 1876

THE MARKED GROWTH IN ARIZONA SETTLEMENT AFTER 1875 AND THE FOUNDING of new towns in many parts of the Territory can be attributed largely to General George Crook's success in subduing the marauding Apaches. Although Indian depredations would not be completely stamped out for another decade to come, it was now considerably safer to farm and mine and do business on the Arizona frontier.

The increased safety of travel over Arizona roads encouraged young Charles Wells to make the gamble of his life—the launching of the Arizona and New Mexico Express Co. Wells, the son of Wells-Fargo express founder Henry Wells, was tired of living in the shadow of a famous father and determined to make a name for himself.

Wells had his father's blessing, but little financial support. He needed some sympathetic suppliers who were willing to risk their money and time in an investment that could prove to be a big winner. He found one in Morris Goldwater.

With the Phoenix store closed, Morris returned to Ehrenberg in the fall of 1875 to devote his time to building up the retail and wholesale businesses there. Joe was spending much of his time in San Francisco at this point, possibly because of Ellen's delicate health and her continuing worry about her husband's safety in Arizona. Mike was on the road a lot, so Morris was left in charge at Ehrenberg.

When Wells approached him about participating in the new express line, Morris offered his help with characteristic enthusiasm.

Long before the first stagecoach of the Arizona and New Mexico Express was ready to roll, Goldwater's had advanced credit to Wells for hay, grain, axes, firewood, leather, blankets, pitchforks, whips, and many other items. Goldwater employees helped dig wells and put up corrals.

Mike and Joe looked on a little nervously as the investment mounted, but Morris assured them that the Goldwater money was safe.

The Goldwater store at Ehrenberg was designated as one of the principal stops on the new line, which accepted its first passengers on January 29, 1876. Morris sold passenger tickets, accepted express, and did all he could to promote the new venture.

But the Arizona and New Mexico Express was born to bad luck. Just before the first stage left Tucson, the firm experienced its first shocking setback: J. G. Phillips, the Tucson agent, inexplicably killed himself. Not long thereafter, a fire (some suspected arson) at Tom Goodman's corral at Ehrenberg burned to death six of the express company's horses.

As revenues sagged below expenses, Wells cut costs and delayed paying his bills. He even took off the man who "rode shotgun" on the stages, a risky move in Arizona in that era.

Morris did not press for payment of Wells's soaring account with J. Goldwater and Bro. By June, the overdue balance pushed past seven hundred dollars.

There was nothing Mike or Joe could do to salvage the situation. On July 15, 1876, the *Arizona Daily Star* of Tucson told the grim story:

> The Arizona and New Mexico Express has exploded and "gone where the woodbine twineth." Too much splurge and lavish expenditures without understanding the country or its requirements.

The Goldwaters must have had a derisive laugh about those "lavish expenditures," none of which were ever made to Wells's best supporter, J. Goldwater and Bro.

Young Wells went home, tail figuratively between his legs, to explain to his father what had gone wrong. His Arizona creditors were never able to locate him thereafter.

Another chastened son, Morris Goldwater, had his self-confidence severely shaken by this second evidence of managerial misjudgment within a year.

As early as 1874, Mike Goldwater had cast covetous eyes on various business locations in Prescott. The *Miner* had reported on February 13 of that year that:

> Mr. M. Goldwater has his eye on a lot for a store which he designs [*sic*] to be erecting here this spring.

But the poor business conditions in the territory that year and funding of several other Goldwater enterprises during that period prevented him from pursuing the Prescott matter further.

Although Mike was not technically a resident of the self-styled "Jewel of Yavapai," he had been a regular visitor to Prescott almost from the founding of the town, a decade before. Undoubtedly, he had more friends there than anywhere else in the Territory.

Until 1876, however, business prospects in new settlements had always seemed more enticing than going into competition with the established firms in Arizona's second largest community. But now it was time for another look at Prescott. Mike was fifty-five (an advanced age on the frontier) and was often referred to in newspaper articles as "the old gentleman." He had suffered a shattered kneecap in a freighting mishap and would eventually get about with the aid of a cane. (In later years, his daughter Carrie told her children that Mike suffered this disabling injury in some sort of attack on his wagons.)

In June of 1876, Mike was in Prescott to look seriously for a place to start another Goldwater branch. He loved the climate of the mountain town, saying that it reminded him of his youthful days at Sonora, and he hoped to settle down in a civilized place for his remaining working years.

Frontier culture flourished in Prescott—music, dramatics, schools, books—and some of the best-educated citizens of the Territory made their homes here. In Prescott, as in few other communities of Arizona in 1876, a man could *live* and not merely exist.

During his June visit, Mike noted that blacksmith James Howey was erecting a two-story brick building on the southeast corner of Cortez and Goodwin streets, across from the town square. It was rushed to near-completion in time to house the town's big Fourth of July celebration, which marked the nation's one hundredth birthday. For the next forty years and more, Prescott would hold many of its biggest social events in the second-story banquet and ballroom of Howey Hall. Mike saw the building as a natural for his proposed general merchandise store, and soon after the Fourth of July, made a deal with Howey.

Mike left Arizona briefly during early fall for a very special trip to San Francisco. Carrie—Sarah and Mike's firstborn—was getting married to a young Jewish businessman named Philip Aronson. When Mike returned to Prescott, preparations were nearly completed for the mid-October opening of the new store. Apparently it was an eagerly awaited event, according to the October 23 *Whipple News* of the nearby Army post:

> It is hoped that the efforts of J. Goldwater and Bro., our new merchants, will soon put an end to some extent to the extortion inflicted upon the helpless people who are forced to make their necessary purchases in Prescott. . . .
>
> It is a fact well known that the prices put upon goods by merchants of this place are outrageous. . . .

On December 14, Morris arrived by stagecoach with his younger brother Sam. There was bad news for the Goldwaters that day: the steamer *Montana* had burned in the Gulf of California en route to the Colorado River. Destroyed in the tragedy were two hundred sixty-seven boxes of merchandise owned by the Goldwaters and destined for Ehrenberg and Prescott. Mike, already financially pressed to start the new store, could ill-afford this new calamity.

But father and sons shook it off, as they had so many other previous setbacks. They were together again, the new store looked promising, and optimism reigned.

Goldwater's new store tried valiantly to serve its varied clientele, from seldom-bathed prospectors to the fashion-conscious wives of army officers and professional men. Morris started an account book on December

14, 1876, and saved it so that future generations could see what sort of business a pioneering store did in that era. His first entry was a sale of one hundred cigars to Joe Crane, owner of the Diana Saloon on Montezuma Street. The second was a box of window glass to Valentine and Windes. Windes was the Rev. Romulus A. Windes, pastor of Prescott's first established Baptist Church and later a Baptist pastor and businessman in Tempe.

Joseph Ehle bought spices for a New Year's cake and "Doc" L. A. Moeller bought some carpet for his house. Kelly and Stephens, news dealers and general merchants, had a snobbish clientele. They bought from Goldwater's five hundred Vanity Fair cigarettes, which nobody but the wealthy and bordello girls smoked. The cowboys and miners on Whiskey Row rolled their own, and most businessmen chose cigars.

Speaking of the bordello girls, it must be noted that "Rosa" quite frequently purchased cases of champagne at forty dollars per case for her customers. She also bought a fancy chamber set for twenty-five dollars. Many of the girls had charge accounts at Goldwater's, and their purchases of fancy clothes are recorded under the names "Miss Nellie," "Miss Katie," "Miss Willie," and others.

The store carried jewelry, toilet articles, perfumes, pocket cutlery, ladies' hats and clothing, tinware, glass, clocks, boots, canned goods, stationery, tobaccos, hardware, paints, farm implements, mining supplies, and almost anything else a pioneer Arizonan could desire.

The store dealt in Yavapai County warrants, too. On July 5, 1877, Goldwater's sold warrants for eight hundred ninety dollars that they had bought just a week before for eight hundred two dollars. Such quick profits made up for spending an hour to make a two dollar sale, and helped equalize the losses from too-generous credit.

Some of the Goldwater losses were more dramatic, such as the one thousand, seven hundred dollars stolen in a stage robbery in early March 1877. With the Indians fairly well under control, masked white men took over the job of making the stage drivers' lives miserable.

United States currency (greenbacks), which had been discounted as much as twenty-five percent a few years earlier, now had regained respect and was discounted at the Goldwater store by only five percent. The store accepted bales of them, along with gold dust, silver, U.S. and Mexican gold coins—and even quicksilver.

In those days, you took your money any way you found it.

Joe Goldwater had not been in Prescott since mid-1872, when he nearly lost his life in an Indian ambush. He had been busy at Ehrenberg, at Parker, and in San Francisco, where we may suppose he was taking care of his wife, Ellen, during an extended illness.

He was in San Francisco in February 1877 as Ellen's illness rapidly worsened. She and Joe had never been very close to the Mike Goldwater family in San Francisco, but surprisingly, they named their only daughter "Sarah." Now there were three young children—Lemuel, Sarah, and Harry—to care for. On February 23, 1877, only two weeks before her fortieth birthday, Ellen died.

Back in Prescott, Mike and Morris were wasting no time establishing themselves in the community. One of the civic groups joined was the Masonic Lodge. Mike had joined the Masons more than two decades before at Sonora, and Morris was anxious to do the same in Prescott. Records of the Prescott lodge show that Morris, then twenty-five, was initiated on February 28, 1877, "passed" on March 14, and "raised" a month later. Both he and Mike became officially affiliated with the Prescott lodge on May 26. On that May evening, in the rooms over the Diana Saloon (now the St. Michael's Hotel at Gurley and Montezuma), Morris Goldwater began six decades of Masonic service that would make him the patriarch of the Arizona lodge.

By early 1877, business was in the doldrums in Prescott but there were those who were predicting that a boom was just around the corner. Machinations were under way in the state legislature at Tucson to spirit the territorial capital back to the pine-scented Mile-High City.

General August Kautz of Fort Whipple, apparently one of those supporting the move, noted in his diary on February 7, 1877, that

> the Tucson people are in a very irritable condition over the loss of the
> capital and are making fools of themselves.

After serving for ten years as the seat of Arizona government, Tucson was indeed irritable over this disastrous setback. Even the consolation of the approaching Southern Pacific Railroad tracks, and attendant prosperity, could not ease the humiliation of the capital move.

For a dozen years, until the growth of the Salt River Valley made the establishment of the capital at Phoenix in 1889 a foregone conclusion, the "Jewel of Yavapai" was also the jewel of Arizona Territory.

As they so often did, the Goldwaters had come to the right town at the right time. Prescott was on the move, and the Goldwaters were eager to be at the head of the parade.

There was nothing but optimism in the progressive mountain town of Prescott. Mike accepted a place on the board of directors of the Prescott Dramatic Society, an enthusiastic band of thespians who staged "East

Lynne" and other melodramas of the period with commendable elan. Mike was not an actor or particularly interested in the theater, but he was in demand as a director because he had a store and would extend generous credit to the Dramatic Society when it needed stage props.

Morris was the rising star of the territorial capital. Energetic, personable, and community-minded, he was on his way to the highest honors the town could bestow.

In September 1878, he was chosen to serve on the committee in charge of welcoming perhaps the most distinguished visitor Prescott had ever hosted: General William Tecumseh Sherman, then commanding general of the United States Army.

Although the many former Rebels in the community were up in arms about the impending visit of "the beast who raped Georgia," the town was determined to show Sherman its very best face.

Only a week later, Prescott welcomed still another famous hero, General John Charles Fremont. The weary old Pathfinder and first Republican presidential candidate had been appointed by President Rutherford B. Hayes to succeed John Hoyt as governor of Arizona Territory.

Gen. Sherman met Governor Fremont in Los Angeles just before the latter departed for Prescott, warning him of the terrible roads and the crude facilities of the territorial capital. So Fremont entered the Territory warily and with a half-formed determination to absent himself from Arizona as often as possible. History shows that Fremont made good on that resolution.

Morris was entrusted with arranging for carriages to transport the celebrities to and from the gala reception and ball for the new governor. In addition, he was on the invitations committee and helped make provision for decorations, as well. Goldwater's provided the wine for the reception, and the bill is recorded in Morris's ledger: one hundred sixteen dollars.

Already Morris was becoming one of Prescott's most familiar figures, a dapper young man whose spectacular mustache more than made up for his lack of stature. He was making friends in high places, and convincing everyone, from Governor Fremont on down, that he was a man to be reckoned with in the future.

As early as a dozen years before, Mike Goldwater had eyed with interest the lots at the corner of Union and Cortez streets in Prescott. When the townsite was laid out, the planners foresaw two fine governmental squares—one for county buildings in the area now occupied by the Yavapai County Courthouse, and the other a block to the east, where territorial capitol buildings were to be erected. Mike reasoned that Union Street, connecting the two town squares, could become the busiest thoroughfare in Arizona.

But that was before 1867, when Tucson mustered enough votes to take the capital away. In the ensuing decade, apparently despairing of being the Arizona capital again, Prescott had sold the Capitol Block to private citizens who built small rental houses on the property.

Then came 1877, the recapturing of the territorial capital, and new blossoming of Prescott's hopes for a capitol square. The city sued to regain title to the square, and many dreamed of an imposing government structure—perhaps with a dome like the one in Washington—in the booming town.

The *Miner* revealed on December 20, 1878, that young Morris Goldwater not only was nursing ambitions in Prescott town politics, but that some thought he was ready for the top spot on the ticket:

> Morris Goldwater has concluded to allow his name to be used in connection with the mayorality at the election in January. Morris has the ability to make an excellent "city dad."

That same edition of the paper carried an even more definite statement of Morris's determination to go for it all in his first bid for Prescott political office:

> At a meeting of the citizens held Monday evening, the following were unanimously nominated for the ensuing election: For Mayor— Morris Goldwater. . . .

Morris was opposed by a popular Prescott businessman, sawmill operator George W. Curtis. Because the incumbent mayor had declined to seek reelection, both felt they had a good chance to win. But Curtis proved to be no match for Morris Goldwater as a vote-getter. The final returns of the January election told the story clearly: Goldwater, 208; Curtis, 114.

Elected with him as town councilmen were Dan Thorne and James Daly, two popular saloon keepers on Whiskey Row. James Dodson was elected town marshal. Dodson numbered among his best friends a young fellow named Virgil Earp, who had failed in his bid to be Prescott's night watchman and so drifted south to Tombstone to join his brother, Wyatt, in an excursion into immortality—the 1881 gunfight at the OK corral.

Morris apparently was acquainted with the whole Earp clan. In a letter to Bert Fireman written seventy-five years later, Senator Henry Ashurst recalled that

> during our 1879 trip to Prescott, I was five years of age, but I well remember Mr. Morris Goldwater and the Goldwater store. . . . I recall

that Morris Goldwater there introduced my parents to General John C. Fremont, Governor of Arizona Territory, and introduced both my father and me to Wyatt Earp and to Wyatt's brothers, Virgil and James, and also to Doc Holliday. They were all in a two-hitch wagon train passing through Prescott en route to Tombstone, which was just beginning to boom.

During Morris's brief campaign for the office of Prescott mayor, his father was busy creating Arizona's first official lottery.

Now that plans were moving for the new store on Union Street, Mike's thoughts turned often to Prescott's Capitol Block just east of the store building. If there was to be an imposing territorial government structure on that block, a lot of money was needed in a relatively short time to get the project moving.

A group of influential Prescott businessmen met to discuss the matter, and before the meeting was over, the Arizona Development Company had been born.

The company had grandiose goals. In addition to raising money for capitol buildings, it proposed to develop toll roads, electric lighting companies, water works, telegraph lines, and more. It was to be capitalized for five million dollars in one hundred thousand shares of fifty dollars each.

It was generally rumored that Governor Fremont not only favored the development plan, but was a moving force behind it. And in the shadows was lawyer Tom Fitch, who readily admitted to being Fremont's best friend in Arizona and exercised alarming power over the Fremont administration.

Fitch, it was commonly believed, persuaded Council President Fred Hughes of Pima County to introduce Council Bill no. 20, "An Act to aid in the construction of Capitol Buildings and for the support of Public Schools in the Territory of Arizona."

What that innocent-sounding bill really did, however, was to establish a public lottery in the territory. The governor was appointed lottery commissioner, and would receive one hundred dollars for each drawing, to be paid by the Arizona Development Company; the bill directed that ten percent would be collected from all prize money for the capitol and school funds. For the first two years, all such money would go to the capitol fund.

It was that simple. The young territory could not afford capitol buildings and other modern improvements, so the money would be raised in one quick effort by offering a sporting chance to Arizonans, who were famous for gambling on almost everything.

"Poker for the public good!" somebody called it, and the phrase caught on.

On March 1 the first newspaper advertisements were placed in journals all around the Territory:

Arizona Lottery
Under the direction of
Governor John C. Fremont
Territorial Commissioner
Michael Goldwater .... President
Bank of Arizona .... Treasurer
In accordance with an act of the Legislative Assembly
of Arizona Territory, and the Proclamation of the
Governor issued thereunder a
Lottery
will be drawn at Prescott, A.T., Wednesday, June 4, 1879.

In his official proclamation, Governor Fremont specified that "the Theatre in Prescott" would be the place where the drawing would be held.

Ticket prices were to be five dollars for a whole ticket, two dollars and fifty cents for a half ticket, and one dollar and twenty-five cents for a quarter ticket. Thus four persons might pool one dollar and twenty-five cents each and buy one chance for the total prize money of thirty-one thousand, two hundred fifty dollars.

The top prize was to be ten thousand dollars and the second prize two thousand dollars. Other prizes ranged downward to ten dollars, of which there were to be one hundred. An elaborate procedure for drawing the winning numbers was publicized: twelve thousand slips of leather numbered consecutively and displayed in a large glass wheel to be sealed by the governor himself.

To guarantee that the plan was fraud-proof, the Arizona Development Company posted a twenty thousand dollar bond with the Territorial Treasurer, and the Arizona Bank was designated to handle all income and approve any necessary expenditures.

Mike Goldwater's breast swelled with justifiable pride. Here he was, elected by his fellow incorporators as president of the Arizona Development Company, and entrusted to run this grand new experiment in public financing. He was a confidant of the nationally famous Governor Fremont, his name was splashed across the pages of every newspaper in the Territory, his business was prospering, and his son Morris was Prescott's newly elected mayor. Surely his cup was running over.

Into each life, they say, some rain must fall. For Mike Goldwater, the year 1879-1880 was one long, drenching monsoon.

It started when the ill-conceived lottery scheme fell into disrepute in

April. What had begun as a triumphant march toward popular acclaim soon caused Mike to retreat ignominiously amidst a hail of hostile fire.

One of the glaring faults of the lottery, of course, was that the Territory was to receive only ten percent of the prize money for the construction of capitol buildings and support of schools. There was a nagging question: How much of the total take was to go to prizes and how much to the Arizona Development Company?

One irate newspaper editor claimed that the company and its incorporators would skim off at least forty percent of the total take. Apparently the plan did have some built-in profits for the incorporators after advertising and other expenses were paid. Mike admitted as much in a letter to the *Arizona Enterprise,* declaring that

> Charley Beach (of the *Miner*) hints that I am getting richer and the people poorer by this lottery. The profits which I have made or may make out of the Arizona Lottery I am ready at any moment to turn over to any benevolent institution in Yavapai County. . . .

Still another seed of the lottery's destruction was the involvement of Governor John C. Fremont and his shadowy cohort, Tom Fitch. Newspapers of Democratic persuasion were out to harpoon Republican Fremont no matter what he did, and they were quick to portray Fitch as a shifty conniver bent only on robbing the public treasury.

It was naive Mike Goldwater's ill-fortune to find himself tarred with the same brush that blackened the reputations of Fremont and Fitch.

Fitch made himself mysteriously scarce when public opinion turned, and the governor left for an extended trip to Washington and the Northeast. That left Mike to take the abuse almost alone through the days of spring and early summer.

Perhaps his most infuriating detractor was James Reilly, fire-eating editor of the short-lived Yuma *Expositor,* who had been against the lottery from the beginning and had even refused the fifty dollars sent him by the Arizona Development Company to cover costs of the first advertisements. Reilly said the lottery caused a "stink in the nostrils of honest men" and ridiculed Arizona Development's efforts, saying that "Arizona people just will not 'develop' worth a cent."

Mike was especially grieved that his old friend Charley Beach of the *Miner* had turned against him in his hour of distress. Beach not only blasted the concept of the lottery, but cast aspersions on the honesty of the men who were involved in operating it.

Mike read Beach's diatribes and angrily withdrew all of Goldwater's advertising from the *Miner* for some three months. The two pioneers crossed the street to avoid each other, and all Prescott watched in apprehension to see how this alienation of two old friends would turn out.

Sales of lottery tickets went well only for the first two or three weeks, or until the newspaper reaction set in. From then on, Arizonans kept their hard-earned money in their pockets. Tucson, one of the areas the promoters had depended on the most, was almost totally hostile to the lottery and the proposed capitol buidings in Prescott. Only a handful of tickets were sold, and the revenue did not nearly match the expense of advertising in Tucson newspapers.

John P. Clum, editor of the *Arizona Citizen* of Tucson, warned Mike to get out of the lottery mess before it engulfed him:

> We are assured by many that Mr. Goldwater is an honorable man; yet if he gets into an unpleasant and unprofitable controversy over the miserable and wrongly conceived lottery business, he will, we feel sure, admit that punishment is not altogether undeserved.

By mid-May, it was obvious to the officers of the Arizona Development Company that they were headed for disaster. Only a few hundred dollars had come into the till from ticket sales, and they were faced with awarding $31,250 in prizes on the fourth of June.

They should have come forward immediately with an admission of failure, returned the money and called the whole thing off. But they hoped for some miracle to save the day. They rushed this advertisement to newspapers around the Territory:

The Lottery heretofore advertised to take place
June 4th, 1879, is hereby postponed until
August 4th, 1879

To be then held at the same place and drawn in the same manner heretofore announced.

ALL TICKET HOLDERS

Desiring to do so may surrender their tickets to J. GOLDWATER & BRO., Prescott, Arizona Territory, and will thereupon receive full cash value for the same.

Mike hoped this generous gesture—offering to refund the money to anybody who wanted it—would end the storm of invective. But it only made it worse. Editor Reilly of the *Expositor* leaped upon it like a wolf on a wounded lamb:

The Secret Out

So that frantic rush for lottery tickets, reported in nearly all the "respectable"newspapers of the Territory, was all a fiction—we might say a deliberate falsehood. They say the sale of tickets amounted to only $6,000. We will bet our last shirt and longest Faber pencil against the *Miner's* best mule team that the sale didn't amount to $600, and if we did not offer such large odds, we would say $60 and feel sure to win. . . .

Hurt and infuriated, Mike burned the coal oil lamp late at night to find some face-saving solution. He did not have to look long, because the U.S. Postmaster General, D. M. Key, put an end to the lottery in early July with an announcement declaring it illegal and forbidding any use of the mails to carry it on.

And so the great Arizona Lottery plan, born in rosy optimism and buried in shame eight months later, passed into history. The Eleventh Territorial Assembly quietly repealed the lottery legislation passed by its predecessor.

Not for more than a century would another lottery scheme win its way through the Arizona Legislature.

How many tickets were actually sold in 1879? People speculated about that for many months, but today we know. Editor Reilly's guess was closer to the actual figure than he could have imagined.

The last entry in Goldwater's ledger, made on June 4, 1879, shows that one hundred thirty-eight tickets had been sold, for a cash total of six hundred ninety dollars.

That troubled early summer of 1879 brought two welcome visitors to Prescott: Mike's brother Joe and his daughter Annie.

Joe had not come to Prescott since the near-fatal ambush of seven years before. He had been in San Francisco, in Ehrenberg and Parker, occasionally out of touch for long periods. Mike found him somehow changed— restless, rootless, looking for some meaning to his life to replace his lost Ellen.

Annie, first of the Goldwater women to venture into the wilds of Arizona, stayed in Prescott just a few weeks and was only too glad to return to San Francisco to reinforce her mother's opinion that Arizona was no fit place for a civilized lady.

With all his other worries, Mike did not need nagging family problems. But Joe's visit reopened the question of how this unhappy younger brother was to be accommodated in the changing Goldwater business. In the old days, before Mike's sons had come of age, Joe's place was secure. But now Henry was running the Ehrenberg store, Morris and Sam were in the Prescott business, and there was no apparent place for Joe.

Mike could almost hear Sarah's voice, rising in pitch during his most recent visit to San Francisco, demanding that he break things off cleanly with "that shifty-eyed brother of yours," who had been drinking more than was good for him, and make the business strictly a venture of Mike Goldwater and his sons.

And so he took the painful step.

The *Miner* of Tuesday, May 18, 1880, carried this advertisement:

Notice of Dissolution

Notice is hereby given that the firm of J. GOLDWATER & BROTHER has this day been dissolved by mutual consent, the said J. Goldwater retiring from the said firm. The business will hereafter be conducted under the firm name and style of MICHAEL GOLDWATER & SON; who, by the terms of said dissolution have assumed all the liabilities and succeeded to all the assets of the said late firm of J. Goldwater and Brother.

Joe and Mike, who had been off-and-on partners since they first opened the saloon at Sonora in 1853, now went their separate ways, never to join in business again.

Joe took his share of the business in cash and drifted off to other things, in San Francisco, Yuma, Bisbee, Benson, Tombstone, Fairbank, and points south. As always, his accursed luck went with him.

Busy as Morris Goldwater was with his mayoral duties and planning for the new store, he took time to sit down with two sheets of lined paper to write a letter to his youngest brother, Baron, in San Francisco. Baron had grown up seeing his father only on rare occasions. Morris could remember too well how he, himself, had longed for his father's companionship and guidance, and he must have felt a kind of paternal affection for Baron, fourteen years younger than he.

The occasion for the letter was Baron's thirteenth birthday, his religious coming of age. Because of its warmth and its insights into Morris's character, Baron preserved and treasured the letter:

Prescott, May 8th, 1879

Mr. Baron Goldwater

My dear brother

Although not too well versed in Jewish theology, I know that there is a special importance attached to one's thirteenth birthday among our people.

It is with pleasure that I congratulate you on having attained this your religious majority. I trust that the years which will pass, ere you can claim to have arrived at man's estate, may prove as free from care and trouble as those through which you have come.

If on that day you can on looking back to the present time, find as little to reproach yourself with as you can find by a retrospection of the past, you will indeed have past a most praise worthy life. It is such a consummation that I trust awaits you, but it is not without great effort on your part that this can be achieved.

I am sorry that from my own experience I can not give you rules that would safely guide you to this much to be desired goal. But I am too well aware of my own defects to think that I could do aught than serve as a buoy on your course to mark some shoal to be avoided.

Nor do I wish to throw you a string of maxims cut from some Poor Richard's Almanac which may be read, thrown aside and never (for some reason or other) be acted upon.

Obedience to your parents and a careful selection of your companions are the only rules which I would urge on you. By a strict attention to these you cannot help being polite, temperate, truthful and industrious, and possessing these virtues you will have all that the world can give of any worth.

It is because I have so strong a belief that by doing all this you will bring pleasure to your parents and those who are dear to you, and honor to yourself, that I so heartily and sincerely congratulate you.

Trusting that He who has guarded you thus far through life may continue to bless and preserve you and endow you with all those virtues which make life worth living, I am

Your loving brother,
Morris Goldwater

Goldwater's new Prescott store building, which had been attracting attention of the populace during nearly a year of construction, was not ready in time for Christmas 1879. Mike and Morris spared nothing in the planning, and they would rather have everything done right than on time.

On December 4, the *Miner* reported that the project was nearly finished:

Goldwater and Bro. new building is gradually drawing to completion, although there is still much to do in the way of finishing touches. This enterprising firm [has] spared neither money nor time in making the most substantial, beautiful and convenient building in this Territory and deserve praise from every property owner in this town. . . .

The Masonic Hall in the upper portion of the building is a perfect gem, being finished in the most elaborate manner. It's worth going to see.

The two contractors were paid a total of thirteen thousand, five hundred nineteen dollars, and there were many incidentals that pushed the cost well over fifteen thousand dollars. The structure was built so solidly that it was still in use almost a century later, and for many years was the home of the popular Studio Theatre.

By May 27, following the dissolution of Mike and Joe's partnership, the *Miner* was referring to the firm as "M. Goldwater & Son." A sign painter was brought in to make the minor adjustment on each end of the big "J. Goldwater and Bro." sign fronting the building.

By this time, Morris had completed his one-year term as mayor and was devoting more time to the business, much to Mike's relief. His two principal concerns in a year as Prescott's mayor were the lack of a dependable water supply and adequate fire protection. The two were part of the same problem, of course, and Morris had warned that one windy night the whole town could go up in smoke before anybody could do anything about it.

But nothing much was done about his exhortations. Only a major catastrophe could stir the people to action, someone said. About 10 p.m. on the night of July 29, 1880, while most of the townspeople were enjoying an ice cream festival at the Methodist Church, that catastrophe occurred.

The fire started in a little dressmaking establishment owned by Miss Mattie Given, located next door to the new Goldwater store at the corner of Cortez and Union. Miss Mattie, it was hinted, was fooling around with some combustible material instead of going to the church function like everybody else.

The *Miner* of July 30 tells the story:

> The alarm of fire was given, and the whole town rushed to where the flames were rolling out upon the night air, carrying destruction in several directions. The fire caught [started] in the building occupied by Miss Mattie Given as a dressmaking establishment and before discovered had gained such a headway that saving the building or contents was out of the question. . . .
>
> Miss Given, of whom Prescott has no more excellent lady, lost all her clothing, household goods and $1,300 in greenbacks, which she had concealed beneath the carpet.

Two buildings next to Goldwater's belonging to Levi Bashford, were destroyed, said the *Miner,* and his loss of some four thousand dollars was not covered by insurance.

The new *Arizona Democrat* of Prescott had the best description of the fire at the adjoining Goldwater's store:

> The Methodist festival hastily dispersed, without waiting for a benediction, and Mr. Charles Crocker the shoemaker, who occupied the

next cottage to the south, hastened home to find the roof afire. . . .

In the meantime, the many buckets had exhausted the water in all convenient wells but that on the plaza, and a general demand for "water" was echoed about. Eight men lugged up a barrel to the roof of the Goldwater's brick store, and just as it got up some misadventure capsized it, and spilled all its contents uselessly.

The wooden cornice and window caps of Goldwater's store began to take fire, and the wooden shed or portico in front of the store was all ablaze. Ropes were attached to its columns and sharp axes were plied to cut them down.

Fifty men manned the ropes, when suddenly the blazing mass fell against the store front and smashed in the doors, so that the total loss of the fine building with all its valuable contents, seemed inevitable.

But the burning timbers were dragged away into the center of the street. . . . Goldwater was not insured a cent.

Disastrous as the fire and smoke damage was to the proud new Goldwater store, (at least three thousand dollars), Mike and Morris were grateful that it had not been worse. They published a card in the next issue of the *Democrat,* thanking all those who worked so hard to keep damage at a minimum.

There was a fascinating postscript in that same issue of the *Democrat,* which had its offices in the same block as Goldwater's. Rev. Adams of the Methodist Church, the item noted, "wants all who couldn't wait for their ice cream last night to come up tonight and eat up several gallons which were left."

7

"Bad Joseph Goldwater"

The cast of Barry Goldwater's family drama is made up of very real people, with strengths and shortcomings that make each character a source of fascination to those who have studied their impact on the development of the western frontier.

Although he played a supporting role as the younger brother of Big Mike, Joe Goldwater made his own mark on Arizona history.

Had he not persuaded Mike to immigrate to America in 1852, there would have been no Goldwater story to tell. It was Joe who financed Mike on his first peddling venture into the wilderness that became Arizona Territory, and it was he who shared with Mike the hardships in several raw Arizona settlements.

Later, it was Joe who carried the Goldwater banner into southern Arizona, living and dying in Tombstone during its wildest decade. Later still, his son Lemuel became wealthy and prominent in southern California.

Yet, the notion has persisted in family lore that Uncle Joe was a black sheep of the Goldwater clan. Certainly there are newspaper headlines to support that thesis. The man was accused of fraud, sued, jailed, shot at, robbed, and generally maligned throughout his Arizona career.

Barry always found his controversial uncle a source of fascination, and he devoted much time over a period of years in researching Joe's stormy life on the frontier. He found that the "black sheep" label stemmed from the animosity that Barry's grandmother, Sarah Goldwater, felt for Joe. Sarah passed that animosity along to her children, and Joe helped perpetuate it with several well-publicized clashes with the law.

Few men in Arizona history seem more prone to have been in the

*wrong place at the wrong time than Joe Goldwater. A black cloud
hovered over him wherever he went.*

*Uncle Joe died in Tombstone in 1889, twenty years before Barry
was born. But his life was one of those which helped shape that of
young Barry, and one that contributed to the building of Barry's
Arizona.*

*Whether he is to be remembered primarily as the stalwart pioneer
described in his many Arizona obituaries, or as "Bad Joseph Goldwater," as the San Francisco* Examiner *once called him, only the future
can tell.*

*One thing is certain: There were few more colorful characters in the
Goldwater drama, which had more than its share of them.*

SAN FRANCISCO–YUMA, 1880

WHEN MIKE AND JOE GOLDWATER TERMINATED THEIR LONG PARTNERSHIP IN
1880, Joe's feelings of rejection were eased considerably by the
small fortune—some sixty thousand dollars—he took with him. Most of
this sum was the settlement Mike and Morris had agreed to pay him for his
share in the J. Goldwater and Bro. enterprises.

Joe had spent much of his time during the past three years in the
commission and forwarding business in San Francisco, and now he was
free to devote all his energies to that developing commerce. He knew the
California suppliers and he knew Arizona business. Both areas of expertise
were helpful in Joe's chosen line of work, the supplying of Arizona stores
with California merchandise.

But first he had an itch that he could not wait to scratch.

The mines of the Castle Dome district of Yuma County were waiting
there to make some brave investor a millionaire, he was certain. So he sank
much of his bankroll in speculative mining ventures that left him almost
broke within the span of a year.

Discouraged but unbowed, he set out to recoup his finances by enlarg-
ing the scope of his commission business in San Francisco. Soon, he was
buying and shipping to a number of firms, both in Arizona and California.

His biggest customer was an old friend, Isaac Lyons of Yuma, who had
suffered business reverses and lost his credit standing with suppliers.
Because the Goldwaters were trusted in San Francisco, Joe was able to buy
on his own credit and keep Lyons's big Yuma store well supplied.

His business dealings with Lyons kept Joe traveling frequently between
San Francisco and Yuma, and nobody thought it unusual that his credit
purchases from San Francisco wholesalers were increasing steadily.

For several months, Joe seemed well on the way to achieving the success in commission trading that had escaped him in mining speculation. But he failed to reckon with the atrocious Joe Goldwater luck.

In late January 1881, some nervous wholesaler was unable to reach Joe in San Francisco and found that he had left the city rather suddenly on business. Inquiries as to Goldwater's destination turned up the disturbing news that he was headed for Yuma, only a few minutes away from the Mexican border.

In a panic, the supplier started the rumor that Joe had skipped town and was on his way to Mexico, leaving thousands of dollars in unpaid bills behind him in San Francisco. The San Francisco *Examiner,* ever ready to suspect the worst about Jewish businessmen, printed a story which hinted broadly that there was serious mischief afoot.

On January 29, the *Examiner* came out with a libelous story that was to derail Joe's financial comeback for years to come:

> Bad Joseph Goldwater
> How He Swindled the Wholesale Merchants of the City
> $100,000 worth of Goods Obtained
> from Hebrew and Gentile Merchants
> Gone Forever
>
> There is weeping and wailing and gnashing of teeth among the wholesale merchants of Sansome, Battery and Front Streets, especially those of Hebrew extraction, over the conduct of Joseph Goldwater, whilom commission merchant, engaged in purchasing goods for the Arizona trade.
>
> Last Saturday he suddenly departed for Arizona, the land of the rattlesnake and tarantula, and on Monday it was whispered that he had been buying heavily on credit within the last 30 days. . . . from Levi Strauss and Co., Weill Bros., Hecht Bros. (and 11 others). . . .

The damaging story called Joe's appearance "not prepossessing," and stated that he was "an unscrupulous operator."

The next day there were newspaper reports that a great number of merchants had appeared at Joe's San Francisco office with bills for goods he had bought. One reporter put the total of Joe's indebtedness at one hundred twenty-five thousand dollars. Undoubtedly, Joe was not in that deep, although he had been trading quite handsomely on other people's money for some time—a practice he believed perfectly proper.

As the rumors grew in intensity and rancor, attorney Joseph Naphtaly was retained by the worried creditors and the San Francisco Board of Trade to find Joe and bring him back for an accounting.

What followed is almost impossible to believe: Capt. A. W. Stone of the

San Francisco detective force also departed for Yuma, and soon thereafter, he was on his way to Prescott to present a request to Governor Fremont for Joe Goldwater's extradition to California to face charges of embezzlement and flight to avoid his creditors.

In company with a sheriff, a deputy U.S. marshal, and the Southern Pacific Railway security chief, Stone arrived by specially chartered railroad engine and car in Yuma and tracked down the unsuspecting Goldwater to the home of Isaac Lyons, where he was having dinner as Lyons's guest.

The Tucson *Citizen* told the lurid story in great detail:

> Mr. (R. H.) Paul informed Mr. Goldwater that he was a deputy United States Marshal and had a warrant for his arrest. Goldwater said yes, he'd go, yet he made no movement in that direction, but gave a sign to Levi [Isaac Levy, a clerk in Lyons's store], who arose from the table and went out the back door. Goldwater was again reminded that his person was wanted, but he made no motion to go.
>
> Paul placed a hat on the prisoner's head, and with the assistance of Capt. Deal, took the resisting offender out of the house. . . .

Levy then came running up, demanded to know where they were taking Goldwater, and said he would not permit them to kidnap him. Levy grabbed Capt. Stone and would not release his hold until Stone drew his revolver.

Levy followed the group of officers to the railroad car, and on the steps of the car he made another attempt to free his friend. Other friends of Goldwater ran to the sheriff's office in search of help, but the California law officers already had the railroad engine moving toward the Colorado River bridge. In a matter of moments, Joe and his captors were on the California side.

Joe was in a state of shock, having had no previous inkling that he was in trouble with the law. After demanding to know what the elaborate capture and arrest was all about, he read the libelous charges against him and swore noisily that he would be suing the San Francisco *Examiner* and his accusing creditors for all the money they had.

Twenty-four hours later, he was in San Francisco, where he was brought before a judge and quickly released on bond.

It is impossible to judge, a century later, whether Joe Goldwater was a victim of gross injustice in the Lyons case, or whether his own actions contributed to his catastrophe. Certainly, he had made some enemies in the wholesale community of San Francisco, as these published quotes from suppliers demonstrate:

> Charles Miller of Huntington and Hopkins: "We never trusted him much and never did entertain an exalted opinion of his honesty."

Mr. Sachs of Schweitzer, Sachs and Co.: "I would not allow him to buy largely from us on credit. I never did trust him much."

Levi Strauss of Levi Strauss and Co.: "We didn't lose much (because we did not extend him much credit). Go across the street and ask Weill Bros." [Weill Bros. would not talk].

Exactly why these merchants did not trust Joe Goldwater remains somewhat of a mystery. He had been buying from them, and paying on time, for many years.

Amazingly, at the time of the February 1881 furor, Joe did not have a single bill overdue!

Contrasting with these views of Joe's character were the dozens of commentaries in the Arizona press after his "abduction" from Yuma. The *Arizona Sentinel* of Yuma had noted Joe's late January visit to that town, adding that "he is his usual genial and happy self, while making others, particularly his lady friends, rejoice."

The *Arizona Silver Belt* of Globe, on February 26, fretted over the way Joe Goldwater's reputation was being unfairly besmirched:

Many sensational, unpleasant and false articles [have been] published about him by the would-be sensational papers of Arizona, charging him with having defrauded creditors in San Francisco to the amount of $100,000. . . . The said obligations, when they became due, only aggregate the insignificant sum of $3,048.09.

Some malicious enemy set the false rumors on foot that he had jumped the country and other injurious, absurd stories.

Even the newspapers that did not leap to Joe's defense were highly critical of the way the California law officers had come into Arizona and spirited him across the border without a chance to defend himself.

Back in San Francisco, Joe Goldwater set about repairing the damage to his reputation and his future business prospects. His first act was to charge into the San Francisco *Examiner* office and demand a retraction of the libelous stories which had been printed about him.

No retraction was forthcoming, but the *Examiner* did consent to publish a statement written by Joe in his own defense:

To the Editor of the Examiner—Sir:

Referring to an article in your issue on January 29, headed "Bad Jos. Goldwater," and knowing your reputation for fairness as a newspaper, I ask that you publish this card as a matter of justice.

First—I was not and am not a resident of Arizona; I have lived and done business in San Francisco for more than five years; my name is on the Register as a voter for that time.

Second—There has not been a time during this period but what I have owed as much or more than I do now, to the merchants of this city.

Third—My credit has been always very good, and I could have bought more goods than I actually purchased during the past six days.

Fourth—At the time I left it was on a business trip, which it has been my custom invariably for the last four years to make from time to time, and I had hardly left my office before attachments were levied on my office, books, papers, etc., by certain creditors. . . .

Finally, my creditors, by their hasty, ill-advised action have ruined my standing and credit as a business man in the San Francisco mercantile community. If they should meet with losses they can lay the blame on their own doors. As far as my own feelings are concerned, if injury has been done, the larger portion has been done to me.

J. Goldwater
Feb. 14, 1881

The criminal charge against Joe was dismissed, since the prosecutor could see that the original premise—that he had skipped out to Mexico— was unsupportable. The harried victim of so much venomous accusation could now breathe a momentary sigh of relief.

But things never went right for Joe Goldwater for very long. Within a week, some of his creditors were devising another means of attack.

Some of his bills were beginning to come due, and none of his creditors was in a mood to give him any grace period. Now, however, he was strapped for cash. He had legal fees to pay, much of his money was tied up in merchandise, and Mr. Lyons was unable to advance him anything on the big bill he owed to Joe.

F. A. Hoffman, one of the San Francisco dry goods suppliers, filed suit in U.S. District Court on behalf of all creditors, claiming Goldwater now owed them about forty-six thousand dollars.

The District Court in Tucson then issued an order requiring the Sheriff of Yuma County to seize the goods in Lyons's big store on behalf of the creditors. The sheriff, probably reflecting the angry mood of the Yuma citizenry, refused to comply with the court order.

When a deputy U.S. marshal attempted to take possesion of the goods, Lyons personally escorted him out of the store and proceeded to place armed men around the store. Even guards from the Yuma Territorial Prison volunteered to take turns in the defense, which was taking on all the trappings of a military operation.

All Yuma watched and cheered as the town prepared to defy what was perceived as an unjust effort by California capitalists to ruin defenseless Arizona merchants.

Deputy U.S. Marshal Joseph W. Evans in Tucson was not about to take this show of rebellion lying down. He immediately swore in a large posse and put the men aboard a train headed for Yuma, which by that time resembled an armed camp. On March 12, Evans's heavily armed warriors arrived and prepared to take over the Lyons store, by force if necessary.

The confrontation did not become another storied gunfight on the streets of a western town, however. Both Joe Goldwater and Isaac Lyons called off their angry guards in the interest of preventing bloodshed, and Evans's men proceeded to strip the shelves of Lyons store preparatory to sending the merchandise to a guarded warehouse.

Meanwhile, Marshal Evans treated Goldwater and Lyons as criminals. They were arrested, marched to the Yuma jail, and locked up. Joe's legal counsel obtained their release, and when Joe arrived in San Francisco to face a judge once more, he was discharged on the grounds that the court did not have jurisdiction. A few days later he was back in Yuma, where he sarcastically informed a reporter that he was "not on my way to Sonora."

Joe Goldwater's years as a San Francisco commission merchant were at an end. His credit had been destroyed, and he was unable to meet his obligations. He made an all-too-familiar trek to the bankruptcy court in San Francisco, where he sadly filed a petition to be declared an insolvent debtor. He listed as the reasons "losses incurred by litigation, payment of interest, expenses of living and losses in mining stock."

To many of his friends, the "losses in mining stock" came as a surprise. It was widely rumored that Joe's fatal weakness for gambling in mining investments had started the devastating rumors of his financial ruin in the first place.

One thing Joe Goldwater was sure about: He did not want to stay in San Francisco a minute longer than he had to. Dead broke, worried, and embittered, he longed to be among friends once again.

He went to Prescott, where he poured out the story of his misfortunes to Mike and to Morris. Then he went to Phoenix, where he looked about for some hint of a road back to financial stability.

Joe had one trump card hidden in his sleeve—a hedge against disaster which he had set up long before the Lyons fiasco. In San Francisco a year before, he had bought and shipped merchandise to an old friend, P. W. Smith, a former partner of Dr. W. W. Jones and now a prominent merchant in booming Tombstone. Smith had needed additional capital, so Joe had made him a substantial loan.

That loan, and the interest it had accumulated, Joe counted on as his last remaining nest egg and his best hope for a new start. He made plans to visit Tombstone to see if Smith could repay the loan in Joe's time of need.

Before he could do that, however, he received another piece of devastating news: On June 22, a fire raged through four blocks of Tombstone, destroying one hundred fifty buildings and homes and causing a loss of more than a quarter million dollars.

Joe did not have to ask whether P. W. Smith's Tombstone properties had been destroyed by the flames. The way his luck had been going, it was a certainty.

Smith had indeed suffered heavy losses, and his burned-out customers were unable to pay him what they owed. There was no way he could help Joe Goldwater now.

One may wonder why Joe—afflicted by fate as painfully as the Biblical Job—did not simply put a gun to his head at that point and end it all. But he resisted that temptation, and soon he had a communication from Smith, inviting him to come to Tombstone to see what might be done to start Joe off on the comeback trail.

He knew little about Cochise County in southeastern Arizona, or its rip-roaring town of Tombstone where the Earps and Clantons were feuding so spectacularly, but he had no choice. It was Tombstone or nothing.

He could not have known that he was to live the rest of his life in Cochise County—to enter business, remarry, and play a leading role in one of the bloodiest sagas of Arizona's frontier history.

Joe Goldwater reached Tombstone in late July 1881, heavy of heart and full of anxiety about the future. He had very little money, even less credit, and he knew virtually nobody in that wild town or the raw mining camps that were springing up along the San Pedro River in Cochise County.

After one night in Tombstone, however, his spirits were a bit higher. This was the most exciting town in Arizona Territory in 1881—crowded with more than six thousand fortune seekers and already well recovered from the disastrous fire that had leveled much of the downtown area only a few weeks before. Most of the buildings were flimsy wooden structures or framed tents, with an occasional adobe or brick building to give a promise of permanency.

Saloons, gambling parlors, and other assorted sin palaces flourished around the clock, and such respectable institutions as churches and theaters were struggling for a foothold. The law, such as it was, often looked the other way when a lusty miner or cowpoke came riding into town looking for a drink and a woman and a fight, not always in that order.

A stage met every train arrival at the nearest railhead, Benson, twenty-eight miles to the north on the Southern Pacific, and Tombstone hotel accommodations were surprisingly good. Joe did not need a hotel because his friend P. W. Smith had lodgings waiting.

Smith had suffered heavy losses in the fire and had considered throwing in the towel. But he still owned a general merchandise store and wholesale liquor business, together with an interest in a branch of Tucson's Pima County Bank. He was determined to start repaying Goldwater some of the money he had borrowed from him.

One of Smith's customers was H. K. Tweed, whose general merchandise store had been hit hard by the fire and who was willing to give up and move on. He still owed Smith for most of his stock, so Smith simply turned the merchandise over to Joe as partial payment of his debt. The Tombstone *Epitaph* announced on July 28 that Joe was taking over the Tweed store and would operate it "in conjunction" with Paul B. Warnekros, one of Smith's clerks.

The J. Goldwater name was still poison to suppliers, so the store was billed as "Paul B. Warnekros Co." The store was successful from the start, and the two partners became the closest of friends, remaining so for years after Warnekros bought Joe out and went on to become a rather wealthy man as proprietor of the Cochise Hardware and Trading Co.

It is probable that Joe was doing business in downtown Tombstone on that afternoon of October 26, 1881, when all hell broke loose near the OK Corral. The trouble between the Earp brothers and Doc Holliday on one side and the Clanton-McLowry gang on the other had been boiling toward an explosion for weeks. During less than a minute of deadly gunfire, Billy Clanton, Tom McLowry, and Frank McLowry were killed, and Virgil and Morgan Earp were seriously wounded.

Hollywood script writers and dime novelists have been milking that dramatic incident even since.

Whether this kind of lawless violence was what turned Joe Goldwater against Tombstone is a matter of conjecture, but we know that he soon left his store there and went into business at Contention, the tiny community which housed ore-crushing mills near Tombstone.

This was a three-partner venture involving some of Arizona's most notorious credit risks. Joseph Guindani had failed in a store operation at Florence in Pinal County two years earlier. Jose Miguel Castaneda had a record of business failures as long as his arm, at La Paz, Ehrenberg, Signal, Phoenix, and points between.

Because there was not a name among them that would entice a wholesaler to ship merchandise to them, they adopted one: "A. A. Castaneda," a name which happened to be that of Jose Miguel's wife, Amparo Arviso Castaneda.

The subterfuge apparently worked beautifully, because they bought on credit, made money, and soon had a second store at Bisbee, twenty-eight miles south of Tombstone across the lofty Mule Mountains. Mile-high Bisbee, just north of the Mexican border, was the site of a big copper discovery, the Copper Queen, and its smelter, both controlled by Ben and Lewis Williams. The Williams brothers were backed financially by an in-law, Judge DeWitt Bisbee of San Francisco, who gave his name to the new camp. Local legend says that Mr. Bisbee never got around to visiting the town named in his honor.

Now things started looking up for Joe Goldwater and his partners. The Bisbee boom was just beginning, and the store was a winner from the first. There was no bank in the new camp, so Joe made arrangements with the Williams brothers that the Castaneda-Goldwater store would cash their payroll checks and offer credit to the miners until the arrival of paydays. It was an arrangement much like that of the Goldwater store at Ehrenberg, and it assured a steady level of business.

One of the historical bonanzas from the arrangement is the collection of several hundred letters written by Joe to his banker, Albert Springer, at Tombstone. They are preserved in the University of Arizona Library and at the Arizona Historical Society in Tucson. The letters were sent from Contention, Bisbee, Fairbank, Crittenden, and Benson—all Cochise County towns at which Joe had stores during the 1880s. Not only do the letters record Joe's business dealings, but they reveal much about the most private feelings of this sensitive, lonely man.

Answering a remonstrance from Springer about Joe's drinking, he wrote "Remember, my boy, if I take a little sherry wine under present circumstances, I cannot forget to act honorably to all. . . . I must frankly say to you that my suffering here is and was on account of my [which I thought] best friends, and I paid dearly, not only with money, but with my honor. . . ."

On another occasion, Joe wrote "I am so anxious to see my children in the city." And on another, "Would be much pleased to have a good meal at your home. I am nearly starved."

Much as he hated his life in the rough mining camps, he could see that he was gradually recouping his reputation and his fortune.

"You know our credit is not A-1," he wrote Springer, "but by making prompt payments, we may regain what we lost."

With the Bisbee store thriving, and Joe and Jose Castaneda serving as bankers for the town, money was flowing in and out of the store in big amounts. The big steel safe in the back of the store was eyed hungrily by many a would-be thief.

In early summer of 1883, Joe took his long-awaited trip to San Francisco and returned with a new clerk—his son, sixteen-year-old Lemuel, who was to be a major force in Cochise County business for a decade to come. "Lemmy" was fascinated with Bisbee, one of the most unusual communities in the West. Homes hung precariously from mountainsides, and the town was bisected by the famed Brewery Gulch, "Where There Is Moonshine Every Day," according to the local slogan. It was a treeless rocky camp with few civilized comforts, but its mile-high elevation, dry air, and cloudless skies made the weather pleasant the year around.

Joe Goldwater was often bored and lonely at Bisbee, but at least there were no hostile Indians, no hounding creditors, and no venomous newspaper reporters to make his life miserable. Business was good, and his bank balance was growing. It seemed that, at age fifty-three, his luck had turned for the better.

But then came the historic evening of December 8, 1883.

The senseless violence and slaughter that has been remembered in Arizona frontier legend as "The Bisbee Massacre" struck without warning on a chilly, moonlit Saturday night. At about 7:30 p.m., as townsfolk were dining in restaurants, shopping for Christmas gifts, or seeking recreation in the saloons, Joe Goldwater was behind the counter of his store. His son Lemmy was attending to a customer and Joe's partner, Jose Castaneda, was recovering from an ailment on a cot in the back room. Peter Doll, the new bookkeeper (formerly of La Paz and Ehrenberg), was at a desk near the front door.

Suddenly two men pushed their way through the front door, shoved wicked-looking pistols at Doll's head, and demanded that everyone put up their hands. It was payday in Bisbee, and the big steel safe was normally bulging with money at this hour.

What happened next is a matter of some conjecture, since several conflicting versions of the tragedy have been reported. Perhaps the most accurate account, however, is that written by young Barry Goldwater for the August 1941, *Desert* magazine, in the days before politics claimed all his time. Consumed with curiosity about the most dramatic moment in the life of his great Uncle Joe, Barry pored over court records, testimony, oral history, and every other source he could find—including the memory of his cousin Lem, who was on the scene when it all took place.

According to Barry's account:

Bursting into the store came two men brandishing pistols. One of the men, Big Dan Dowd, was masked. The other, a light-complexioned, debonair man wearing a moustache, was unmasked. He was Tex Howard.

Shoving their pistols at Peter's head, they commanded: "Hands up!"

Surprised, Doll at first didn't comply with the command, but upon more insistence from Big Dan and Tex, up went his hands.

As he stood there, arms raised, he noticed three other masked men, Red Sample, Bill Delaney and Yorky Kelly, had entered the store and had forced the customers and other employees into assuming the same defensive position Doll had taken. One of the newly arrived masked men rushed to the back of the store, and, as new customers arrived, in ignorance of what was going on, the other bandits forced them to put up their hands.

Doll was ordered to open the safe, but said he didn't know how. Howard, who appeared to be the leader, then spotted Joe Goldwater and recognized him as the boss. With pistols at his head, Joe was ordered to open the safe. Barry's narrative continues:

Joe answered with the trace of Polish accent he always retained:

"You come in here and say 'hands up' and my hands go up. Then you say 'open the safe.' I am no magician. Tell me how to do it."

Howard's answer was curt: "If you don't open that safe, I'll blow the top of your head off."

"Who then will open the safe? What will you gain by that?"

Another bandit gruffly ordered him to get the payroll out of the safe. A challenging smile crossed Joe's face as he still gambled for time.

"That's where you get fooled. The stagecoach is late. The payroll is not here."

But the hour of truth had arrived. The menacing pistols convinced Joe that he should open the safe.

While Joe was stalling for time, hoping that the local law would arrive, the bandits outside the store were getting nervous. Sample and Kelly had gone back out the front door and were pacing up and down. A passer-by, Johnny Tappenier, stopped short in his tracks, and when he made a move to run, one of the outlaws fired two shots at short range. Tappenier staggered a few steps and fell dead.

From then on, it was open season on the streets of Bisbee.

A stage driver, D. Tom Smith, heard the shots as he ate in a nearby restaurant. Rushing out, he caught a bullet squarely in the head and died instantly.

The bandits then began firing at anything that moved. The third victim was Mrs. W. W. Roberts, a pregnant newcomer from New York. A wild bullet caused injuries that took her life, and her child's, before midnight. Barry's account described the final fatality:

The Grim Reaper's special representatives were not through. James A. Nolly, trying his best to gain a place of protection, was wounded seriously in the left breast. He managed to run to Bob Pierce's Saloon, where he collapsed. . . . He died the next day.

This shooting didn't take long—maybe five or six mintues—but that short space of time had brought death to four innocent people and robbery to the store.

While the outside shooting was in progress, Joe was forced to empty the safe's contents into the gang's jackets. Not content with what little loot the safe offered, one of the masked men went into the back room where Castaneda lay sick. Forcing him to sit up, the robber extracted a bag of gold from under his pillow—a bag he had slipped there for safekeeping when the rumpus started.

Unfortunately for the outlaws, they had planned their robbery on a day when the stagecoach carrying seven thousand dollars was late, and the Goldwater store lost only about six hundred dollars. It was a pittance to stack up against the killing of four people and an unborn baby. And there was more dying to come.

The gang escaped the two posses that rode out after them as soon as the alarm was sounded. One of the reasons for their escape was that a hastily deputized posse leader, John Heath, proved later to be one of the ringleaders of the robbery. Heath led his horsemen on a fruitless chase in the wrong direction.

Joe Goldwater was the center of attention in Bisbee for weeks to come. Stories about his cool behavior under stress were told all over southern Arizona, and some, such as Joe's reported remark to the departing killers that "it will be a cold night. Maybe you'd better take some blankets," became legends.

Later, when the killers were rounded up and brought to trial, Joe made a wisecrack in court that has become cherished in the history of Arizona frontier justice. Called to the witness stand and asked to raise his right hand to be sworn, Joe raised both hands high above his head.

"One hand is all that is necessary, Mr. Goldwater," said the judge.

"Your honor," he replied, "when I see any of those gentlemen around [pointing to the defendants], I generally hold up both."

All five of the outlaws who participated in the robbery and killings were found guilty and sentenced to death by hanging, a sentence that was carried out before a month had passed. Even before that, John Heath came to his untimely end. Heath, who had only recently arrived in Bisbee, became involved with the others and helped plan the payroll robbery. But because he did not actually hold a gun (he was playing stud poker nearby when the robbery began), he was let off with a sentence of twenty years in the Yuma Prison.

Bisbee folks thought that punishment was too lenient, however. Barry Goldwater concluded his story with this description of Heath's demise:

> On Washington's Birthday of 1884, the people acted. More than fifty armed men rode over the Mule Mountains into Tombstone (where Heath was being held in jail) early that morning. In Warnekros' store they obtained a short rope, one made to stand the strain of a steer suddenly jerked to a stop. . . .
>
> By the time people really got to stirring in Tombstone that morning, John Heath had space between his feet and the ground. Another victim was chalked up for the Grim Reaper.
>
> At the coroner's inquest on the body so suspended, the report of Dr. George E. Goodfellow was read: "I find that the deceased died of emphysema of the lungs, which might have been caused by strangulation, self-inflicted or otherwise."
>
> With the subsequent hanging beside the Tombstone Courthouse of the five principals on a special yellow pine scaffold, which, in droll parlance might have been described as a five-holer, the affair of Saturday night, the 8th of December, 1883, was closed. It had taken the lives of nine men, one woman and an unborn child, to close a bloody chapter of Arizona's history.

In the pre-dawn chill of February 18, 1885, a homeward-bound bartender discovered a fire burning in a pile of trash between the Goldwater-Castaneda store and Pierce's Saloon in Bisbee. He fired his pistol to awaken the town, but the citizens who rushed to the scene had only the water in two barrels to fight the blaze. Within minutes some gunpowder in the store went off with a thundering blast that scattered flaming missiles all over the middle of town. Several small fires resulted, but they were soon extinguished.

According to the Tucson *Citizen,* the store and merchandise sustained a loss of twenty thousand dollars, a much more serious catastrophe than the Goldwater fire at Prescott five years before. It was too much for Jose Miguel Castaneda to accept, and he immediately withdrew from further participation in the management of the Goldwater-Guindani-Castaneda enterprises.

Joe continued to manage the rebuilt Bisbee store, Lemmy took over the Fairbank wholesale operation, and Guindani ran the store at Contention. In 1887, Joe's younger son Harry made the traditional Goldwater trek from

San Francisco to Arizona. He was assigned to work under Lemmy at Fairbank.

Meanwhile, Joe's health began to fail. Several of his letters to banker Springer mention his continuing headaches and lack of energy. "Send by driver one bottle of the stuff [medicine] you use," he wrote Springer, "even though it is a very hard substance to get down." But he continued to work as hard as ever.

Soon the headaches and fever, diagnosed as malaria, grew so debilitating that he had to move from Fairbank into Tombstone, where he stayed at a hotel to be near his doctor and his friends, the Castanedas. Jose Miguel's wife, Amparo, and her mother, Manuela Arvizu, brought him homemade soup and gave him the sympathy and kind attention he had longed for.

Mrs. Arvizu was a year or two older than Joe, but she appeared much younger at fifty-eight than he did at fifty-seven. A handsome woman, now widowed, she was seen in Joe's company with increasing frequency. Theirs was not a romance of youth, but Joe and Manuela found joy and comfort in one another.

On October 16, 1887, they were married in San Francisco, probably at Mike's home at 716 O'Farrell Street. Mike, recently retired from his Arizona businesses, was a genial host, and his wife, Sarah, tried to hide her resentment at Joe for marrying outside his faith.

Certainly Manuela was not after Joe's money. She signed a prenuptial agreement that stated that, when he died, she would receive only one thousand dollars. The rest of his estate was to go to his three children.

It was not long before that estate of some twenty-five thousand dollars was sorrowfully divided. On August 29, 1889, the Tombstone *Prospector* noted:

> Joe Goldwater is lying at the residence of A. A. Castaneda in this city
> in a very precarious condition. His health had been poor for some
> time past, and his present illness may result fatally.

Two days later, at age fifty-nine, Joe Goldwater died.

When he got the news, Mike let his memory roam to the moment in 1850 when the ragged, half-starved Joe had knocked fearfully on his door in London . . . to the pleading in his voice when he urged Mike to leave his wife and two children to gamble on striking it rich in California . . . to Sarah's anguish when the two brothers decided to go. He remembered old times: their early partnership in Sonora . . . the elegance of the Bella Union Hotel . . . heated arguments over business policy . . . the Indian ambush near Prescott . . . the family tensions that spanned thirty-five years.

For Joe, life had been one part accomplishment and nine parts disappointment. His really happy days had been few, indeed. But there were those who remembered that life as one of significant pioneering. Tombstone's *Prospector* published an editorial about Joe Goldwater that was reprinted in several other territorial newspapers. It said, in part:

Joseph Goldwater, one of Arizona's pioneers, died in this city Saturday afternoon after a brief illness. He occupied a place in Arizona's history which few men now living can claim. He came to the territory early in the 60's and began business at La Paz on the Colorado. . . .

His life was full of hardship and bitter experience. He was not a man who courted the friendship of everyone, but those whom he counted on as his friends were true as steel. He braved Indian outbreaks, and outlaws time and again robbed him of the fruits of his toil. But he never looked back or uttered a word of complaint. . . .

His many acts of charity and kindness toward those who were in need are monuments to his memory.

Joe would have laughed ironically at the praise heaped upon him in death by the San Francisco newspapers. The man who was crucified in the press there only eight years before now took on the mantle of a great pioneer of the West.

The San Francisco *Chronicle* said of him on September 6:

Joe Goldwater was one of the pioneer merchants of Arizona and for a number of years was associated with his brother Michel in Prescott. In the latter part of the sixties, it was very much a matter of life and death to travel in northern Arizona. Joseph Goldwater never hesitated, however, in his business, and until his death he had scars of Indian treachery on his body. . . .

Goldwater was known by almost every resident of Arizona for the last twenty years, was social and liberal and helped many a poor miner and hungry man. He was most popular where best known, and his last sleep is but a rest from a varied and tumultous life.

Manuela Arvizu Goldwater, who had buried two husbands, lived on almost forty more years—past her ninety-ninth birthday. She died May 16, 1928, at Nogales and was interred at Benson in the Castaneda family plot.

Lem took over the responsibilities of the family business in Cochise County. The Bisbee store had been sold and the Contention store closed by the time Joe died. Lem and Harry settled with Guindani and went on their own, taking over the Benson store and selling out the Fairbank operation.

Three years after their father died, they sold the Benson store to none other than Jose Miguel Castaneda, who operated it and the Virginia Hotel in Benson for many years thereafter. Lem later made a fortune manufacturing "Boss" overalls in southern California, established the Bank of Anaheim, and was a founder of the Cedars of Lebanon Hospital.

The question of where Joe Goldwater should be interred seemed thorny for a time, but Lem begged Manuela to let his father be buried in the family plot, beside Ellen, in the Hills of Eternity Cemetery. With her usual concern for the feelings of others, Manuela gave her permission.

So Joe Goldwater, his tumultous life and notorious bad luck now at an end, was buried in the peaceful greenery of a San Francisco resting place—his head to the east, toward Jerusalem.

8

Wild and Woolly Politics

Barry Goldwater was born and bred for politics as surely as a thoroughbred horse is destined for the Kentucky Derby. His zest for competition, his natural affability, and his ambition to reach for the highest star were all legacies from highly political forebears.

From 1874, when Mike, Joe, and Morris ran for office in the wild Arizona Territory, the Goldwaters were fascinated by the excitement of election campaigns and the satisfaction of public service. As Barry declared in his decision to run for Phoenix City Council in 1949, "there has always been one, and sometimes two, Goldwaters damned fools enough to get into politics."

Many of the Goldwaters dabbled in politics, but it was the indomitable Morris who made a life work of it. Mayor of Prescott for twenty years, territorial legislator, vice president of the Arizona Constitutional Convention—these and many other public posts were his over a span of half a century.

Because Morris was like a father to young Barry, it was only natural that he would imbue his eager nephew with his love of the political arena. Although Morris was a powerful force in the Arizona Democratic Party for much of his life, he espoused many of the conservative principles that later made Barry the leader of America's Republicans.

How Morris built his remarkable political career, and passed along his political fervor to his willing nephew, makes a story of major significance in the history of American politics.

PRESCOTT, 1885

FEW ARIZONANS OF THE 1880s AND 1890s CAPTURED THE PUBLIC FANCY SO COMpletely as did W. O. (Buckey) O'Neill.

Born in St. Louis in 1860, admitted to the bar in Washington, D.C. as a callow youth, and an Arizonan by way of Honolulu, Hawaii, Buckey did almost everything with a touch of the spectacular. He was a frontier sheriff who trailed his man for weeks through trackless wilderness—a judge who played no favorites—an editor who wrote it like he saw it—a big, handsome brute who had half the female population of Arizona swooning. He was a politician, a volunteer fireman, an organizer of militia. And he seemed always to be competing with Morris Goldwater in each of these endeavors.

Buckey's name was noised around as a political contender after an 1883 trial at the Yavapai County Courthouse, in which his skill as a shorthand reporter took a back seat to his talents as a bare-knuckle brawler. It was a case involving water rights—always an emotional issue in Arizona Territory—and the defendant's lawyer made his legal point by hurling an inkstand with unerring aim at the head of his opponent. Within seconds, fists and curses were flying all over the courtroom.

O'Neill sprang gleefully to the aid of the plaintiff's attorney, Clark Churchill, and bashed people with reckless abandon. Knives appeared, and then guns. Before the riot was quelled, a rancher named McAteer was dead and several others, including O'Neill, had suffered serious wounds. The courtroom was a heap of broken furniture, and blood splotched every wall. The decorum of the legal process was often disturbed in such fashion in the Prescott of the 1880s.

As owner and editor of the Republican-leaning *Hoof and Horn* newspaper, O'Neill soon came into conflict with Democratic chairman Morris Goldwater, who suffered more than once from Buckey's editorial jibes. And as a political aspirant from age twenty-six, the big Irishman helped cool many a Democrat's ambitious plans.

When he decided to run for probate judge in 1886, he published his announcement with typical O'Neill candor and charm. It said, in part:

> It is a soft berth, with a salary of $2,000 per annum attached. While in the way of special qualifications I have no advantage over 75% of my fellow citizens in the County, yet I believe I am fully competent to discharge all the duties of the office in an efficient manner. If you coincide in this opinion, support me, if you see fit; if you do not, you will by no means jeopardize the safety of the universe by defeating me.

Who could vote against a man who talked like that?

Some Democrats, fearful of O'Neill's growing popularity, anonymously circulated a venomous broadside charging him with being a drunkard, an inveterate gambler, and a libertine. Charley Beach of the *Miner* put his finger on the truth when he wrote the next day that "this will boomerang upon its authors and elect W. O. O'Neill probate judge."

Certainly, Morris Goldwater was afraid that might happen. He rushed into print with a statement addressed to Buckey, declaring that the Democratic organization had no connection with "the slanderous and cowardly attack which has been made from some anonymous source on you as the republican nominee for probate judge. . . . It merits the just censure and condemnation of all fair-minded men."

But Morris's disclaimer did not completely soothe Buckey's feelings or make the two fast friends. Their heated rivalry would burn for more than a decade to come.

Morris was an organizer of the "Prescott Rifles" militia company. O'Neill restructured the Milligan Guards into the rival "Prescott Grays." Morris was a founder and lifelong member of the Dude Fire Hose Company. O'Neill was an organizer of their arch-rivals, the Toughs.

Regardless of what one of the energetic, ambitious men set out to do, it seemed the other was in the way. But when Buckey used his personal popularity to organize a company of the Rough Riders for Spanish-American War duty, Morris gave him every support possible. And when they brought Buckey's lifeless body down from San Juan Hill a few months later, Morris was the first to offer his services to erect a memorial to Buckey O'Neill and his intrepid comrades. With his friend Robert E. Morrison, Morris led the campaign for funds to commission sculptor Solon Borglum to create a masterful equestrian statue.

That remarkable statue, the pride of Prescott, stands today at the north end of the Courthouse Square. It is not only a memorial to a flamboyant hero, but to his rival, Morris Goldwater, who submerged personal animosities to honor a great Arizonan.

Both Morris and Buckey were, of course, involved in the machinations of the immortal Thirteenth Arizona Territorial Legislative Assembly, celebrated in history as "The Thieving Thirteenth." No other legislature in Arizona annals was wooed more shamelessly by eager lobbyists, and no other group of lawmakers entertained themselves more boisterously, operated more scandalously, or did more lasting good for Arizona in so short a time.

Morris labored quietly, and at little personal gain, as chief clerk of the House of Representatives. The bills passed by the House were written in his fine hand, and his name is attached to many a document of the session. Buckey O'Neill managed to enrich his depleted coffers during the session, which ran from January to mid-March of 1885. His *Hoof and Horn* journal received some lucrative printing contracts, and his service as a lobbyist for a Cochise County group brought in an undisclosed sum.

Lawmakers, lobbyists, and the press took over Governor Fremont's former home (now preserved as a historic site across the street from the Sharlot Hall Museum in Prescott) and turned it into a house stocked with good liquor, cigars, and fine foods.

Spirits and tempers ran high, both in and out of the legislative sessions, held in the just-completed Prescott City Hall (since razed for the present Yavapai County Building). There were fist fights in the House chambers and along Gurley Street, a challenge to a duel, and threats of chastisement from a senator with a bull whip.

To close out the session in memorable style, the legislators and their lobbyist friends held the most lavish stag party in territorial annals. The scene of this grand event was Howey Hall, the former Goldwater store. Buckey, who planned the affair, set the type himself for the menus, which were printed on embossed satin. The finest delicacies and liquors were served, and flowers were imported from California. It was in a euphoric haze that the lawmakers returned to their deliberations the next morning.

But what amazing results they obtained from their wheeling and dealing! They passed enabling legislation to connect the Southern Pacific with the Atlantic and Pacific Railroad, via Prescott. They established the Territorial Insane Asylum in Phoenix (with a huge one hundred thousand dollar appropriation, largest of the session). They passed a modern public school code, made the first serious move toward women's suffrage, funded roads and bridges, and created both the University of Arizona at Tucson and the Territorial Normal School (now Arizona State University) at Tempe.

It was in a spirit of contrition for their many sins that the legislators approached the final day of the session. Representative Selim Franklin of Pima County, youngest of the group at twenty-five years of age, expressed that feeling in his last-moment plea for establishing the University of Arizona:

> The 13th Legislature has been the most energetic, the most contentious, and the most corrupt that Arizona ever had. We have been called the Fighting Thirteenth, the Bloody Thirteenth and the Thieving Thirteenth. We have deserved those names and we know it.
>
> We have employed too many clerks, we have subsidized the local press to cover up our shortcomings, and we have voted ourselves additional pay in violation of an act of Congress.
>
> But here is an opportunity to wash away our sins. Let us establish an institution of learning. . . . For your own salvation, you *must* vote for this bill.

Obviously, there were a number of solons who felt in need of salvation.

They washed away their sins, approved the creation of the University of Arizona, and within hours, the Thirteenth Legislative Assembly was history.

During the rolicking sessions of the Thieving Thirteenth the host city's mayor was none other than His Honor Michel Goldwater. Wearying somewhat after twenty-two years of mercantile pioneering in Arizona, Mike was strongly considering retirement when a citizens committee called on him at the end of 1884 and urged him to run for mayor. Flattered by their expression of confidence in his ability, he agreed to put Sarah off a little longer and stick around Prescott for his first and last serious venture into the political arena.

He had been a highly popular man in Prescott (at least until the disastrous Arizona Lottery incident) and more than five years had elasped since then. Mike longed to test his popularity once more.

The election of January 1885 was a close one. The incumbent mayor, butcher J. L. Hall, had a host of friends and was a good campaigner. But Mike had even more support. The final tally was: Goldwater two hundred eighty-nine, Hall two hundred thirty-two.

Mike threw himself into his new duties with total devotion. He set out immediately to clean up Prescott in a dozen ways: he pushed through an ordinance barring the amateurish "B" girls from the bars of Whiskey Row (a measure enthusiastically supported by the professional prostitutes, whose cribs were located a block to the west); he drew criticism for supporting a measure to build an expensive wooden fence completely around the courthouse square to keep out stray cattle; he gained passage of an ordinance to provide wooden crossings at the downtown street corners.

His most controversial piece of legislation, however, was his pet ordinance, which required all property owners in the central city blocks to construct wooden sidewalks in front of their lots at a cost of about twenty dollars for a fifty-foot front. That raised a howl of protest from many who had extensive land holdings but were not planning to develop them in the near future. It would mean bankruptcy for some, it was claimed. But Mike stuck to his guns, not too diplomatically, and strained many an old friendship in the process.

It was soon evident that Mike was not the smooth politician that Morris had proved to be. He took hard-nosed, no-compromise positions on almost everything, and his reservoir of good will on the council was rapidly drying up. Nonetheless, he plunged ahead. He got a music stand built on the Courthouse Square for band concerts . . . had a lamp post placed in front of the city hall . . . built a new bridge across Granite Creek. It was his war against stray dogs that was his undoing.

Unhappy with the way Police Chief James Dodson was enforcing the stray dog ordinances, Mike called Dodson to task at a council meeting. Dodson responded with a few choice insults aimed at His Honor, and the war was on. Fed up with the irritations of high office, Mike wanted a showdown. At the next council meeting, he confronted the council with an ultimatum:

> Whereas, on the evening of July 7, 1885, at the sitting of the Common Council, and during the session thereof, James M. Dodson, Chief of Police of the City of Prescott, did in the presence of the Mayor and Common Council of the said city of Prescott, use insulting language to the said Mayor, and likewise act disorderly and improper.
>
> Therefore be it resolved that said James M. Dodson be fined the sum of $100 and that he be suspended from office until he pay such fine and appear before the Common Council with proper apologies for his said conduct.
>
> Michel Goldwater, Mayor

Dodson had friends on the council, too, and others felt a one hundred dollar fine was pretty stiff for a man making only one hundred fifty dollars a month. The fine was reduced to fifty dollars, and even that drew bitter argument.

A partial victory would not soothe Mike Goldwater's hurt. When the vote was complete, he submitted his resignation and walked out. The stunned councilmen voted not to accept it.

Efforts to get him to reconsider were to no avail. Three weeks later, the council met again, but Mike was not present. This time his resignation was read and accepted. The brief seven and one-half month administration of Mayor Michel Goldwater was at an end.

Again Mike's thoughts turned to sweet retirement, and within a year, he had made arrangements to sell his entire interest in the Goldwater business to his son Morris. All Mike received in the sale was $11,858, surely a pittance for all the those years of labor and of danger.

Mike Goldwater, at age sixty-five, was free of his Arizona business and civic responsibilities for the first time in a quarter century.

Sarah . . . blissful retirement . . . his grandchildren . . . the life of a patriarch in the Jewish community of San Francisco . . . it all stretched out invitingly for the battle-scarred old frontier warrior.

He had earned his rest.

Even before the fire of 1880, Morris Goldwater had been concerned about developing a dependable water supply for the village of Prescott. During his first term as mayor in 1879, he had initiated planning for new wells and water storage. In 1880 and 1881, as a leader in the formation of the Hook and Ladder Company, he encountered repeated frustration as he tried to fight fires with water pumped by hand from the four wells in the central plaza. He became convinced that only with a pressurized water system could Prescott have any real protection against disaster by fire.

To gain a power base for advocating such a water system, Morris ran for the Common Council at the end of 1881 and was handily elected. All through 1882, he preached his familiar sermon about water needs. And in November of 1882 he ran successfully for the Council, the state legislature's upper house. In the Twelfth Territorial Council in February 1883, he pushed through legislation enabling towns in Arizona to bond themselves to build water systems and other needed improvements.

The fruits of that effort were immediate. On February 27, 1883, Prescott officially became a city and redoubled its search for solutions to its water problem. Despite city leaders' best efforts, the water crisis hung like a sword over the head of Prescott. On January 11, 1895, when he was inaugurated to the second of his many terms as mayor, Morris Goldwater spoke out in frustration:

> Our present system of waterworks is a decided failure. It was a folly or fraud to begin with; it has been a failure and an expense since its inception. Today, after a cost of over $100,000, it gives no water fit for a human to drink; it is insufficient for garden irrigation or sprinkling purposes, and necessity only compels its use for bathing. At the time water is most needed, we have it not.

In the view of many, effective development of solutions to Prescott's water problem began at that moment. Soon, plans were in motion to impound the waters of Pott's Creek and Aspen Creek, and far-sighted people were looking beyond the city in search of dependable water sources. But the voters were loath to approve financing for a really adequate water supply.

They were, that is, until the fateful night of July 14, 1900, when the granddaddy of all Prescott fires raged through the center of the city and destroyed most of the business section. Only three weeks later, a new bond issue of one hundred thousand dollars was approved by Prescott's citizenry. Morris continued to take the lead in solving Prescott's ever-continuing water problems. On December 29, 1923, the City Council celebrated the completion of a new dam and storage lake. Resolution no. 72 honored Morris for half a century of leadership and labor on behalf of Prescott water self-sufficiency. It stated, in part:

> Whereas, as a result of the building of said dam there is now

impounded the waters of Banning and Groom Creeks, forming a beautiful lake, which is and always will be a credit and asset to the City of Prescott.

Now, therefore be it resolved, that the name be known as Lake Goldwater, in honor of Morris Goldwater, Mayor of the City of Prescott.

Lake Goldwater it still is today—as fitting a tribute to one man's wise foresight as Arizona can boast.

Along with all the other fire companies, the volunteer group that the Goldwaters belonged to, the Dudes, fought valiantly on the night of July 14, 1900, when Prescott suffered its worst fire (see appendix). Connell's history says:

This night Prescott had its biggest fire, and there was no water available to fight with. A few dry years had dried up most of the water sources and it was necessary to resort to dynamiting the buildings in the path of the fire, in order to halt its spread through the city. Three and one-half blocks of business and residential buildings burned for a total loss of one and a half million dollars, which was less than 50 percent covered by fire insurance. More firewater went down gullets than was put on the fire.

All of Whiskey Row was destroyed, along with many buildings to the north of the Plaza. But the Goldwater store, hardest hit in 1880, escaped the 1900 conflagration unharmed.

Mike had two ventures into politics, Joe made occasional entries into the political arena, and Henry had short-lived ambitions as a public servant. But for half a century—until Barry Goldwater decided to run for the Phoenix City Council in 1949—Morris carried the Goldwater political banner almost alone.

First elected mayor of Prescott in January 1879, Morris was never out of office for long. When Prescott celebrated its Centennial in 1964, Ray Vyne nominated Morris for that city's "Man of the Century" award, listing these highlights of a distinguished political career:

•1879—Mayor of Prescott
•1883—Served in Upper House (Council) of Twelfth Territorial Legislature
•1884—Yavapai County Board of School Examiners (six years)
•1885—Clerk of the House in Thirteenth Territorial Legislature
•1888—Chairman of Territorial Democratic Central Committee
•1890/94—Two terms on County Board of Supervisors
•1894—Member of Territorial Board of Equalization

- 1894-97—Mayor of Prescott
- 1898-01—City Councilman
- 1899—President of the Council in the Twentieth Territorial Legislature
- 1905-13—Four terms as Prescott mayor
- 1910—Vice President of Arizona Constitutional Convention
- 1914—President of the Senate in Second Arizona State Legislature
- 1919-27—Mayor of Prescott

Even the careful Mr. Vyne did not list all of Morris's public service activities. It could be added that he was appointed to the Tempe Normal School Board of Visitors in 1910-1911; that he was a leader in the ill-fated effort to bring the transcontinental railroad through Prescott in the early 1880s; and that he was a tireless promoter and investor in the successful scheme to build the narrow-gauge Prescott and Central Arizona Railroad (known as the Tom Bullock Line) connecting Prescott with the main line to the north in 1887.

Add to that his service to the Dudes fire company, his monumental career as a Masonic leader, his leadership in forming the Prescott militia, his decades of labor as secretary of the Arizona Bankers Association, and untold other endeavors, and one marvels anew at the unbelievable energy and devotion of this remarkable man.

Morris made his first bid for major territorial office—President of the Council (Senate)—against an Arizona legend, George W. P. Hunt of Gila County in the Twentieth Assembly of 1899. Hunt had powerful backing for the post, but Morris went into the Democratic caucus and handed Hunt one of his few political defeats. In that session, today's Northern Arizona University was born, plans were mapped for obtaining Arizona statehood, and Santa Cruz County was created. Morris's efforts on behalf of women's suffrage fell short, but not by much.

It was during his term on the Territorial Board of Equalization that Morris's sense of humor often got the board through tense deliberations on tax assessments.

Looking around the room during a meeting in Phoenix one day, he was struck with the diversity of the board's makeup. In mock seriousness, he said:

> This board needs to be reorganized. We have three Jews and two Mormons. What do you say we put a white man on the board?

His remark was widely quoted in territorial newspapers, and nobody seemed to be offended. The *Miner* reported that "the board burst into laughter and six bottles of soda were ordered up."

One of the fascinating anecdotes of the Goldwater political saga concerns a little Italian-American boy who came to Prescott as a ten-year-old when his father, a career army bandmaster, was transferred from Fort Huachuca to Fort Whipple in 1892.

The boy grew up in Prescott, attended Washington School there, and was graduated from that school in 1898, just before his father was transferred by the Army to a post in Missouri. He knew Baron and Henry Goldwater, and developed a special admiration for Morris, who was mayor of the city during much of that period. Later he moved to New York City, and became one of its most famous mayors.

Morris was delighted to learn of his young friend's rapid rise to prominence, and the next time he was in New York, he knocked on the City Hall door marked

Fiorello H. La Guardia

Mayor

"Tell Mayor LaGuardia that Mayor Goldwater is waiting out here to see him," Morris instructed the secretary. Within minutes, the mayors of New York City and Prescott were embracing and remembering the old days when the West was wild.

Arizona citizens had chafed under territorial status for thirty-five years when Buckey O'Neill helped organize the Arizona contingent of the Rough Riders for the war in Cuba. Repeated attempts to push statehood bills through Congress had met with defeat, and the outlook seemed as bleak as ever.

Perhaps, reasoned Buckey and his mates, a spectacular showing by Arizona patriots in the Spanish-American War would give statehood chances a solid boost. But all that the Arizonans got from their heroism was a bit of flowery publicity. The statehood issue still languished, and little support was accorded it.

Start of construction of the Roosevelt Dam on the Salt River gave exciting new promise for prosperity and population growth in the irrigated empire of central Arizona. Another move for statehood was launched, but easterners could not imagine such a sparsely populated land qualifying for such exalted status.

A compromise was offered: How about lumping the statehood aspirations of Arizona with those of New Mexico. The capital would be Santa Fe, but at least Arizona would be part of the Union.

A vote was held to test the acceptance of the joint-statehood idea, and it came out exactly as might be expected: New Mexico heavily endorsed it, and Arizona turned it down flat.

Morris Goldwater, along with other Arizona political leaders, kept the wires and mails busy with messages urging Arizonans to hold fast for separate statehood. When Congress finally passed the enabling legislation for Arizona statehood in 1910—nearly half a century after the creation of Arizona Territory in 1863—there was wild celebrating in every city and settlement from border to border.

Now it was time to put aside sectional and party animosities, to gather the most competent leaders in the territory to hammer out a constitution for what soon was to be the forty-eighth state of the American union.

Who would lead that constitutional convention? Many had aspirations for the presidency of that historic gathering. George Wiley Paul Hunt, the rough-talking dynamo from Globe, coveted that high honor with all his being. And Morris Goldwater admitted that he would not turn it down if his fellow Arizonans offered him the mantle of convention leadership.

An Album

Michel Goldwater, circa 1880

Michel and Sarah Goldwater,
circa their fiftieth wedding
anniversary, 1900

Sarah Goldwater (Mrs. Michel), about the
time of their marriage

Young Joe Goldwater,
circa the 1860s

Young Henry Goldwater, in Prescott

Lemuel Goldwater, Joe's son, shown in
later years in California

Morris Goldwater, with Masonic decorations

Josephine Williams, upon
graduation from nursing
school

Baron Goldwater,
circa 1910

Goldwater annual picnic; Baron Goldwater is in top row center

Josephine Williams (later Goldwater) in
Chicago before departing for Arizona,
1903.

Graduation day for the young Goldwaters: Barry (top), Carolyn (left), and Bob (right).

"My two Barrys": Jo Goldwater titled this photo of Baron and young Barry, taken about 1912.

Cadet Barry Goldwater, Staunton Military Academy, Virginia

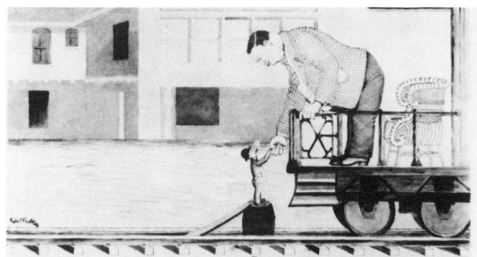

THE PRESIDENT TOLD MR GOLDWATER IT WAS MOST GRATIFYING TO SHAKE
THE HAND OF A MAYOR WHOSE VERY NAME INDICATES THE MONETARY STAN-
-DARD OF THE NATION AND THE FOUNDATION PLANK OF THE PROHIBITION PARTY.

Cartoon depicts Morris Goldwater welcoming President Taft to Prescott, 1909.

Phoenix main street, 1872

Goldwater's Prescott store, built 1879

Bella Union Hotel, Los Angeles, about 1855, where Mike and Joe
Goldwater had business operations

Goldwater's Phoenix department store, mid-1930s

Baron Goldwater residence, 710 N. Center Street, Phoenix, circa 1920

The Barry Goldwater family: (top row) Michael, Joan, Barry Jr.; (bottom) Margaret, Peggy, Barry

Pilot Barry Goldwater prepares to fly jet aircraft

The Phoenix Thunderbirds: (l-r) Len Huck, Barry Goldwater, Paul Fannin

Barry Goldwater with Lyndon Johnson

Barry Goldwater with Senator Everett Dirksen, 1964

Former president Dwight D. Eisenhower and Barry Goldwater, 1964

Ronald Reagan with Peggy and Barry Goldwater at the 1964 Republican
National Convention

9

Chasing Rainbows

The first Goldwater to play a role in national affairs, and the first to become seriously involved in western reclamation projects, was not Barry, but his Uncle Henry Goldwater, who came onto the Arizona scene three decades before Barry was born.

This little-known member of the illustrious family was an older brother of Barry's father, Baron; Henry came to Ehrenberg as a boy, ran a Prescott cigar store for a time, and broke away from the family business on several occasions to make it on his own.

Barry's notable career in Arizona water legislation, and particularly his long battle on behalf of the Central Arizona Project, was foreshadowed by Henry Goldwater's 1885 efforts to create an irrigated agricultural empire in Arizona's Yuma County. It took amazing foresight to picture that barren desert country as a green paradise of citrus groves and cotton fields, but Henry's dream has long since become a reality.

Even earlier, Henry made his mark in Arizona history by blowing the whistle on white-collar crime in the U.S. Post Office. As the youthful postmaster of Ehrenberg, he discovered that unscrupulous contractors were defrauding the federal government of millions of dollars in what has become known as the "Star Route Scandal." Summoned to Washington, D.C., to tell what he knew about the machinations in the delivery of rural routes, he contributed to the downfall of several wealthy contractors and two United States senators (see appendix).

Barry Goldwater knew very little about his Uncle Henry until he became engrossed in researching the history of his family. The story that was pieced together by his investigations and those of other researchers make Henry come alive as a warm and earnest personality who played a role on the stage of Arizona history.

We see in Henry a passionate youngster whose dreams of glory and gold never came true. He was very different from his father, Mike, and his brothers Morris and Baron, who stuck tenaciously to a task until it was completed.

Henry was a butterfly, flitting from one promising flower to another, never staying long enough to find sustenance in any of them. Yet he helped build Arizona Territory, as did his community-minded wife, Julia. Henry and Julia are part of the intricate tapestry of Barry Goldwater's heritage.

Today we are reminded of them by the beautiful Victorian home they built in the mid-1890s on an eminence overlooking the city of Prescott. The Henry Goldwater House has been restored and will be maintained as a historic structure.

Perhaps this narrative will help restore Henry to his rightful place in the history of early Arizona.

PRESCOTT, 1884

IN 1884, HENRY GOLDWATER WAS FOND OF HIS FOUR BROTHERS, BUT HE DID NOT have an exalted opinion of any of them.

He respected Morris, of course—more as a wise old uncle than a brother. But he considered his eldest brother, six years his senior, much too bound up by feelings of family responsibility and civic duty. Morris's idea of a good time was to spend an evening with a new telescope and its associated lenses that he had bought from a scientific catalog. Morris was always buying some new gadget from a catalog.

At the other end of the age spectrum was Baron, eight years Henry's junior. Baron was an obedient sheep, following the wishes of Morris and his father in all things. Yes, Baron—work hard, keep your nose clean, and you'll be a partner before any of the rest of us.

Sam, a year older than he, was a more regular fellow, but his goals were too low. Sam seemed completely happy in that smelly little cigar store, making small bets and cleaning out cuspidors. Gambling was all right, but a real man should gamble for higher stakes than Sam did.

Then there was Ben, having a ball over in California and living the life Henry would like to live. Ben was now a traveling salesman for B. Blumenthal and Co., one of the nation's major makers of gloves. He didn't have a really solid income, but he was going places and seeing things.

Who was the Goldwater brother with imagination and foresight, the one destined for big things in this world? Henry himself, of course. Oh, he had run into some bad luck at Ehrenberg, at Parker, at Howells, in the forwarding business, and in some mining ventures. But he was the one with *big ideas,* and one of these days he'd make a fortune off one of them.

In 1884, Prescott was too small to hold Henry Goldwater. Railroad building in Mexico was very big at the moment, and he decided to get in on the rewards. Family friend E. J. Bennitt, the civil engineer and former Goldwater's clerk, had been surveying railroad rights-of-way in Mexico only two years before. Bennitt could put Henry on the inside track to success.

So Henry soon found himself in Mexico City, looking for an executive job in railroad building. Before long, he was not only unemployed, but broke and too proud to write home for money. With help of a friend, he got a job as a clerk in a small railroad depot in Guanajuato, making seventy-five pesos a month. Those were barely subsistence wages, however. Soon Henry was on his way to Yuma, where Abe Frank (with some urging from Morris) had offered him a job in his store. By August 1885, Henry had talked his way into the job of postmaster at Yuma, his third (after Ehrenberg and Howells) such post in Arizona.

Soon he was envisioning great possibilities for irrigated farming in the Yuma area, and putting his money into a stock company that built canals and dams, called the Mohawk Valley Canal Company. That and other Yuma irrigation projects enthralled and impoverished Henry for several years. (It was more than seventy years later that the federal government made a success of the Wellton-Mohawk Project, a program strongly supported in the U.S. Senate by Baron's son, Barry.)

As was often the case, Henry Goldwater was simply a man ahead of his time. His vision of an irrigated empire around desolate Yuma must have seemed laughable in the late 1880s. But one has only to visit the amazingly prosperous Yuma County agricultural empire today to see how prophetic Henry's plans really were.

Henry and his fellow investors failed only because they did not have enough capital or enough technical know-how at that time. But many thousands of Arizonans can be grateful for their foresight.

Like so many ambitious men who lived along the Colorado River, Henry took many a flyer in gold-mining ventures, none of which ever paid off. At the time, each was a sure thing, but somehow they never panned out the way everybody expected. Henry's wages in Frank's Yuma store were modest, and he never was able to save anything.

Viewing the situation with growing concern, newly retired Mike wrote to Morris in Prescott in 1888, urging that he persuade Henry to come back into the family business.

Like the prodigal son, Henry came back.

Not only was he welcomed by Morris and Baron, but he was made a partner in the firm. Again the signpainter was called in, this time to make the sign on the Prescott store read "M. Goldwater and *Bros.*"

Tired of wandering, Henry entered into the family business gratefully and with enthusiasm. Always a personable young man who made friends easily, he was a real asset to the Goldwater firm. And in 1889, he fell in love.

The young lady was Julia Kellogg, a pretty school teacher from Keokuk, Iowa, whom every young swain in town was courting. She had everything— brains, good looks, a sweet disposition, amazing loyalty—everything, that is, except the Goldwater family's religious faith.

Here was the crisis Mike and Sarah had dreaded for so long. Their loving son was in love with a gentile, and determined to marry her. When Sarah became convinced that Henry was really going through with the marriage, she sorrowfully began the Jewish rite of "sitting shivah," usually reserved for a death in the family.

Morris was called into the controversy and asked to do what he could to avert this tragedy. After a long talk with Julia, Morris reported to his relieved parents that Julia had agreed to embrace the Jewish faith and to be married by a rabbi. The ceremony took place in Chicago on October 27, 1893, and was conducted by Rabbi Emil Hirsch. So it was that the first of the Goldwater sons to marry did not, after all, disappoint his parents by marrying outside the faith.

Henry could not have chosen a more completely wonderful mate. Carrie's daughter, Evie Aronson Margolis, remembered her sixty years later as "the sweetest thing in the world." Mike was pleased with his new daughter-in-law, and even Sarah was not unhappy with her. Julia supported Henry in all his ambitious enterprises, followed him hither and yon, and did without many of the essentials of life in the lean years.

Not many months after their marriage, they moved into a spacious new house (now a Prescott showplace) at 217 East Union Street on Nob Hill. Henry was able to provide Julia with a part-time cook and maid. He became treasurer of the prestigious new Prescott Club, and Julia was known for her energetic support of civic causes. She and Henry had no children.

Her favorite charity, by all odds, was the public library that she and her friend, Mrs. E. B. Gage, worked so hard to establish in Prescott. Hearing that wealthy Andrew Carnegie was distributing his millions across the nation in support of free public libraries, she wrote a personal letter to the great philanthropist, stating Prescott's need in these words (and with a few errors in spelling):

Prescott, Arizona
June 1, 1899
Mr. Andrew Carnagie
Pittsburg, Pennsylvania
Dear Sir:
Your well known philanthropy has prompted me to appeal to you in the interest of a truly charitable work.

In our little town of 3,000 inhabitants, we have after much effort and work established a library of nine hundred volumes—good, readable books in good condition; but we have no endowment. . . . It is our aim and hope to make the library free and to maintain a free reading room.

Prescott has a large floating population of young men, many of whom cannot afford to keep their own homes lighted and heated. They have no recourse but the saloons and "dives," for there are no innocent amusements in the town.

If we could get an endowment of $10,000, or even $8,000, we would at once make the library free. . . .

Julia Kellogg Goldwater

Carnegie, whose riches from America's steel industry established sorely needed libraries from coast to coast, replied to this plaintive appeal from Arizona Territory. If they could raise four thousand dollars in Prescott for the public library, the Carnegie Foundation would match it, he said.

Julia Goldwater was ecstatic. She and her co-workers canvassed the town with missionary zeal, and raised the money. The *Journal-Miner* of November 18, 1899, noted that "these ladies are actuated by a desire to maintain not only an institution of benefit to all, but a retreat likewise to those who under present conditions are compelled to wander aimlessly about."

On December 28, the *Journal-Miner* proudly announced that:

Mrs. E. B. Gage and Mrs. Henry Goldwater, who have labored persistently and gratuitously in the cause of a public library, are on the eve of seeing their labors fulfilled. . . . They have succeeded, so it is said, and the county officials will donate a strip somewhere on the Plaza for the purpose and on the completion of the plans of the building.

Succeeded they had! Prescott will always owe a debt of gratitude to Julia Goldwater, who wrote to Andrew Carnegie on a long chance, and came up with the money for a library that has developed into one of Arizona's best.

Many people have wondered how Henry Goldwater managed to appear so prosperous, even in times when he was deep in debt. In the mid-'90s, when Morris and Baron were residing in Prescott boarding houses and living as simply as monks in a monastery, Henry had a grand house on Nob Hill, a fine carriage, and membership in the best club in town.

One of the sources of Henry's prosperity was the money he managed to borrow from others. Julia's family in Keokuk was generous, too. And when the money the Kelloggs sent was not sufficient, Henry sometimes borrowed more. Henry felt confident that these borrowings would be repaid, with handsome interest, the first time one of those "can't miss" business deals came through.

Henry was one of those who urged that Goldwater's make a second venture into Phoenix after the territorial capital was moved there in 1889. Julia always told her relatives that the entire Phoenix project was Henry's idea. But it was his younger brother Baron who developed the plan for the Phoenix store, and was selected by the family partners to be the manager when the store was opened there in 1896.

It was a severe blow to Henry's pride, and he started looking around for new worlds to conquer. By the end of 1901, he had decided to leave Prescott. His sister Annie had married Ralph Prager, member of a Portland, Oregon, clothing store family, and Ralph gave Henry the managership of a new Prager store in San Francisco. It was not a success.

As his niece, Evie Aronson Margolis, later explained,

> Henry was sweet and lovable, but full of crazy ideas for making a fortune. One time he would be investing in bees, another time in strawberries, and almost invariably his plans would end in failure. He was a man chasing rainbows. . . .

Henry entered partnership with a man from South America to build furniture in a Richmond, California, plant. He moved to Aberdeen, Washington, and worked as an accountant. In 1916, he was granted U.S. patent no. 1045695 for a T-square for draftsmen, with features not found on any other.

Early in 1917, with the faithful Julia at his side, he was back in Arizona, this time dabbling in mining promotions on the desert between Quartzsite and Bouse, near the La Paz of Mike's pioneering fifty years before.

A year later he was in Los Angeles, installing a cost system for a film laboratory. The owners urged Henry to stay and grow up with the movie industry, but he was restless and moved on to what he considered bigger prospects.

That's the way it went with Henry and Julia, living precariously from year to year, from one crushed hope to another.

Morris never ceased to worry about his younger brother, and, on one occasion in 1918, he wrote to Baron in Phoenix to see whether they might find a place for him there or in Prescott. The Goldwater family ties were as strong then as they are today. But Henry's pride was as unquenchable as ever. If such an offer was ever made, he turned it down.

As Henry Goldwater moved into his sunset years, his resemblance to his father became increasingly remarkable. One national magazine later ran a picture of Henry under the mistaken assumption that it was Mike. But the resemblance was physical, only. Somehow, the tenacity and the hard business sense that characterized the father were not passed along to the son.

Henry died September 22, 1931, at age seventy-three in Los Angeles, and his ashes were placed in the Goldwater family plot in Hills of Eternity Cemetery, San Francisco.

Today Prescott's ornate Henry Goldwater home, now restored to all its Victorian grandeur, is one of the few Arizona monuments to the lovable fellow who chased rainbows with so little success throughout his long career.

10

Baron and the Phoenix Store

In his love of politics, gadgetry, Masonry and adventure, Barry Goldwater more nearly resembles his Uncle Morris than his own father, Baron Goldwater. Because Baron did not spend an inordinate amount of time with his three children, and because he died while Barry was only a college freshman, father and son did not have as close a relationship as Barry later had with his Uncle Morris.

But anyone who wants to understand Barry Goldwater must first understand Baron. The man who fathered Barry, extricated him from many a youthful scrape, sent him to military school for a more disciplined regimen, and served as his male role model in his formative years, played a leading part in the young man's development.

Barry Goldwater has only admiring words for his father, whom some might consider neglectful of his boisterous children. Barry regarded Baron with great respect. The elder Goldwater, it must be remembered, reached the age of fifty while Barry was a child of seven, and his prominence on the Phoenix business scene made him seem somewhat grand and remote to the youngster.

Still, father and son did share some interests, among them a love of boxing. Barry was an avid participant in the manly art, but Baron preferred to sit at ringside at the Phoenix boxing cards. So regular an attender was he that the local promoter, wishing to show his respect after Baron's death, announced a moment of silence, followed by a symbolic "counting out" of Baron Goldwater with a slow count to ten.

More important was Barry's appreciation of his father's genius as a merchandiser. Although the youngster did not spend much time in the Goldwater store, he was there enough to learn something about the business and to make a decision that he would one day follow in his father's footsteps as head of the store.

Baron (more commonly called Barry) served as a role model in community service, too. Much of young Barry's later enthusiasm for leadership roles in Phoenix can be traced to his father's civic and charitable activity.

It was Baron Goldwater who established the family in Phoenix, and it was he who transformed a frontier general store into one of the nation's best-known and most fashionable department stores. He was one of the builders of modern Phoenix, and his story deserves to be better known.

PHOENIX, 1896

MORRIS GOLDWATER HAD AN EXCELLENT MEMORY. HE COULD STILL PICTURE vividly the frustrations of 1875, when he had labored into the night and on Sundays in a losing battle to make a success of the first Goldwater's store in Phoenix. When approached with the idea almost twenty years later, he could not see the family going back to the scene of that earlier disappointment. The Goldwater store had prospered in Prescott, and Morris was not at all certain that Phoenix had the great future some optimists were predicting for it.

With Mike long-since retired from management, the mantle of seniority was on Morris's shoulders, and it was up to him to counterbalance the expansionist ardor of his younger brothers, Henry and Baron.

Family tradition credits Baron with changing Morris's mind, and with the kind of spectacular stroke that has always been a hallmark of the Goldwater family.

It was in 1894 that Baron challenged Morris to a game of casino to settle the issue. The elder brother's defenses evidently had been considerably weakened by that time, so Morris was willing to leave such an important decision to the gods of chance.

Baron won the game and the decision was made: M. Goldwater and Bros. was headed for Phoenix. A formal partnership agreement to launch the new enterprise was signed by Morris, Henry, Baron, and E. J. Bennitt, the Goldwaters' Phoenix banker and later Barry Goldwater's godfather. Thus Bennitt became the first non-Goldwater since Bernard Cohn in 1867 to be admitted to the exalted status of partner in an enterprise of the Michel Goldwater family. A former New Yorker, he came to Arizona Territory in the early 1880s as an engineer and surveyor, and worked for the Goldwaters, both as a consulting engineer on some of their mining interests and as a clerk in the Prescott store. Bennitt's guidance, and his ability to introduce Baron and Morris to Phoenix business leaders and their wives, was invaluable.

The only decision that remained was that of who should manage the new Phoenix store. Henry, who was older than Baron and who had some experience in managing his own businesses, believed he should be chosen for that important assignment. But Morris saw in Baron a young man of unusual talents as a merchandiser. Moreover, he was steadier than Henry, and showed more likelihood of sticking it out through the probable disappointments of the early years of the new enterprise. Henry would have to remain in Prescott. Bennitt evidently agreed, and Baron got the nod, much to the chagrin of brother Henry, whose heart was never in the family business thereafter. He again started looking about for greener pastures.

More than a year was consumed in scouting the capital city for the most favorable location, sizing up competition, assessing the market, and preparing the building and stock for the grand opening.

In early spring of 1896, the capital of Arizona Territory was little more than a frontier village with fewer than ten thousand residents within and beyond the city limits. Streets were dusty or muddy, depending on the weather; there were stables and blacksmith shops downtown; open canals lined by trees gave the town a rural look. Phoenix depended principally on the surrounding irrigated farming oasis, on business, finance, and government (the territorial capital had been wrested from Prescott in 1889).

There was little demonstrable need for another dry goods store in the dusty little capital. There were seven stores vying for the business of milady and her family: Goldberg Bros., the Bee Hive Store, Alkire's, The Hub, Phoenix Dry Goods, Ike Diamond's, and Sam Korrick's New York Store.

Phoenix enjoyed a surprising amount of "culture"—amateur theatricals and musicales, touring artists, concerts by local bands, lectures, and revival meetings—and sporting events galore. Baseball was popular, and the Phoenix Indian School had recently organized a football team. Later in 1896 at nearby Tempe, a young science teacher named Frederick M. Irish organized the first Territorial Normal School football team, which has since evolved into the Arizona State University Sun Devils.

Air conditioning, sadly, was four decades in the future. As a result, nearly every Phoenician who could afford it left the valley during much of the blistering summer. In many families, Dad was forced to sweat it out at home while Mom and the kids took off for Prescott, a mountainside tent, or a cottage on a Southern California beach.

But even in summer, Phoenix was fast becoming the hub of territorial political and commercial activity. Baron Goldwater was more than willing to brave Phoenix's one-hundred-ten-degree temperatures and frontier crudities to grow with this exciting new city-to-be.

With Morris and Bennitt, during early 1896, he scouted the tiny down-town area, essentially three blocks in any direction from the intersection of Washington and Center streets. The store location that seemed to meet all the necessary criteria—proximity to foot traffic, an empty and available building, and reasonable rental cost—was one in the Fleming Block, at eighteen and twenty North First Avenue.

Opening the Phoenix store was a worrisome undertaking for a family grown comfortable in familiar Prescott, where they knew everybody and what merchandise they were likely to buy. Phoenix was an alien territory, with a very different climate, clientele, and merchandising strategy. Bennitt, who knew Phoenix people, was a key man in those first days of the new enterprise.

Morris and Baron worked feverishly to have the new store open by the advertised date, Saturday, March 21, 1896. Maddeningly, several of the key lines of feminine clothing that they hoped to feature did not arrive at the depot as scheduled. They considered postponing the opening until all the merchandise was on hand, but decided to open the doors on the twenty-first as promised.

The *Gazette* ran an article under its "Brief Mention" heading on opening day:

> We are in receipt of an invitation from M. Goldwater and Bros. of No. 18 and 20 North First Avenue, asking us to visit their new store on Saturday next. The invitation says that we and our friends and our friends' friends will be welcome at all times.
>
> While the firm is in Phoenix to do business, it hopes at the start to impress on the minds of all that visitors as well as customers will always be welcome. In quality of goods, the newness of ideas; in completeness of assortment; in everything that tends to make a store a "thing of beauty," the aim is to be now as ever "The Best Always."

Note the reference to the famed Goldwater's slogan: "The Best Always." It had been used as a watchword of quality, and as an advertising standby, at least as early as 1885, and it was painted prominently on the front of the Prescott store, along with the name "M. Goldwater and Bro., Dealers in General Merchandise."

Family tradition says that it was Morris who first suggested using the slogan "The Best Always," and it was he who perpetuated it until his dying day in 1939. Both Bob and Barry remember that in later years Uncle Morris "would raise hell with us" if they inadvertently omitted it from a store advertisement.

Most of the record of that historic opening day comes to us from the pages of the *Gazette,* which covered commercial activity in greater detail. Its Sunday, March 22, story published a few hours after the last straggler had left the store, captures some of the excitement of a grand opening in a town hungry for excitement:

The First Day
Goldwater Bros. New Dry Goods
Emporium Now Open

If there is one thing more than another dear to the feminine heart, it is an opening day at a dry goods store, and especially when everything is known to be new from the eastern markets.

For this reason, yesterday, which was the day announced for the doors of the Goldwater Bros. store to be thrown open to the public, was a red-letter day in the business history of Phoenix. From an early hour, a continued crowd of people thronged the building and admired the many handsome and useful goods displayed on the counters.

It was meant to be a reception day, and was. But the sales made auger well for the future of the firm in this community. A description of the store is useless and must be seen to be appreciated.

Dutifully appreciative of the *Gazette's* editorial attentions, Goldwater's ran much of its early advertising in that newspaper, including an announcement repeated five times in successive issues, that new dry goods were expected every day.

"Come at any time during the day or evening," read the ad, "provided the electric lights do not go out, and look at the store and goods. Doubtless there will be some articles which will interest visitors as they are in keeping with our motto, 'The Best Always'." It was also pointed out that Goldwater's had a telephone—number 154.

What a wonderland of new merchandise, especially for the ladies, awaited the visitor to that pioneer Goldwater's store! Ladies' suits, two dollars each . . . fine kid gloves, one dollar and ten cents per pair . . . colorful shirtwaists, lacy kerchiefs, ribbons and lace, accessories . . . summer underwear . . . corsets, one dollar . . . fancy parasols. From the beginning, and for a half a century thereafter, piece goods formed a major part of the offering. In one early clearance-sale advertisement, the store offered dress goods at an astoundingly low price: twenty-five yards for a dollar!

From the beginning, Baron stressed customer satisfaction at almost any cost. Goldwater's was going to earn a reputation as a store of quality, dependability, and honest dealing.

Some six weeks after the euphoria of the opening-day extravaganza had passed, Baron ran the following advertisement outlining his business principles.

Watch The Store Grow

Note the active, thrifty, progressive look of things. You have confidence in the reliability of our statements. . . .

We won't sell you cotton for wool, or jute for flax. The meaner sorts of merchandise we have no time to bother with. Neither have you, if we judge our trading public right.

Clean, honest, reliable stuff at the lowest prices is what intelligent buyers are looking for. We want none other.

Remember, we give your money back if you are not pleased with the purchase. Try us with your next mail order. The thousand and one "little things" it always pleases a lady to find are to be had at our "notion counter."

M. Goldwater and Bros.
18 and 20 North 1st Ave.

"Pleas[ing] a lady": in those three words, Baron Goldwater summarized what was to be his life's work. Here was a man who truly admired and appreciated women, and who spent most of his days on earth romancing them with special attention and merchandise most dear to the feminine heart.

The Phoenix Goldwater's store was to be noticeably different from its Prescott parent in several ways. Mike and Morris's store had served the pioneer's need for everything from shovels to sunbonnets. Almost from the first day, Baron's character was embossed on the Phoenix store, which set out to gain trust and confidence, but didn't mind beguiling with the latest temptations from New York and the Continent.

What sort of young man was this Baron Goldwater, who brought a new dimension of merchandising to the Goldwater operation, spread the family influence to the new capital city of Arizona, and became a recognized leader in Phoenix financial and community affairs?

He was a handsome young man in early 1896—not quite thirty and still regarded by his parents and elder siblings as the baby of the family. He stood just under five feet, ten inches, weighed about one hundred sixty-five pounds, had blue eyes, dark hair that later became a distinguished grey. He dressed impeccably, had his nails manicured, and even used cologne.

Born May 8, 1866, in Los Angeles, he lived with his mother and attended school in Los Angeles and San Francisco during his father's long periods in Arizona where he was laying the foundations of a mercantile empire.

But like his brother Morris—fourteen years his senior—Baron could hardly wait to leave the dreary schoolroom and win his spurs in the real world of business. Morris had been sixteen when he joined the family business, and Baron was the same age in 1882 when he made the trek to Arizona Territory to take his place with Mike and Morris in the Prescott store. Henry was still trying to make it on his own in 1882, and did not return to the family fold until early 1888.

Unlike Henry, the sometimes-rebellious one, Baron was an obedient and attentive son who buckled down and directed his energies to one purpose—learning the mercantile business. One of Baron's little-known activities was as a dealer in fine pianos. Newspaper items of the late 1880s confirm that he had pianos shipped to Prescott on a steady basis, apparently as a private venture unconnected with the store, and ran a regular advertisement for this enterprise.

Whether it was pianos or ladies' underwear, Baron seemed to have a God-given ability to sell merchandise, and knew it. By the time he was entrusted with the management of the Phoenix store in 1896, he had made several buying trips to California and the East, and had proved himself adept at choosing lines that would sell. He was a wizard with figures, too. Associates often marveled at his ability to scan a column of sales totals and point out errors without resorting to an adding machine.

Most important of all, he demonstrated unusual ability in getting along with employees, suppliers, customers, and almost everyone else. Both Mike and Morris, whose tendencies toward brusqueness sometimes caused minor irritations, became admirers of the young man's natural flair for human relations.

Once he had the new store operating smoothly in Phoenix, Baron began to take part in the civic life of his adopted town. In just over a year, he was elected a director of the Phoenix Chamber of Commerce and was in demand for special civic projects. His long-time friend and competitor, Chet Goldberg, recalled in later years that Baron was a "good community service man, but he really was a lone wolf when it came to business." Baron went his own way on closing hours, merchandising, promotions, and many other matters.

Baron, who had made a lengthy buying trip in early March just before the Phoenix store was opened, was off again to New York in mid-July. This time, according to the *Gazette,* he was gone nearly two months. As he would do many times in coming years, Morris came down from cool Prescott to the worst of the Phoenix summer and took over management of the new store in Baron's absence. Although Morris had enjoyed his buying trips to New York, he was now too deeply involved in local and state politics (he was at that time a member of the Territorial Board of Equalization) to be away so long. To Baron, then, fell the responsibility of buying for both the Prescott and Phoenix stores.

By Christmas of their first year in Phoenix, Goldwater's was adding new lines with some frequency. A new department devoted entirely to neckwear and accessories opened, and the housewares department was enlarged. The store's eminence in cosmetics and toilet articles, which was to gain national note, had its beginnings at this time. It started with what seems today to be a questionable thesis: "Toilet articles are cheaper in our store than in a drug store," but prices seemed to bolster the argument. Some bath powders sold for five and ten cents a can, and Vasoline was a nickel a jar. Even the more expensive soaps and facial preparations were less than twenty cents.

Baron set the styles for the women of Phoenix for many a year, and he often set the pace for men, as well. Chet Goldberg credits him with being the first Phoenix businessman to break away from wearing suits in the summer heat and going to work in a short-sleeved white shirt and necktie. Succeeding generations of Phoenix males, even with air conditioning, have reason to bless him for that.

It was not long thereafter that Baron started to arrange exclusive contracts with many of the top-line cosmetics firms.

"At one time," recalls his son Bob, "Goldwater's had exclusive rights in Phoenix for most of the major lines—Elizabeth Arden, Helena Rubenstein, Dorothy Grey, and several others. People in New York must have thought we had a store in Phoenix as big as the May Company or Marshall Field. It was because of Dad's persuasiveness, and his good representation of the lines, that we were able to lock up these lines for so many years."

It was during the fall of 1898 that Baron decided the store must be moved to larger quarters. Despite everything his staff could do to use each inch of space in the First Avenue building, it became increasingly cramped as the popularity of the store increased.

His search for new quarters took him less than three blocks east to an available building with a sales floor twenty-five feet wide and one hundred thirty-six feet deep at 134 East Washington Street. Baron had a rear balcony installed, providing room for a mezzanine of sorts. Moreover, there was a basement at the site, and this space was used as a storeroom.

As soon as the Christmas holiday rush was over, Goldwater's staff started moving merchandise to the new location.

In its edition of January 3, 1899, the *Gazette* ran this plug for the new store:

A Store To Be Proud Of
M. Goldwater and Bros. New Establishment

The Store to be Opened Today for Public Inspection

The Stocks as Well as the Store Are the Finest in the Territory

When M. Goldwater and Bros. open their store at 134 East Washington Street this morning, they will open the finest equipped store in the territory. Not only will they open the finest store, but they will offer for sale the finest stock as they adhere to the high quality standard which they have set for themselves since their advent in the Phoenix mercantile world three years ago.

The object sought by Messers. Goldwater in moving from their old location into their present quarters was more room and a store which would be equipped to better advantage and wherein their fine stocks of dry goods, ladies' suits and wraps, fancy goods and art ware might be shown. . . .

There are several skylights through which the bright Arizona sunlight streams, and at night over a hundred incandescent lights will shed their rays on the fine goods. . . .

There were the festivities always associated with Goldwater's openings—music, entertainment, and general gaiety. Although a store twenty-five feet in width seems incredibly cramped by today's standards, the new location did offer more floor space and a site a bit closer to the heart of downtown business activity.

The years 1897 and 1898 brought a double dose of sadness to the Goldwater family.

First, Baron's brother Ben died on July 13, 1897, in Prescott. Only thirty-three at the time of his death, Ben was two years older than Baron. He had been a traveling salesman until moving to Prescott in 1895. The Prescott *Journal-Miner* had this to say of the young man's demise:

> Ben F. Goldwater died Sunday at noon at the residence of his brother, Henry Goldwater, of consumption. He came here two years ago suffering with the disease, apparently in its last stages, but he was benefitted by the climate and no doubt prolonged his life for several months.
>
> Brothers of the deceased residing in Arizona are Morris, Henry, and Barry Goldwater, prominent in mercantile circles here and in Phoenix, who have the sincere sympathy of the entire community in their bereavement.

Tuberculosis, known in that era as "consumption," claimed another brother, Sam, fifteen months later. Like Ben, he had moved from California to Arizona in a futile attempt to cure the dread disease, but came too late.

Arizona newspapers announced Henry's departure from Prescott on

February 15, 1902. The partnership consisting of Morris, Henry, and Baron M. Goldwater, under the name M. Goldwater and Bros., was dissolved. Henry was leaving for the West Coast, and Morris and Baron continued as partners under the same firm name.

The younger of the two remaining Goldwater brothers was busily growing up with Phoenix, a town that pleased him more with each passing year. At the turn of the century, Baron was living at 128 East Adams Street, not much more than a block from the new store. Let others worry about owning carriages or one of those newfangled automobiles—Baron Goldwater would walk. Unlike Morris, he detested machinery. Never did Baron learn to drive a car, even when he later relented and bought one. The family handyman, LeRoy, drove him when the occasion demanded. And after Baron's marriage, his wife Jo usually took the wheel.

Not only did Baron disdain driving, but refused to concern himself with anything mechanical—automobile engines, furnaces, plumbing, or anything else.

"I never saw him hammer a nail or tighten a screw," says his son Bob. "He liked to watch boxing, but he wasn't interested in outdoor sports. I'm told he played only one game of golf, and after hitting several balls out of bounds, he threw his clubs into a canal and never ventured onto the course again."

Baron had his own interests, and they were many. He enjoyed social events and travel, if it was first class. He loved good food, properly served, and fine wines. He was a loyal Elk and a member of the Phoenix Chamber of Commerce board. There was no more constant patron of the Arizona Club bridge and poker tables than he. Charitable projects of many kinds found him a willing worker and a generous giver. In 1900, he was one of the founding investors in the Iron Springs Outing Club, which built a popular Arizona resort near Prescott.

"I'm sure the man gave away more than he kept in this life," one of his old friends declared after his death.

One of his early interests was community health care. When the Sisters' Hospital (now St. Joseph's) encountered financial difficulty in late 1898, Baron banded with other Phoenix community leaders to find a solution.

His duties at the store, his busy social life, and his community service kept Baron Goldwater occupied from early morning to evening. Unfortunately for him, he never devoted his time to investing in valley real estate or growing industries. (Those who did—men such as Harry and Newton Rosenzweig's father, Isaac—amassed ranches and building lots and other properties that tripled and quadrupled in value when boom times came.) Baron chose not to enter into such speculation, and even rented his store building and his home. That he might have become a rich man with a few well-chosen investments is beyond denying. Whether he would thus have been a happier man is open to conjecture.

The store at 135 East Washington, opening in conjunction with the new year of 1899, was an almost instant success. Business was good as the decade of the Gay Nineties approached its close, and Phoenix was alive with optimistic talk—talk of a great new dam that might soon be built at the confluence of the Salt River and Tonto Creek, creating a storage reservoir and guaranteeing both an agricultural boom in central Arizona and a barrier against the ruinous floods that periodically plagued the Valley; talk of new business ventures; even discussion of Arizona statehood, thought to be just around the corner.

After three years at the helm of Goldwater's Phoenix store, Baron had developed a solid self-confidence. Moreover, he had convinced Morris that he could handle any problem that might come up. That was fortunate, because 1899 was the year in which the Hon. Morris Goldwater was elected president of the Council (now called the Senate) of the Territorial Legislature. Although his legislative duties kept him in Phoenix for weeks at a time, Morris was so involved in problems of government that he stayed out of Baron's hair. Much as he loved and admired his older brother, Baron felt a certain relief when Morris was not looking over his shoulder.

Baron's reputation as a businessman and civic leader was exceeded only by his fame as Phoenix's most eligible bachelor. He was by now in his late thirties, trim and good looking as ever, a fabulous dresser, charming company at any social event, and the target of many an ambitious husband hunter.

Whenever Baron visited San Francisco, his mother and sisters managed to introduce him to eligible Jewish girls. Like Morris, he had patiently warded off such introductions for years. In Phoenix, he enjoyed the company of many a charmer, but was never tempted to pop the question.

His parents hoped that all their children would marry in the Jewish faith, but so far, of the five sons, only Henry had married at all. As they reached the twilight of their lives, Mike and Sarah sadly accepted the fact that they would never see a grandchild named Goldwater.

The death of Mike in San Francisco in 1903 removed one of the last ties to Baron's and Morris's tenuous Jewish heritage. Since his retirement from the family business in 1887, Mike had been living a well-earned life of leisure and community service in San Francisco with Sarah. He had come to Phoenix to see the new Goldwater's store in June 1896, but had not visited Arizona often since that time.

The details of Michel Goldwater's death and funeral were told in the *Arizona Republican* of April 21, 1903 (note the misspelling of the first name):

Michael Goldwater Dead
The Passing of an Arizona Pioneer in
San Francisco

Barry Goldwater of this city received the painful news yesterday morning that his father, Michael Goldwater, died in San Francisco Sunday evening at 10:15 o'clock (April 19).

Michael Goldwater was one of the earliest pioneers of Arizona and one of her best known and most highly respected citizens. He came to the territory in the 60's, shortly after the war, first engaging in business at Ehrenburg [sic], on the Colorado River, with his brother Joseph, now dead.

When he arrived the only town of any moment in the western part of the territory was La Paz, some distance south of Ehrenburg and near the Colorado. . . . Mr. Goldwater, besides keeping a store at Ehrenburg for many years secured contracts from the government for supplying the military posts in central and northern Arizona, with provisions for man and beast and in carrying out these contracts did an immense freighting business west from New Mexico supply points.

About 1874 he opened a store in Phoenix, still maintaining his Ehrenburg house. . . . After several years he closed it up and opened a store in Prescott, also closing up the Ehrenburg store. The Prescott store was managed till about 14 years ago, when he retired from business and returned to San Francisco, his family home. . . . Mr. Goldwater had reached the advanced age of 83 years and in view of the fact that about three years ago he suffered a stroke of paralysis, his death was not especially surprising, though he was till recently enjoying a fair measure of health.

It was two years after Mike's death that Baron, thirty-nine and assumed by all to be an incurable bachelor, met the young lady who was to change his life completely.

Josephine Williams was her name and nursing was her profession. Like so many Arizonans of the early 1900s, she had come to the territory from the Midwest with respiratory problems. But now she had won out over the disease that doctors said would end her life within six months, and she was a popular member of the Phoenix social set. Almost from the moment she met Baron Goldwater at his store on East Washington, she knew that this was the man for her.

"Every woman in Phoenix was after him," she declared later, "but I got him!"

11

Families

"All that I am, or hope to be, I owe to my angel mother," Abraham Lincoln once declared. Barry Goldwater's mother, Josephine Williams Goldwater, was regarded as something less than angelic by many of her Victorian contemporaries. But there is no doubt that she shaped Barry's life as surely as Lincoln's mother shaped his.

Jo was one of a kind: a spunky individualist who refused to conform to the stuffy moral code of her day. She smoked and had an occasional drink; she swore when she felt like it, wore trousers, and did many other things that ladies of her station were not supposed to do. But in the really important areas of living—caring, loving, achieving, serving— Jo was truly an angel. Few mothers gave themselves more completely to their children than she.

Barry, Bob, and Carolyn can reminisce for hours about growing up in Jo Goldwater's home, and about the sheer joy she brought to their adventuresome young lives. "Mungie," as they called her, took them camping in the wilderness, crammed them and their friends into a car for trips across the desert to California, taught them golf, and gave them the moral sustenance that has fed them all their lives.

Baron Goldwater married Jo Williams a few months after his brother Morris had broken his vow of bachelorhood by marrying his Prescott landlady, Sarah (Sallie) Fisher. Both marriages helped change the course of the Goldwater saga, and thus of Arizona history.

Until the two middle-aged bachelors took wives, the Goldwater story in Arizona had been almost exclusively a male narrative. Mike's wife, Sarah, refused to set foot in Arizona, except for a brief visit after Mike retired. To her, the territory was too uncivilized for any proper lady. Joe's wife, Ellen, never came to Arizona at all. Of Mike and Sarah's five sons, only Henry married before their parents' death, and they soon left Arizona for California.

In sharp contrast, both Morris and Baron's wives spent most of their lives in Arizona. They loved this raw land, and they gave all their energies to building and civilizing it.

Barry Goldwater cherishes the memories of his mother, who will always be honored as an authentic frontier character and a pioneer builder of Phoenix. Much of his own record of achievement and public service has roots in Jo's guidance.

PHOENIX, 1906

SARAH GOLDWATER ALWAYS WANTED HER SONS TO MARRY IN THE JEWISH FAITH, and (as was evident in the case of Henry's marriage) made it clear that she would be deeply hurt if they did not follow her wishes in this matter. Whether or not Morris and Baron delayed marriage because of their mother's feelings is debatable. but the fact remains that they did not marry until after her death in San Francisco on May 27, 1905.

After many years of boarding at the home of Mr. and Mrs. John L. Fisher, 240 S. Cortez Street, Prescott, and following a nine-year wait after Mr. Fisher's death, Morris told Baron in June 1906 that he was going to marry his landlady, Sarah (Sallie) Shivers Fisher, who was a Protestant.

Upon receiving this news, Baron wrote Morris a letter, on M. Goldwater and Bro. stationery, June 7, 1906. One of the few surviving pieces of correspondence between the brothers, it overflows with genuine love:

My Dear Morris:
Dear brother and friend, accept my most sincere and hearty congratulations. God bless and keep you and bestow on you the many blessings you so well deserve. May your every wish, and for years to be, be realized. . . . I want to embrace and love you. How much you have been and always will be, to me, you will never know.

I am happy to learn that you are to have a home for yourself, and a good wife. . . .

Why don't we go [to San Francisco], have your last batchelor [*sic*] "bout" together? We can say nothing of your [marriage] intentions if you think best. . . .

Again I congratulate you. My love to my future sister and yourself.
Your loving brother,
Barry

Who was Sarah Shivers Fisher, Morris's intended bride and the lady the Goldwaters remember as "Aunt Sallie?" She was born in Missouri in 1859 and came with her family to the Prescott area in 1862, before the creation of Arizona Territory. She married John L. Fisher, a Chino Valley merchant and later Prescott mayor, when she was sixteen and moved with him to Prescott.

Sallie, a large woman with a hearty laugh, loved to talk, especially about her pioneering days in early Arizona Territory. Morris's sisters evidently thought she lacked the learning and finesse to be Morris's wife. Evie Aronson Margolis remembered that her mother "always felt Sarah was a good, wholesome influence on Morris, but on the other hand, she was a poor cook and not a very good housekeeper."

Morris was serving one of his terms as mayor of Prescott in 1906, so it was impossible for him to have much of a private life. His decision to go on rooming at the Fisher home so many years after the death of Sarah's husband caused whispers of disapproval from some Prescott residents. There are old-timers who declare that the City Council went so far as to make a resolution that the mayor should either marry the lady or move out of her home, in the interest of civic propriety.

Morris heard the rumors and sensed the disapproval, but he went serenely on his way, living at the Fisher home as he always had. Finally, more for Sarah's sake than to appease the Prescott citizenry, Morris asked the lady to set a date.

Apparently wishing to avoid a big wedding in Prescott, the pair went to Los Angeles for the ceremony, which was performed by a Protestant minister on September 19, 1906.

The *Arizona Republican* of the following day had this to say about the wedding:

> GOLDWATER-FISHER—Hon. Morris Goldwater and Mrs. J. L. Fisher were married in Los Angeles yesterday by Rev. E. W. Meaney. The function was a private family ceremony, attended only by a few immediate relatives. Mr. and Mrs. Goldwater will return to Prescott about October 1.
>
> Mr. Goldwater is one of the most prominent and successful businessmen in Yavapai County and is Mayor of Prescott. The bride has also lived in that city for many years and is well-known and popular.

Back in Phoenix, Baron's romance with nurse Josephine Williams was the talk of the town. From the moment in late October 1903, when she had arrived in Phoenix on the caboose of a freight train, Jo Williams earned a reputation for individuality and for daring.

No prisoner of Victorian mores, the spunky little lady from the Midwest lived life to the full and did pretty much as she pleased. Part of her zest for living could be traced to the reason she now lived in Phoenix: her doctors in Chicago had sent her to Arizona to die of tuberculosis, and they hadn't been optimistic that she had many months left to her.

Jo had bounce and zing, an independence that no one could saddle, and a willingness to try anything once. Although she never weighed as much as one hundred pounds until her children came, she often braved the unfamiliar Arizona desert and mountains on camping trips. She walked unafraid down dark Phoenix streets to care for patients, and she could put the huskiest man firmly in his place if the occasion demanded.

She had first set up housekeeping in Phoenix in a tent on the desert north of the city—a precaution expected of all sufferers from tuberculosis—and soon was helping to alleviate the suffering of the friendless "lungers," whose plight kept them separated from the rest of society like so many lepers.

A poverty-stricken young physician, Dr. R. D. Craig, watched her appreciatively and one day asked if she would accept special nursing assignments. By that time, she had won her own battle against tuberculosis (if she ever really had it), and was able to pass the physical examination for nurses.

She is sometimes characterized in biographical sketches as a nurse at St. Joseph's Hospital. In later years she said that was not true, that she was never on the St. Joseph's staff, but did take special nursing assignments there on occasion. So compassionate was she that several of her patients fell in love with her and proposed marriage. Jo sometimes has been called "the first registered nurse in Arizona Territory." That also is untrue, although she certainly was among the early R.N.s in Arizona.

With her health, her confidence, and her bank balance restored, Miss Williams moved into town. The Phoenix City Directory of 1905 shows her living at 303 E. Monroe St. City life required some new clothing, and for that she went shopping for dress goods at Phoenix's premier store, M. Goldwater and Bro.

Fortunately for future Arizona history, Baron Goldwater himself chanced to wait on her. He was as charming, suave, and persuasive as she had been told he was, and she particularly liked the way he parted his dark hair in the middle. There was something in his manner that suggested their relationship might move on beyond that of merchant and customer. "I thought he was fresh," Jo recalled later, "but he *was* a charmer."

During the ensuing weeks, Baron Goldwater wanted to know a lot more about this fascinating little newcomer. What he saw, he liked immensely: although tiny, Jo gave an immediate impression of personal strength and restless energy; her eyes were green; her long hair auburn; her smile infectious. He was to learn much more about Jo Williams and her family as their relationship warmed to romantic proportions.

Bowen, Illinois, a village of some two hundred inhabitants, did not keep official birth records before July 1, 1877. And because the town has no record of a daughter being born at Bowen to Robert Royal Williams and Laura Smith Williams of that community, it was assumed that Josephine was born before that date.

Highly sensitive about her true age, because she always seemed much younger, Jo kept it a secret from even her closest friends until her death. Then family records revealed that she was born at Bowen, in Carthage County, some one hundred twenty miles north of St. Louis, on March 19, 1875, and baptized Hattie Josephine Williams. She was the youngest of six Williams children, four boys and two girls.

Her father, a farmer who reared his family in the devout ways of a Presbyterian home, took pride in the family tradition that claimed descent from the colonial American hero, Roger Williams. Her mother's family had come from Missouri.

When Jo was still very small, the Williams family moved on west in the spirit of the late 1870s. They settled on a farm near McCool, in York County, Nebraska, about thirty-five miles west of Omaha. Jo spent her childhood there and attended high school at nearby Waco, Nebraska.

Then came the first big experience in her life: moving from the farm to Chicago, America's great inland metropolis, to attend nursing school. Life at Illinois Training School for Nurses was as exhausting as it was exhilarating for the young Nebraskan.

There were several complications for her at nursing school. First, she found she enjoyed the bright lights and fun of Chicago more than courses in anatomy and hygiene. Second, she had nurtured dreams of being a concert pianist, and it was hard to give up her piano. Finally, she admitted years later, "I had a lot of trouble trying to keep my hair under my cap, and the supervisors insisted that I must."

She had completed her training and was in practice as a nurse when a visit to her doctor brought the news that she had contracted tuberculosis. In those days such a diagnosis was almost a death sentence. There was little that the science of medicine could do about the dread disease except send the patient to a warm, dry climate, prescribe complete rest, and hope for the best.

A friend made arrangements for her to take the train to Phoenix, which she believed to be somewhere out in Arizona Territory where the Apaches killed most of those poor souls which the rattlesnakes overlooked. To spare her family unnecessary worry, she wrote them that she would be gone awhile, accompanying a patient to sunny Arizona.

A trip to Phoenix by rail from Chicago involved leaving the Santa Fe main line at Ash Fork and taking a feeder line one hundred twenty-five miles on to Phoenix. But someone had blundered, and there was no Phoenix ticket awaiting her at the Ash Fork depot.

Low on funds, but high in adventuresome spirit, the tiny nurse grabbed her suitcase and started walking southward along the railroad tracks. What she hoped to accomplish even she was not sure. But providentially, a freight train lumbered alongside her a moment later and a helpful brakeman hauled her aboard the caboose, just behind a string of fragrant cattle cars.

That's how Jo Williams, future wife of the capital city's leading merchant, made her debut in Phoenix.

It was in the fall of 1906 that Baron Goldwater gave up his lifelong struggle against matrimony and asked Jo Williams to be his wife. Because she believed in honest relations between men and women, she did not blush, faint, or act surprised. And because he was forty and she thirty-one, she could see no reason for delaying the wedding.

She had no family in the territory, but was determined to be married in a church. So it was decided that the wedding would be held in St. Luke's Episcopal Church, Prescott, on New Year's Day, 1907, with only family and close friends in attendance.

But there was the important matter of assembling her trousseau. Fully aware of her limited means, Baron offered to let her pick out any apparel in the Phoenix store for the wedding trip.

"I told him nothing doing," Jo related in after years. "Until I was Mrs. Baron Goldwater, I was determined to buy all my own clothes. So I bought some red silk over at Korrick's, where it was cheaper, and found a lady who made up a dress from it. I also had her make my wedding dress. Then I was ready to go to Prescott and get married."

Baron's letter to Morris, outlining the wedding plans, has been preserved:

My dear Morris:
Hope you and Sallie are well. Now, about the wedding. My idea in being married in Prescott was to insure my brother Morris' attendance—absolutely nothing else.

Our plans—to be married in the Episcopal Church, Father Bennett "executioner." Then to your home. Sallie, Morris, Liz, Gus, Miss Ironsides, Jo's brother, Mr. E. J. B. [Bennitt] if he can come. Don't want any strangers. Of course if Sallie and you wish anyone else, you invite them in your name.

We think you had better send announcement cards here [Phoenix], as we wish same mailed before starting. Think this answers all questions. . . .

Love from Jo and myself to you and Sallie.

Yours affectionately,
Barry

(P.S.) Will you please obtain License?

Apparently Baron was more than willing to let Morris take care of all the wedding arrangements.

The Prescott *Journal-Miner,* in its edition of January 1, 1907, made note of the wedding:

> B. M. Goldwater, brother of Morris Goldwater, Mayor of Prescott, and Miss Josephine Williams will be united in marriage at St. Paul's Episcopal Church in this city today. Rev. Father Bennett will officiate.
>
> Mr. Goldwater is one of Phoenix's leading merchants, while the bride is one of the more popular belles of the capital city.
>
> After the ceremony, Mr. and Mrs. Goldwater will leave for New York to spend their honeymoon, making their home later in Phoenix.

[Church records show that, contrary to the *Journal-Miner* report, it was St. Luke's, not St. Paul's, Episcopal Church. The Minister was Rev. Fredrick Trotman Bennett.]

On the first day of January 1907, a driving snowstorm made travel on the streets of Prescott all but impossible. The only cabbie in town had closed down for the duration of the storm, but he could not turn down Mayor Morris Goldwater's urgent request to drive the bridal party to the church. After the ceremony, everyone returned to Morris and Sallie's home for a wedding feast.

And then Mr. and Mrs. Baron Goldwater, starry-eyed and excited as teen-aged newlyweds, boarded the train for a honeymoon in New York City. If their bliss were to be interrupted occasionally by Baron's purchasing visits to dry goods manufacturers—well, what must be, must be.

The saying that "opposites attract" was never more true than in the case of Baron and Jo Goldwater.

Here was Baron: devoted to his business and community, sartorially impeccable, carefully conservative, conscious of his public image, reluctant to get his hands dirty or leave the niceties of civilization. And here was Jo: peppery, loving the outdoors, willing to experiment with almost any new idea or device, casual in dress, a bit too profane for the tastes of some Phoenix matriarchs, so honest and direct that she sometimes strained the bounds of diplomacy.

Later, more differences would surface, particularly in their relationship with the children. Jo joyously hauled them around town, romped with them, taught them games, took them camping in the wilderness, drove them to California when that was a dangerous undertaking.

Baron loved the children deeply, but in his own way. A man who admired order and propriety in all things, he was often disturbed by their rowdy play, their noisiness, and their undisciplined grubbiness. He hated camping and working up a sweat in sports. Little wonder that his children remember him as loving but a little distant—the man who stayed in Phoenix to mind the store while they romped off with Mungie on another exciting lark.

But it was this remarkable number of differences in Baron and Jo Goldwater that enabled them to give their children such a rich genetical inheritance.

The newlywed Baron Goldwaters returned from their lengthy New York honeymoon and settled down in a small house at 818 North Second Avenue, Phoenix. One of the oddities of Baron Goldwater's character was that he never chose to own a home of his own. Although eminently able financially to buy a house, he preferred to let a landlord worry about holes in the roof, leaky plumbing and the like.

Sometime in mid-1908, after Jo had learned that their first child was on the way, they started making plans to move into an even larger home, owned by their friend E. J. Bennitt, at 710 North Center Street (now Central Avenue), just north of the site where the Westward Ho Hotel was erected some twenty years later.

Jo recalled later that Bennitt did extensive remodeling of the house at North Center in preparation for the newlyweds' occupancy. It was a big, roomy home with a spacious yard, bedrooms upstairs, a basement, an attic, and a barn in back. To Baron and Jo's three children, that house would hold a special place as the only home they would know until they became adults. The house facing on Phoenix's main traffic artery amid beautiful ash trees and pleasant lawns, was long ago demolished to make way for commercial development.

Different as they might be in many respects, Baron and Jo Goldwater had one glorious area of agreement: they both loved parties. Both enjoyed dancing, the company of light-hearted friends, and a cheering nip from the flowing bowl. Their social life was as busy as any couple's in Phoenix, and they were particularly fond of the Phoenix Country Club crowd, several doctors and their wives, and a few of Baron's business colleagues.

Their home was a favorite party site, and the Goldwaters were known throughout Phoenix as generous and considerate hosts. Even when they were not at home, it was common knowledge that the Goldwater house was open to any friend who might be walking by. (Such naive hospitality— a certain invitation to burglary today—was common in pre-World War I Phoenix. People simply did not lock their houses. The story is told of one prominent Phoencian who sold his house, and when asked for his door key, had to admit that he hadn't seen it in years.)

For two years, Baron and Jo lived a carefree life, unencumbered by family responsibilities. But on January 1, 1909—their second wedding anniversary—their first child was born, in the bedroom at 710 North Center. It was a boy, and he was given his father's nickname, Barry. There was no doubt as to the child's middle name. It would be Morris, after Baron's beloved older brother. Morris, fifty-six and never to have children of his own, was delighted by the honor.

Once their family was started, the Goldwaters wasted no time in adding to it: Robert Williams Goldwater (known as Bobby until adolescence) was born eighteen months later, on July 4, 1910; the third and youngest of the Goldwater children, Carolyn, was born at the Prescott home of a family friend, Tom Campbell (later to be Governor of Arizona), on August 13, 1912. Carolyn was named for her great aunt Carolyn Goldwater, the first child born to Mike and Sarah Goldwater.

Three memorable events in the history of Phoenix occurred during that period.

The capital city welcomed Arizona Statehood on Valentine's Day, February 14, 1912, with noisy celebrations, feasting and drinking, and a parade from the Ford Hotel to the Capitol Building at 1700 West Washington. Bulky, mustachioed Governor George W. P. Hunt insisted on walking all the way to demonstrate that he was a man of the people.

Master Barry Goldwater, age three, served on Statehood Day as ring bearer at the first wedding held in the state of Arizona. The ceremony united Joe Melczer and Hazel Goldberg, whose eldest son, Joe Jr. is Barry's attorney and lifelong friend.

A year before, former President Teddy Roosevelt had made the long trek up the Apache Trail to star in gala dedicatory ceremonies for the Roosevelt Dam on March 20, 1911. Roosevelt, in magnificent understatement, told the throng after the ceremony that "with this new dam you may have as many as seventy-five to one hundred thousand people living in the Salt River Valley." The dam opened up a new era for central Arizona. It enabled citizens of the area to open new acreages to agriculture, tamed the ruinous Salt River floods, and brought new prosperity to Phoenix and Maricopa County.

But the event closest to the heart of Baron Goldwater was the opening of his grand new store at 33 North First Street on December 31, 1909. It was the most spacious Goldwater building yet, and the first constructed of reinforced concrete in Phoenix. Owned by Dorris-Heyman Furniture Company, it was rented to Goldwater's, and would be the location of the store for the remainder of Baron's life.

The opening of the new store on New Year's eve was a long-heralded social event, covered in a twenty-inch article in the *Arizona Republican* of January 1, 1910. Excerpts follow:

Formal Opening of
New Goldwater Store
Public Reception Last Night
Was a Brilliant Scene
New Business House Is a Veritable
Palace of Feminine Finery

M. Goldwater and brother ushered in the New Year festivities last evening with a spectacular function when "Your" store was formally opened to a curious and admiring public. It was decidedly a social event, but by no means an exclusive one.

All evening there was a moving procession of carriages and automobiles in front of the big white building, and the wealth and beauty of the city attired in gorgeous costumes and accompanied by attentive escorts came to pass judgment on Arizona's newest and finest store. . . .

All were greeted warmly at the door by Barry Goldwater, the manager of the store, for whom the occasion was one of satisfaction and flattering success. . . . Nothing was for sale—last night.

It could be said that Carolyn Goldwater's birth, which completed Baron's family, rounded out his life from that day forward. During the space of half a dozen years he had found a wife, started and completed his family, settled down in his permanent home, and moved his store to its permanent location. He would make no changes in any of these vital elements of his life during the nearly seventeen years remaining to him.

Two other facets of Baron's daily living pattern were also in place by this time: his visits to the Arizona Club for cards or conversation, and increasing involvement with the corporate affairs of the Valley Bank of Phoenix. It was the latter that was soon to present him with one of the great crises of his life, and to add some grey to his well-tended hair.

This was not today's giant Valley National Bank, it must be noted, but one of the smaller financial institutions that later merged to form that bank. Baron's friend, E. J. Bennitt, one of the early officers of the Valley Bank of Phoenix, paved the way for Baron to join its board of directors not long after he arrived in Phoenix. By 1914, it was the largest bank in the new state, and Bennitt had moved up to become president.

Many knowledgeable people had been saying for years that this bank was overloaned, and that many of those loans—such as those to proprietors of valley ostrich farms—were of questionable soundness. By the fall of 1914, the bank was facing a crisis as Phoenix real estate hit a slump and valley agriculture was in a depressed state.

The *Arizona Republican* of November 11, 1914, shocked its readers with an ominous banner headline: "Valley Bank's Doors Closed for the Time." The worried officers and board of the bank knew they faced the wrath of their depositors, which included most of the prominent individuals and business firms of Phoenix.

For the next fifty-one days, Phoenix talked of little else. Jo Goldwater and her children saw little of Baron, who was closeted in endless sessions with his fellow board members, trying desperately to find fresh capital and avoid the total collapse of the Valley Bank of Phoenix.

Coming to the rescue at last were the chief stockholders of the Gila Valley Bank and Trust Company of eastern Arizona, who agreed to put up enough capital to prevent disaster. Baron and his fellow board members were assessed twelve thousand five hundred dollars each in the financing package, which represented a major sacrifice for most of them.

On December 31, 1914, a new bank opened its doors in Phoenix. Born of a merger between the Gila Valley and Phoenix banks, it was christened The Valley Bank. R. E. Moore of the Gila Valley bank was named chief executive, and there was a new twelve-man board of directors.

Smiling with relief after his close brush with catastrophe was Baron Goldwater, whose appointment to the board of the newly strengthened bank was evidence of the high regard in which he was held by the Phoenix financial community. Baron remained a member of the Valley Bank board, and a principal stockholder, until his death. Then his son, Bob, took his seat on the board and served for four decades more.

From the early days when Mike and Joe served as bankers for their pioneer communities, to Morris's half century of service as an officer of banks and secretary of the Arizona Bankers Association, through the modern financial leadership of Baron and Bob, the Goldwaters have been Arizona's bankers.

Barry Goldwater's childhood was one long, glorious caper—a combination of Mark Twain's *Huckleberry Finn* and Thomas Bailey Aldrich's *Story of a Bad Boy*. He had to sample every sensation and every minor sin at least once, and his adventuresome spirit led him into predicaments.

Barry remembers the years between 1912 and 1922 with remarkable clarity, and he recorded some of those memories in an article for the Arizona Historical Society.

His mother's patriotic fervor was one of the first images implanted on the mind of a boy just turned three, as he recalls in these words:

> The very first thing I can remember is Mother taking the flag down and sewing two new stars on it for New Mexico and Arizona. I would like to know where that flag went, because it would be a curiosity now. The flag was always on the flagpole in front of the house on the days it should be. My mother was very religious in seeing that this was carried out.

When the children were old enough, Jo took them regularly to the Phoenix Indian School at Center Street and Indian School Road—now in the heart of Phoenix, but then "way out in the country"—to watch the retreat ceremonies and lowering of the flag. Jo also taught her children about nature, and instilled in them a life-long love of the outdoors. They learned sports from her, and she gave them free rein to play almost any noisy game they chose, inside or outside the house.

Barry waxes poetic in his recollection of his boyhood home:

> I remember Central Avenue as Center Street and its being unpaved, with ditches on either side. On the banks of these ditches grew the beautiful ash trees that once lined Central and made it, to my memory, the most beautiful street I have ever seen. . . .
>
> We used to run up to the corner every morning to be carried on the shoulders of Aaron Goldberg, whom we called "Ba," and Celora Stoddard's father. I can see these men yet, and other fine old men of Arizona, as they walked past our house on their way to work. And I can remember them coming home in the evening, as they stopped by the house to have a drink with my father. Some of them didn't even bother to knock, because they knew they were always welcome. They knew where the bottle was, and just went in and helped themselves.

When America entered World War I in 1917, the Goldwater children staged mock war games and paraded with American flags. Baron sold war bonds as vigorously as he sold women's clothing, and he virtually turned over the store to the Red Cross for the duration.

As Phoenix waited breathlessly in the fall of 1918 for news that the Armistice had been signed, the national epidemic of Spanish influenza hit the city with terrible force. A call for nurses was trumpeted in the daily press, and Jo Goldwater was one of the first to offer her services. She was already supervisor of the surgical dressings department of the Red Cross, but gladly took on her duties to assist the flu victims. Before Jo and her colleagues could return to their normal pursuits, the flu epidemic had killed more than two hundred Phoenicians.

Much to the annoyance of Baron and his friends, Arizona voted in Prohibition even before the nation adopted it in 1919. Barry's father had long enjoyed a regular afternoon ritual: stopping by his favorite downtown saloon at the end of the day, putting a foot on the shiny brass rail, and ordering a bracing libation.

When Prohibition closed down the saloon, the owner presented Baron with the brass rail on which he had spent so many happy hours. He carried it home over his shoulder, and Jo enshrined it in the basement of their home. When she moved to a new home in Country Club Manor, she made sure the rail went with her, to be installed in a place of honor in her dining room.

Adventures in the back country and long auto treks across rough desert roads were part of the agenda for the Goldwater children as soon as they could walk. Onlookers must have gaped in wonder as Jo packed the car for such a trip.

It was a scene wrenched from the pages of *The Grapes of Wrath:* a big, overloaded touring car with two spare tires hung at the rear, a canteen stuck at a rakish angle between them . . . bedrolls and tarps and cooking gear protruding from the left fender . . . three young children tugging at a mother wearing khaki pants, leggings, and a disreputable hat . . . all preparing to head across the desert toward California.

But the year was 1919—not 1932—and these were not the Joads of Oklahoma but the Goldwaters of Arizona: Josephine and her three lively youngsters, Barry, Bob, and Carolyn.

Many fortunate members of Phoenix's upper class escaped the summer heat in rented cottages along Southern California beaches in that era, but they made the trip in style, by Pullman car and diner. Not doughty Jo Goldwater and her brood.

Half the fun of the annual California trek was getting there—that meant cranking up the big Chalmers touring car and striking out across the desert for another adventure in the outdoors. Because the trip could not be made in a single day on the roads of that era, Jo and her children took tarps and sleeping bags and camping gear along. When the sun began to set, she simply pulled off the road and they all pitched in to set up camp. Never mind the rattlesnakes, the scorpions, or the Gila monsters—the Goldwater family was on vacation and the wild creatures would have to move over.

It was a noisy, happy crew—singing, arguing, and hoping to get safely through the next sand bar or mud hole. There was no air conditioning in the Goldwater car, of course, but the wind streaming in onto young bodies perspiring in 110-degree heat kept things tolerable.

Where was papa Baron? Likely as not, he was in New York City on one of his frequent buying trips. Much as he loved his family, his ideas of fun did not include roughing it amid the cactus and the greasewood. He was content to bid them all a fond farewell and then get on with more genteel living.

On occasion, the Goldwaters took along one or more of the children's friends, and Jo later recalled that more than once she had to call long distance from some desert filling station to inform parents that their children were on their way to California.

Once on the beach, she rented a cottage and settled down for weeks of uninterrupted fun. She would put on her knee-length bathing suit, and with children screaming in delight behind her, would dive headlong into the biggest breakers that crashed in from the Pacific.

There were always exciting things to do on those beach vacations, and the three children grew up as a closely knit unit. Today, Carolyn speaks fondly of those adventures, and declares proudly that the three Goldwater siblings have missed only one Christmas together—when Barry was in India during World War II—in all those years.

From the day in 1903 when she arrived in Phoenix on a caboose behind a cattle car, Josephine Williams Goldwater did things just a little differently from most people. She put little stock in proper breeding or social position, but treated everyone with the same frank, open friendliness. If skirts hampered her outdoor activity, she wore trousers or knickers. If she chose to set the air ablaze with some colorful bit of profanity, she let 'er rip. Above all, she was herself, with no fakery or prudery in sight.

She was a lady of many names: Josephine or Jo to friends, Jo-Jo to grandchildren and a few intimates, and "Mungie" to her children. Why "Mungie?"

"It's a combination of Mother and Angie," she once explained. "Angie was our maid when the children were very small. They loved her dearly and saw her more than they did me. So they called me Mungie."

All but Barry, that is. He always abbreviated it to "Mun."

Mungie's philosophy of child rearing was not taken from the commonly accepted book. She was permissive to the extreme, and the Goldwater children grew up having just about anything they wanted and doing just about anything they pleased. Carolyn is quick to point out that there were well-established limits, in her case, on hours to be home and on kinds of permissible activity. The children were not allowed to hurt each other or those around them. But beyond those comfortable parameters, almost everything they wished to do was allowed.

They had all the clothes and playthings any child could desire, and were usually the first kids in town to own any new item on the market. Baron brought home presents from his travels and surprise gifts of many kinds for his children.

In 1920, his father gave Barry a crystal radio set. With careful tuning on a good night, he could pick up Los Angeles stations. The boy became fascinated with radio, and not long thereafter built his own transmitter, operating his amateur radio station "6BPI" from the garage loft. While still only twelve years of age, he assisted radio shop owner Earl Neilson in setting up Phoenix's first commercial radio station, KFAD. Ham radio has been a vital part of Barry's life ever since. He has become America's best-known ham, and he looks forward with great anticipation to the rare hours when he can get behind a mike and chat with fellow radio buffs around the world.

Because Baron was a partner in the Rickards-Nace Theaters, he provided unlimited free movie passes for his children and their friends. There also were passes to boxing matches, and to the popular Riverside Park swimming pool. Needless to say, the Goldwater kids did not lack for companionship.

How did all three avoid being spoiled rotten beyond belief?

The secret was Mungie. She gave them unlimited love and encouragement, took them on countless trips, went hunting with them, and demonstrated by her own example what a grown-up should be.

All three of Mungie's children remember that morning of May 1, 1921, as though it was yesterday—their father coming to breakfast with his injured arm in a sling and wearing a grave expression on his face.

"Your mother and I were in an automobile accident last night," he told them, "and she was hurt. She will be in the hospital for a while."

Baron and Jo had been invited to a party in Mesa, and Jo, as usual, was at the wheel. With them in the Goldwater car was a close friend, Dr. Robert Brownfield, a Phoenix physician.

As she later remembered the nightmare, Jo was driving, talking and laughing, when a horse and buggy suddenly loomed in front of the headlights. Fighting the wheel in an effort to avoid a collision, she felt the car skidding out of control and finally flipping over on its side.

When the police arrived, they found both Jo and Dr. Brownfield crushed in the wreckage. Because the doctor was more seriously injured, physicians at the hospital worked feverishly over him for half an hour before giving serious attention to Jo. It was an almost-fatal mistake.

Dr. Brownfield had suffered such massive injuries that he was dead within a few hours. But Jo's body was nearly as badly crushed.

"All her ribs were broken," remembers Bob, "and because of the delay in treating her, they never did heal properly. She suffered from the results of that accident for years to come."

It was not just her ribs. There were serious internal injuries, and it was many months before Josephine Goldwater was able to resume her active life once more.

The Goldwater home was the clubhouse for the notorious Center Street Gang, as rough and ready a group of young athletes and pranksters as ever allied themselves against the world.

Baron had a garage in the rear built that provided shelter for four vehicles, the two family cars and two trucks used by the store. Above the garage was an open space apparently designed for just such an assemblage as the Center Street Gang. Leaders in the gang included Barry and Bob Goldwater, Harry and Newton Rosenzweig, Bob Lewis, and several others. They staged track meets, boxing matches, baseball games, bicycle races, swimming meets, mudball fights, and other competitions. Their arch rivals were the Third Avenue Gang and the Truesdale Gang on First Street.

Both Barry and Bob became good boxers. A ring-wise older man conducted boxing classes for young boys in the back of a drugstore at Monroe and First Avenue, and both boys profited from his instruction. Later, their coach's son, John Henry Lewis, became light heavyweight boxing champion of the world.

Bob Goldwater later became a one hundred sixty-pound class boxing champion at the University of Illinois. But Barry's enthusiasm for the fistic sport was dimmed considerably by an incident that involved a future Arizona governor and U.S. senator, Paul Fannin. Barry and Paul were watching a professional boxer named Kid Parker work out, and Barry agreed to step into the ring with the pro. He made the mistake of landing an early blow on Parker, who pounded Barry unmercifully for the rest of the single round of their uneven contest.

"Sonny, don't ever do that again," Parker warned the groggy youngster.

"And I never did," Barry recalls.

Swimming was more to Barry's liking. He became captain of his military school swimming team, and later was a freshman swimmer at the University of Arizona. One day, all three Goldwaters entered a major meet at the Tempe Beach swimming pool and amassed more points than any four-man team in the competition.

Golf was Jo Goldwater's game, and enthusiasm for it still burns bright in the hearts of her children and grandchildren.

It all started, surprisingly enough, in Prescott in 1899, when some hardy souls began playing the game on a makeshift course. Before the year was out, according to yellowed newspaper reports, Phoenix sportsmen decided they would not be outdone by Prescott. They started a desert course, with sand greens, west of Phoenix on Van Buren Street. One of the early directors of the Phoenix Country Club was Baron Goldwater. Baron and Jo were habitues of the club and participated in most of its social events long before Jo was bitten by the golf bug.

The club moved north of town, to a site on North Center Street and the Arizona Canal, just after the turn of the century, and its handsome clubhouse was a Phoenix social center until the club was moved to its present site at Thomas Road and Seventh Street in 1920.

Carolyn recalls her mother telling how she started playing golf:

"She was knitting at home one day, when friends came by to urge her to join them in a golf game. She found out in a hurry that she was good at the game, and soon she agreed to enter a tournament at Phoenix Country Club. I still have the trophy she brought home for winning the 1918 women's championship at the club."

Bob recalls that Phoenix Country Club pro Lewis Scott gave Jo her first lessons, and that soon Scott was teaching Barry and Bob the rudiments of the game. Willie Low, a more recent pro at the club, also was one of their favorite teachers.

All three Goldwater children became excellent golfers. Carolyn still plays a good game; Barry was good enough to win the Phoenix Open Pro-Am event with Sam Snead in 1940; and Bob was, for decades, one of the top amateur golfers in the West.

Jo wasn't bad herself. Before she put away her clubs she had won both the Arizona and Southwest women's championships.

Everybody, it seems, has a favorite story about that "unforgettable character," Jo Goldwater. Hulda Skov of Benson had one that illustrates Jo's character to perfection.

Through long practice on some rugged desert courses, and with great personal dedication, Hulda was able to shock the favorites and capture a championship in a state women's golf tournament. But she felt uncomfortable at the party after the competition because she was a country gal who did not fit easily into the company of country club sophisticates.

Hulda recalled later that she was standing alone, ignored by the women at the club after the tournament. She was about to leave the party when she turned to find the socially prominent Jo Goldwater approaching with a smile.

"I liked her immediately," she says, "and she sort of took me under her wing until I made some new friends. She seemed to understand that I felt out of place in that company, and she made sure I felt at home."

Hulda Skov never forgot that bit of human kindness from a great lady.

As far as Jo Goldwater was concerned, her children had the talent and the spunk to achieve just about anything they set out to do. And she was very nearly right. Carolyn won student honors throughout high school and college, Bob was both an outstanding scholar and athlete, and Barry—well, Barry had his strong points, too. But scholarship and deportment were not among them.

He was often in some boyish scrape: shooting a cannon over the Methodist Church one midnight, for example . . . embarrassing female visitors at the Goldwater home by planting a loudspeaker at the base of the bathroom toilet . . . putting rocks in his sack to beat other boys in a cotton picking competition . . . using his growing skill as a photographer to shoot people in compromising situations at parties.

While Bob skipped a grade in school, Barry barely got by. Had it not been for the special tutoring of his all-time favorite teacher, Mrs. Mabel Hancock Latham in the seventh grade at Kenilworth School, Barry might not have made it as far as high school. It was not that he couldn't make good grades, but that he was too interested in other things to take time for study.

In the fall of 1923, when he enrolled at Phoenix Union High School, he was frankly spoiled and self-centered. Winning the election as freshman class president did not reduce his ego, and he playfully barged through that first year without opening a book. By the end of his freshman term, he had several teachers and the principal of Phoenix Union High agonizing over his puerile pranks and his poor grades.

"One day, the principal called my father into his office and suggested as diplomatically as he could that I should plan to attend some other school in my sophomore year," Barry recalls. "Dad took the hint, and started looking into military schools. He chose one of the best—Staunton Military Academy in Virginia—and the decision did a lot to shape the rest of my life."

It is sometimes said that going to Staunton made Barry Goldwater's career possible. The military regimen focused his wild energies and taught him self-discipline for the first time. Without the Staunton years, the diverse Goldwater talents might well have been dissipated and a future leader lost in anonymity.

Mungie protested that she wouldn't see her son for months on end, but she could see the wisdom in sending him to the East. Barry recalls that his father arranged to go to New York at a time when he could accompany his son on the train to Virginia.

"I remember that I met a boy on the train—Bucky Harris—who was also going to Staunton," says Barry. "We were playing poker with some others, when Dad walked up in his dark suit and derby hat and asked if he could join the game. Harris glared at him and said 'no.' Dad left, a little angry, and I asked Harris why he had been so rude. 'I can spot a card shark every time,' he said, 'and believe me, that man is one of them.'"

When the train arrived at Staunton, Baron said goodbye to his son at the station and said "You're on your own now." Barry walked two miles to the school, carrying his bags, and began a new chapter of his life.

Back home in Phoenix, Bob was starting to make his mark at Phoenix Union High School, then one of the nation's largest high schools. He had skipped a grade in elementary school, so he was barely thirteen when he began his freshman year.

Although smaller than Barry, he was in superb physical condition. Already one of Phoenix's best golfers, he set about to win letters in almost every team sport and to establish himself as a good boxer, as well. At sixteen, he won both the Arizona and Southwest amateur golf championships. Before he graduated in 1927, Bob had quarterbacked the football team, captained the basketball team, led his class in scholarship, was elected student body president and "Most Popular Boy," and won all three of the coveted awards offered to seniors. One of them, established at Phoenix Union by his father only the year before, was the Goldwater Cup for outstanding student activity, service, and scholarship.

It was a tough act for Carolyn to follow, but she soon established herself as one of the better students and class leaders of the school. In dramatics, in sports, in the classroom, and in the social whirl, Carolyn had few equals.

"Carolyn was an ordinary teen-aged gal, full of all the fun and nonsense of that age," her mother said in a later interview. "She was always happy, optimistic, and eager to give life all she could give. She was a joy!"

Jo's children occupied much of her time in the 1920s, but she always seemed to find hours for social events, for golf, and for charitable community service. She took her children to the Episcopal Cathedral regularly, and the family later gave major gifts to the church.

One story she loved to tell in later years involved a children's class at the church, members of which were supposed to have a monogram on their sweaters. Unhappy with the monogram which was chosen, young Barry declared that he wanted a "P" on his.

Why?

"For 'Piscopal,' of course," he replied.

Jo and Baron could be counted on to be among the donors to almost any major fund drive in Phoenix, but they shunned publicity about their giving. Health care was one of their major interests, as evidenced by Baron's early support of the Sisters' Hospital (now St. Joseph's) and Jo's frequent volunteering for health-related services. In later years, when Franklin D. Roosevelt's polio became a national concern, Jo paid for the first iron lung in Arizona, but would not allow grateful polio fighters to put her name on the donor's plaque.

Their charities were not confined to major projects, either. Rummage sales, for example, could always count on the Goldwaters for gifts of clothing.

"Phoenix must have had some of the best-dressed poor people to be found anywhere," Jo once told an interviewer. "Baron loved new suits, which he often had made at Wanamakers in New York. He'd wear them a while and then give them away."

The good economic times that began while Calvin Coolidge occupied the White House continued into the first year of the presidency of Herbert Hoover. The Roaring Twenties had enriched the Goldwater coffers considerably, because many people could afford the quality fashions that the store made available.

Jo and Baron had only one child at home after 1927, since Barry was away at Staunton Military Academy and then at the University of Arizona, and Bob had entered the University of Illinois. Only Carolyn, finishing her high school career and looking ahead to college, was still at home in the big house at 710 North Center Street.

Baron branched out with a small shop in the elegant San Marcos Hotel in Chandler, and then started taking increased interest in the construction of the magnificent Arizona Biltmore resort. The extent of his financial interest in the Biltmore has not been recorded, but it is certain that he was one of its prime movers. Long before the Biltmore was opened in February 1929, north of Phoenix on 24th Street, Baron started planning for a major new Goldwater's shop off the hotel lobby.

Not long before her death, Jo remembered those days.

"He had no business getting so involved in the hotel and the new store there," she declared. "He had been battling angina pectoris for ten years, and had gone twice to California hospitals for rest and treatment. Overwork was something his heart really didn't need."

But Baron Goldwater was weary of following doctor's orders—no alcohol, no excitement, plenty of rest—and wanted the Biltmore store opening and style show on March 5, 1929, to be a splashy success. He worked night and day on that opening, and that evening he donned a tuxedo and went down to the Biltmore early to welcome the expected throng. He enjoyed every minute, but he drank too much and stayed up far too late.

"He woke up feeling uncomfortable the next morning," Jo recalls. "I was playing in a golf tournament at Phoenix Country Club that morning, but I had a strange feeling that I was needed at home. So I left the club early, and when I got home he told me he thought he might be dying. Early in the afternoon, he was gone, following a massive heart attack."

Jo made arrangements for the funeral service in the Episcopal Cathedral, and for cremation and a private family service at Greenwood Memorial Park in Phoenix. The *Arizona Republican* (March 7) said of Baron:

> Baron "Barry" M. Goldwater, 62, resident of Arizona for the past 40 [*sic*] years, died at his home, 710 N. Central Avenue, at 2 o'clock yesterday afternoon as the result of a heart attack. Mr. Goldwater was one of the best-known residents of Phoenix and a pioneer merchant of the city. . . .
>
> Mr. Goldwater was prominent in the development of the civic and business life of the community and was especially active in the social and club life of Phoenix. He was secretary and treasurer of the Goldwater Company and held memberships in the Phoenix Country Club and Arizona Club. He was a stockholder and director of the Valley Bank for many years. . . .

Baron left everything to Josephine except a $10,000 trust fund to care for his sister, Elizabeth. Morris was named executor of the estate. At age sixty-two, Baron Goldwater joined the growing roll of departed Arizona pioneers. Beginning with that day in 1882, when he was a sixteen-year-old eager to experience frontier life while the Old West still lived, he had cast his lot with the builders and shapers of a new land.

Because he was essentially a private person, and one who left no treasury of written records, he has not been as well known to history as have others in his family. But he left an admirable legacy, a mercantile empire that has expanded to neighboring states, institutions that he nurtured, worthy charities, and a family that has brought honor and fame to the Goldwater name.

It was fortunate, perhaps, that Baron did not live to experience the disappointments and calamities of the Great Depression. Soon the carefree, affluent days would be over, and the trials of belt-tightening would begin.

Josephine survived her husband by more than thirty-seven years, refusing to grow old in anything but chronology. Devoted to her city, her friends, her charities, her children, and her grandchildren, she became famed well beyond the borders of Arizona.

There will not soon be another quite like her.

12

A State is Born

It might be argued that Barry Goldwater's natural instincts would have led him eventually into the political arena. Outgoing, handsome, ambitious, and sincerely concerned about the operations of government, he might well have had a political career, even without the influence of his Uncle Morris. But with Morris as his model and advisor, it was a sure thing that Barry would carry on the Goldwater political tradition.

After his father's death in 1929, Barry became even closer to his Prescott uncle, who introduced him to many of the Arizona political powers of the day. Everywhere he went, Barry heard Morris spoken of with the deepest respect. Not only in state government was he a man of renown, but also in Arizona Masonry and banking, as well.

Little by little, Barry pieced together the full story of Morris's role in the building of the Democratic Party in Arizona and of his leadership in writing the state's constitution. As vice-president of the 1910 Arizona Constitutional Convention, he was a potent force in erecting the structure of government which has served Arizonans to this day.

Barry and subsequent researchers have uncovered correspondence that verifies that Morris was offered powerful support to run for the U.S. Senate against Henry Fountain Ashurst, and for other high offices. After his term as president of the Council (Senate) of the 1899 territorial legislature, he developed a following that might have taken him to Washington, or perhaps to the Arizona governor's chair.

Morris, however, liked small-town living, and could never picture himself in a metropolitan setting. London and New York and Washington made him uncomfortable, and even Phoenix was too large for his taste. He liked being a merchant who gave his time to government service, not a full-time politician.

Like many builders of Arizona, Morris had been promoting state-hood for Arizona Territory since the 1880s. Finally, in 1909, after years of disappointment, statehood hopes burned bright at last. Popu-lation of the territory was growing fast, the economy was healthy, and advocates of joint statehood for Arizona with New Mexico (with the capital at Santa Fe) had been effectively silenced. Now Roosevelt Dam was well on the way to completion, promising new prosperity for the Salt River Valley.

In October 1909, President William Howard Taft and an impressive entourage visited Arizona Territory to determine first-hand whether it was indeed ready to join the proud Union. That visit set the stage for the drama of the Arizona Constitutional Convention, in which Morris Goldwater was to play a leading role.

PRESCOTT, 1909

THEY WERE AN ALMOST LUDICROUS PAIR: TINY MORRIS GOLDWATER, AT FIVE FEET, four inches and under one hundred forty pounds, shaking hands at the podium with President William Howard Taft, six-feet-plus and three hundred twenty pounds.

The date was October 12, 1909, and the place was the Masonic Hall in Prescott, where the Past Grand Master of Arizona Masonry was introducing the bulkiest U.S. President in history to the assembled brothers of Aztlan Lodge number one. Mayor Goldwater was his host in Prescott, and Taft, himself a Mason, accepted Morris's invitation to speak to the local lodge.

President Taft was in Arizona to see for himself whether this noisy, demanding territory had the leaders, the citizenry, and the resources to qualify for statehood. Although Taft was a conservative Republican, and Republicans had been opposing Arizona and New Mexico statehood for years, he was willing to believe his own eyes and ears. So he came west to let those Arizonans and New Mexicans try to change his mind.

Such genial hosts as Morris Goldwater did their best. Taft was so pleased with Morris's hospitality that he presented the Prescott mayor with a signed personal calling card, explaining that it would give him immediate admittance to the White House whenever he might be in Washington.

Morris treasured that card—as he did a similar one given him by President Theodore Roosevelt—all his life.

Although they were brothers in Masonry, Goldwater and Taft were not in tune politically. Goldwater was a Democrat, a low-tariff man, and a dyed-in-the-wool westerner. Taft's interests lay with the industrial East, and he was a conservative who viewed with alarm the progressive experimentation that was going into the new state constitutions in the West.

In his Prescott speech, President Taft gave Arizonans stern warning: when you achieve statehood, do it with a conservative constitution, one without newfangled, radical ideas. Otherwise, I'll veto it and send it right back to you.

"Progressive" Democrats, as they liked to call themselves, had other ideas. Given a chance, they would draw up an Arizona constitution containing all three radical instruments which Taft deplored: initiative, referendum, and recall.

Morris's position was about midway between Taft's and the Progressives, who were led by the Territorial Council President, George W. P. Hunt. Although conservative and frugal by nature, Morris was a good Democrat and a good westerner. Perhaps more important, he longed for Arizona statehood so badly that he wanted to avoid the wrath of Taft and the Congress.

In less than a year, he would be in the thick of an emotional battle over which philosophy would prevail.

A man can be a very big fish in his small pond, and still not be known far beyond the borders of his home town. Important as Morris had been in Prescott for so many years, he needed a vehicle to promote his territory-wide visibility.

His two previous terms in the Legislative Assembly had helped, as had his service on the Territorial Board of Equalization. But neither of these gave him half the name identity around Arizona as did his yeoman work in the Masonic Lodge. From the day he joined the Prescott Lodge in 1877, he devoted incredible numbers of hours to the Masons' charitable and ritualistic activities.

"Morris will never marry," a female friend once remarked. "He's already married to the Masonic Lodge."

He was elected Worshipful Master of the Prescott Lodge in 1880, and was accorded the rare honor of re-election the following year. When the Arizona Grand Lodge was organized in 1882, Prescott's brotherhood became Aztlan Lodge number one—a salute to its longevity.

Morris was the prime mover in the founding of the affiliated Order of the Eastern Star in Prescott, and is still regarded as the "father of the Eastern Star" in Arizona.

In 1887, he was elected Deputy Grand Master of the Arizona Grand Lodge and persuaded the order to hold its 1888 conclave in Prescott, where he was elected Grand Master, the highest office the Grand Lodge can bestow.

One of his many duties as Grand Master in 1888-1889 was to preside at the laying of the cornerstone for the first building (now called Old Main) at the University of Arizona in Tucson. (Forty years later, his nephew Barry would be reminded of that fact when he enrolled at that institution.) During Morris's term, he established the Masonic Widows and Orphans Fund, which has aided unfortunates for decades.

Visiting every Arizona community with a Masonic lodge—every town of any size—he made lasting friendships and became known as a man of wisdom and good will.

Twelve times after his term as Grand Master, he was named Grand Lecturer, continuing his travels around Arizona. In 1900, as Grand Lecturer, he helped launch the new Tempe Lodge number fifteen, and there met young Carl Hayden, son of his father's old friend and freighting competitor, Charles Trumbull Hayden. Carl already had political ambitions, and a dozen years later began his fifty-seven-year career in the Congress of the United States.

Morris proudly accepted his installation as thirty-third degree Scottish Rite Mason in a December 1903 ceremony held in San Francisco. And in 1919, he and his closest friend, Tony Johns of Prescott, were selected to represent the Arizona Grand Lodge at the Peace Jubilee conclave of international Masonry in London.

So it was that, sixty-five years after crossing the Atlantic with his mother in a westerly direction, he returned for the first and only time to the country and city of his birth. Morris found London weather miserable, the people a bit stuffy, and whiskey hard to get. As soon as the ceremonies were at an end, he was eager to start home.

Writing to his wife, he declared that:

> My mother took me away from here sixty-five years ago, Thank God, and if it pleases Him I am going to take myself away as soon as possible and never hope to come back.

For the rest of his days, he was honored as a grand old man of Arizona Masonry. Although he would bristle at the notion that his Masonic friendships were ever used for political purposes, there is no denying that Morris, the Mason, helped make possible Morris, the Politician.

Congressional passage of the Enabling Act for separate New Mexico and Arizona statehood in June 1910 brought joy to the long-suffering citizens of both territories. President Taft supported the act and repeated his charge that the constitutional conventions authorized by the act should avoid the populist fever that was then sweeping the West. As a former judge and future U.S. Supreme Court justice, he was particularly hostile to any provision calling for elections to recall judges.

The president watched with keen interest the elections of delegates to the constitutional conventions, knowing that the men elected would determine the nature of the constitutions they would produce. The returns from the special September election in Arizona filled him with foreboding. Instead of the even party split that had been predicted, Arizona voted to send forty-one Democrats and only eleven Republicans to mold its new state constitution.

And what Democrats the voters selected! In almost every county, Progressives won clear-cut victories over conservative Democrats, and organized labor was able to elect its people in many a key race.

"Radicals Control Convention," shouted the Arizona *Journal-Miner.* "Democrats Will Write the Constitution." And an editorial comment by the worried *Journal-Miner* editor on September 14 said: "If the Democrats carry out their campaign promises, statehood will be lost."

But all the delegates were not young radicals. Yavapai sent a well-seasoned delegation, including the seventy-six-year old A. A. Moore, a thirty-four-year resident of Arizona; Judge Ed Wells, for forty-six years an Arizonan (and the only Yavapai Republican); and Morris Goldwater, forty-three years an Arizonan and second only to Wells in territorial longevity.

Morris was immediately touted around the territory as a strong candidate for the presidency of the Constitutional Convention. He was the favorite of many Democratic conservatives, but it was not hard to predict that the Progressive victory at the polls made organized labor's George W. P. Hunt the man to beat.

Several other candidates vied for support, but when the Democrats caucused just before the October 10 opening of the convention, Hunt won hands down. There was a contest for the presidency on opening day, with the Republicans nominating Judge Wells, but everybody knew the die had been cast.

Meeting in one hundred-degree weather in the House of Representatives chamber of the Capitol in Phoenix—without air conditioning—the wool-suited delegates sweated through the voting. It went exactly along party lines—forty-one votes for Hunt, and eleven votes for Wells. Later, the conservative Democrats got their sop with the selection of Morris Goldwater as vice president.

The fifty-two founding fathers of the new state were a fascinating collection of Arizona's meritocracy. Cochise County—Arizona's most populous county in the 1910 census just compiled, with 34,591 people to Maricopa's 34,488—sent ten delegates. Maricopa had nine. Other counties, in order: Yavapai, six; Pima, five; Gila, five; Graham, five; Yuma, three; Pinal, two; Navajo, two; Coconino, two; Apache, one; Mohave, one; and Santa Cruz, one.

The convention included three future Arizona governors: Hunt, Dr. B. B. Moeur, and Sidney P. Osborn. Mulford Winsor, a political power for two decades, was there. So was Dr. A. M. Tuthill, later General Tuthill, long-time Arizona Adjutant General.

It is interesting to note that there were fourteen lawyers in the group, as well as thirteen ranch and stockmen, five merchants and assorted others, including a minister and a mechanic.

Like his fellow delegates, Morris Goldwater was besieged with letters and telegrams urging him to support one faction or another. The Prohibitionists and the Women's Suffrage people were the most active petitioners, with organized labor not far behind.

On August 20, in answer to a strident prohibition letter from an Anti-Saloon League leader, he wrote.

Sir:

Am in receipt of your circular letter dated August 16. I have read the same with great care, but am unable to decide whether it is intended as a threat or a bribe.

I do not concede that *you* have any right to ask me what I am going to do, if elected, nor shall I enter into any argument with you.

But that your mind may be at rest, I answer NO to your inquiry.

Morris Goldwater

Morris, who enjoyed his tumbler of bourbon several times each day, was never very polite to those who would take it away from him. He was more charitable to the women's suffrage advocates, and was generally supportive of the exciting new efforts for grass-roots government.

The minutes of the sixty-day Arizona Constitutional Convention make formidable reading, but there are a few light moments—many of them engineered by Morris Goldwater of Yavapai.

On opening day, October 10, delegates were wrangling about how much to pay stenographers, pages, and other convention employees. The delegates, who took home only four dollars a day, were more generous with their hired help. Morris asked to hear a repeat of the salaries to be paid, and then got off his first knee-slapper of the conclave:

MR. GOLDWATER: Mr. President, the pages will receive five dollars per day. I move that I resign from this Convention serving as a member at four dollars a day and be hired as a page! (laughter).

One of his early resolutions was one calling for the privilege of members with prepared speeches to file a typewritten copy with the secretary, and thus have them published in the *Journal.* He added:

Be it further resolved that the secretary be authorized to insert at
such intervals as he may deem proper, in said speech, these words in
parenthesis: "hear, hear," "applause," "loud applause," and "laughter." (laughter).

Delegates were grateful for Morris's wit. It was an awesome task, this
writing of a constitution to govern a state for decades to come, and
tempers grew frayed. Often a gentle quip by the man from Yavapai broke
the tension and got everybody smiling again.

President Hunt appointed him chairman of the standing Committee on
Ordinance, and the minutes show that Morris was the man most often
called upon to chair the Committee of the Whole when the President
stepped down. His was a wise and steady hand in a convention loaded
with hot-heads and prima donnas.

With all the fanfare about radicals in the convention, its output was
surprisingly sound. There were some controversial labor propositions
passed: the eight-hour day for employees of the state and its subdivisions
. . . forbidding of employer blacklists . . . workman's compensation for
injuries and illness . . . employer liability provisions. Child labor (under
fourteen) was outlawed during school hours, no liquor was to be sold to
Indians, and a corporation commission was established. Women's suffrage and prohibition were defeated.

These were relatively insignificant compared with the three incendiary
populist issues: the initiative, by which voters could originate legislation;
the referendum, which gave voters a chance to rule on the Legislature's
laws; and the most controversial of all, recall of elected officials including
judges.

Republicans had promised to oppose all three, and President Taft had
given fair warning that he would veto any constitution permitting recall of
judges. But the Democrats ruled supreme, and the recall provision was
approved, thirty-eight to nine, with several delegates abstaining.

Next day the convention chaplain, in his opening prayer, said:

Lord, we hope that President Taft will not turn down the constitution
for a little thing like the initiative and referendum. Lord, don't let him
be so narrow and partisan as to refuse us self-government!

In the final days, with the hard decisions made, Morris almost caused an
impasse over a surprising issue: the new Great Seal of Arizona. Like many
old-timers, he wanted the basic Arizona Territorial seal retained, with a
"Great Seal of the State of Arizona" encircling it. But Maricopa delegates
argued for a new seal that showed Arizona as a farming state, with the still
unfinished Roosevelt Dam prominently in the center. Angrily, he declared:

It seems to me that any man who has lived in this territory as long as I have can continue to live under it [the territorial seal] until he dies, without hurting anyone.

He could see no good reason to put a water storage dam on the seal, especially since, in his view, the Roosevelt Dam "has caused more trouble to this convention and the county of Maricopa than any benefits it has had." But the new seal, with dam, prevailed. Morris's view is understandable; his Arizona was one of deserts and mines and forests and he could not be expected to see the future in irrigated farming.

Because Congress had appropriated only one hundred thousand dollars for the convention and specified a sixty-day maximum for it, the delegates worked night and day in the last weeks to hammer out the final document. There was little time for pleasantries. When one member proposed to send good wishes to the New Mexico constitutional convention, which was in session at the same time, President Hunt replied in characteristically grating style: "They started two weeks before we did, and they haven't sent us any good wishes. Why should we give them any honors?"

At last, on December 10, the job was done, and the twenty-five thousand-word document was ready for signing. It was approved by a vote of forty to twelve. Only one Republican—John Langdon of Gila—was willing to put his name on it. On the Democratic side, everybody signed except Ellinwood of Cochise.

It was Morris Goldwater who made the motion to adjourn the historic session. He took one last look at the room which had been his virtual prison for two months and then stopped by 710 North Center Street to say goodbye to Baron, Josephine, twenty-three-month-old Barry, and five-month-old Bobby before he boarded the train for Prescott to pick up his life once more.

Arizona's voters went to the polls and gave overwhelming approval to the new constitution. Morris's efforts on behalf of ratification are reflected in an August 1911, letter from W. Maxwell Burke, a Phoenix attorney:

Allow me to congratulate you upon the successful conclusion of your fight for the Constitution without mutilation, which you helped to frame.

Although the document was a bit too populist for his taste, Morris used all his influence to win acceptance for it. But there was a big cloud on the horizon—William Howard Taft. He had neither forgotten nor forgiven, as he demonstrated by sending the constitution back to Arizona with a demand to remove the judge's recall provision. Observers cautioned Arizona's Democratic leaders that the big man meant business, and that failure to heed Taft's warning might set Arizona statehood back many years.

The president did say that he did not seriously object to any other feature of the new Arizona constitution, and that he would sign a statehood bill as soon as Arizona voters went back to the polls and eliminated the offending provision.

It was with joyous hearts that Arizonans obliged Mr. Taft, returning to the polls in the fall of 1911 to eliminate recall of judges from their new charter. The joy came from two sources: (1) they were taking the last step on the long road to statehood, and (2) everybody knew they would vote recall of judges back into the constitution as soon as they were safely in the Union. That they did, and there was nothing President Taft could do about it.

As it turned out, Taft's recalcitrance was a big boon for the Democratic Party in Arizona. So angry were Arizona voters with Taft and the Republicans that they defeated GOP candidates with monotonous regularity for years.

At 10 a.m. on February 14, 1912, the President signed the bill creating the forty-eighth state. George W. P. Hunt walked his mile to the Capitol ceremony inaugurating him as Arizona's first governor and celebrations erupted throughout the new state.

On the north lawn of the Courthouse Square in Prescott, Morris Goldwater presided over the ceremonial planting of "The Statehood Tree." Marked by the prominent sign, that tree still spreads its ample branches and invokes memories of one of Arizona's proudest days.

13

Fighting the Tide of Depression

Financial disaster had been no stranger to the Goldwaters. Barry was well aware of his grandfather's bankruptcies in California, of Joe Goldwater's business failures, and of the banking catastrophes (his father's and Morris's) that had threatened to darken the Goldwater name.

But Barry had no way of knowing, as he took over the management of the family department store in Phoenix, that the newly arrived Depression was to be the worst in American history. Although Phoenix was not as hard-hit as many other cities, the Goldwater store management was sorely tested as it struggled to survive the storm.

The Depression years brought Barry Goldwater face to face with economic reality. The rich kid who had never worried much about money was now the boss, responsible for the livelihood of scores of Goldwater employees. He soon discovered how hard it was to turn a profit in such a depressed economy.

It was a testing time—a belt-tightening time—and it helped shape the character of the future senator.

With all the stringencies of the 1930s, Barry managed to grow and learn, and to have an adventurous good time. Somehow he found time to explore Arizona, learn first-hand about its Indian culture and its colorful history, fly airplanes, brave the Colorado River rapids, serve in the National Guard, and take community leadership positions.

Also during the thirties, he married Peggy Johnson, and they started their family. With all its fears and hardships, it wasn't such a bad decade for him.

PRESCOTT–PHOENIX, 1925

THE GREAT DEPRESSION CAME EARLY FOR MORRIS GOLDWATER. HIS STORE AND his other investments had weathered the brief post-World War I recession with little difficulty. In late 1925, America was at the height of its Roaring Twenties prosperity. But it was a different story for cattlemen in Yavapai County, and for the bankers who financed them.

Few men were more deeply embroiled in livestock loans than Morris, who at that moment was president of the Commercial Trust and Savings Company of Prescott, a director of the Prescott State Bank, and vice-president of the Bank of Jerome. From the day in 1893 when he became founding vice-president of the Prescott National Bank, he had given much of his life to banking. He had helped organize the Arizona Bankers Association, and served as secretary of that organization longer than any other man.

At age seventy-three, Morris Goldwater was one of the most trusted father-figures in Arizona. For fifty years, after some minor failures as a youth, he had enjoyed almost unbroken success in business and in politics. Widows and young people and corporate executives—everybody—trusted his business judgment and his integrity.

So it came as a traumatic shock to all who knew him when, in November 1925, the Arizona Bank Examiner's office audited the books of Morris's three interlocking banks and found those institutions wanting. Like the Valley Bank of Phoenix a decade before, they had been too generous with their loans to local agriculture. It required only a prolonged drought or a sharp dip in cattle prices to land all three banks in very hot water. When both calamities occurred at once, and some rather shoddy management practices came to light, the examiners closed the doors on November 25, 1925.

R. N. Fredericks, Morris's good friend and Masonic brother, had been particularly close to the daily management of the banks, and he took their failure so personally that he became ill a few weeks later and died (of a broken heart, some said) in less than two years. Morris suffered the tortures of the damned, but did not show his anguish.

His files contain sheaves of letters and telegrams from distraught depositors, from worried family and friends, and from angry townspeople. An even larger number were supportive. Governor Hunt reaffirmed his faith in Morris's integrity, as did Masonic officials and civic leaders.

Particularly distressing to him was the fact that the Masonic Lodge faced major losses in the collapse, and that the City of Prescott had put its funds and its trust in his bank. Before it was over, the lodge had brought a "friendly" suit to recover its money and a group of angry Prescott citizens demanded his recall as mayor.

So humiliated was Morris that he turned down the Masonic Grand

Lodge's offer to make him treasurer. "While I have done nothing discreditable," he wrote, "my appointment would be criticized by many. I much prefer to drop out of sight." For the first time in memory, Morris Goldwater chose not to attend the next convention of the Arizona Masonic Grand Lodge.

Much as it wounded his pride, the bank debacle did not have a long-range effect on Morris's personal popularity. He continued to receive honors and accolades for more than a decade to come.

This bitter failure only proved that even Morris Goldwater, later to be revered as Prescott's "Man of the Century," was human after all.

Back in Phoenix, the Depression approached in a more leisurely fashion. For a year and more after Baron Goldwater's death in March 1929, business at Arizona's premier department store stayed at near-record levels. But there were subtle signs that hard times were coming.

"Women who had always bought six pairs of hose at a time started buying only one or two," Barry Goldwater remembers. "When I'd ask them why, they would say 'my husband says times are getting bad and we must economize.' People talked themselves into a business slowdown."

Bob and Barry had talked things over after their father's funeral and decided that Barry should leave the University of Arizona and start preparing to take his place in the store. He had made a scholastic comeback at Staunton Military Academy, and had been chosen the outstanding cadet in his 1928 graduating class. For a time, he had wanted to enter West Point. When he enrolled at the University of Arizona in Tucson, he was immediately elected president of the freshman class and pledged to Sigma Chi fraternity. But Barry was not cut out for the academic life, and he thirsted for the challenges of the real world.

Sam Wilson, long-time manager of the Goldwater store under Baron Goldwater, took over the top executive role after Baron's death and started grooming Barry for a management position. Wilson was a conscientious taskmaster, and he made sure there was no easy "boss's son" road to the top for the twenty-year-old neophyte.

Barry's first assignment was in piece goods, a major department of the store in 1929. From the beginning, it was evident that the youngster could sell. Wilson looked on in amazement as women congregated around the piece-goods counter to hear him expound on the excellence of this fabric or that.

Next came ready-to-wear, and again he was a success. During one Christmas season, he set a store record of two hundred four sales in a single day. Wilson moved Barry here and there in the store, always with the aim of preparation for executive positions. When he had sampled all the sales jobs, and some of the office work, Barry was assigned to buying, and spent several months in New York learning the ropes.

Goldwater's had always taken the lead in merchandising innovations, such as Baron's much-praised pneumatic tube system for cash transfers and the town's first elevators. Barry's pranks with the tube system became a part of the Goldwater's legend, especially the time when he put a dead mouse in the tube and sent it racing off to cashier Clara Mains. Mrs. Mains's shriek could be heard all over the store, as could her screaming pursuit of the young culprit.

"Barry had some great ideas," recalls his brother Bob. "He put in the electric eye door at the store, another Arizona first. I can still see [people] sitting on the curb, watching that door open and close when people came through. They thought it was some kind of magic.

"Barry was the merchant, and I was the finance man," Bob adds. "He could sell anything—still can—and such innovations as his Desert Fashions and style shows; Little Pedro, our advertising symbol; his branding iron patterns for piece goods; and his sales promotions were all winners."

Probably the best-remembered idea spawned by Barry Goldwater the merchant was his "Antsy Pants" men's underwear. He had white cloth imprinted with huge red ants and ordered men's undershorts made from it. Orders poured in from around the nation.

When Sam Wilson resigned and married a rich widow, Barry became boss at the Goldwater store. Despite the tightening grip of the Depression, Goldwater's held onto its Phoenix leadership during the 1930s. Barry didn't fire any long-time employees, although everybody took pay cuts, and he actually improved employee fringe benefits. By trimming expenses in every area of the business, Goldwater's managed to break even during the worst years. But it took management and clever merchandising to do it.

Through the darkest of the Depression years, Barry Goldwater took time from business to cultivate his love of Arizona's Indian culture. When he was only seven years old, the future Senator Goldwater made his first trip to the Hopi village of Oraibi, a community continuously inhabited for more than a thousand years. His guide was John Rinker Kibby, who had a deep admiration for the Hopis and collected their Kachina dolls, replicas of Hopi gods.

Kibby introduced Barry to the wonders of Arizona's Indian reservation life and interested him in starting his own Kachina collection.

"I remember buying my first doll with an empty toothpaste tube," Barry recalls. "Each time I returned to the reservations, I would buy or trade for more dolls. Probably the most I ever spent for one was three dollars."

By 1940, Barry had an impressive Kachina collection. One day he called

Kibby and offered to buy his dolls, but Kibby's price was beyond Barry's capability. When he returned from World War II service, he called Kibby again and learned that his old friend was now married. Moreover, his wife was demanding that he get his collection out of the house.

"Kibby offered me the whole bunch, plus a lot of other Indian artifacts his wife was tired of looking at, for $1,200," says Barry. "I jumped at the chance."

Barry Goldwater thus became the owner of the largest collection of authentic Kachinas in existence. As more and more people grew interested in the colorful dolls, the Goldwater collection climbed in value (several hundred dollars each in some cases) and became an Arizona resource. About four hundred of them were later placed on display at the Goldwater's Phoenix store, and some have since been sold. Many of his favorite Kachinas are still proudly displayed at his Phoenix home.

Barry has been going back to the Indian reservations with regularity ever since he was introduced to the world of the Hopis, Navajos, and Apaches. He always took his camera with him, and his collection of slides and photographs of Indians and their homeland is one of the best. Organizations all over the state clamored to see his slide shows, and his travels for such speaking engagements gave him exposure which would later boost him to high elective office. Many of his dramatic photographs of landscapes and Indians found their way into *Arizona Highways* magazine and into a notable book of his photo artistry entitled *Arizona Portraits.*

Among the voluminous photographic files of the Goldwater family are many pictures of Barry and Bob camping, playing golf—even deer hunting—together. But there are no pictures of Bob scaling mountain peaks or risking his neck with Barry in the roaring rapids of the Colorado River.

"Barry can have all of that stuff he wants," says Bob. "I'm more of a room-service man, myself."

No adventure was too dangerous or too exhausting for Barry in his youth. Sometimes it seemed to his family and friends that he was determined to see how far he could go without killing himself.

Certainly, his 1940 river expedition with the Nevills Party must find a place in that latter category. Norman Nevills of Mexican Hat, Utah, headed the party, which traveled 1,463 treacherous miles in small boats from Green River, Wyoming, to Lake Mead between June twentieth and August twenty-third.

Barry's diary of that memorable voyage down the Green and Colorado rivers, a pioneering feat in those days, and many of the photographs he took en route have been published in book form by the Arizona Historical Foundation (1970) under the title *Delightful Journey.*

"In a lesser and latter-day sense, the journey duplicated the boat trip of the intrepid one-armed explorer Major John Wesley Powell seventy-one years earlier," he wrote later. "We had the benefits of his pioneering, and that of others who preceded us."

Barry, who joined eight other river rats at Green River, Utah, on July 10, had planned and prepared for months. Still, the trip taxed his endurance to the limit as the party battled blazing heat, fearsome rapids, and constant drenching; the wild ride through approaches to the Grand Canyon and down the Colorado took the party to the depths of that magnificent gorge.

Barry, who once escorted "Believe It or Not" Robert Ripley down the river, returned to the Grand Canyon again and again. During a flight over the eastern end of the canyon in 1951, he saw to his amazement the shadow of what appeared to be a natural bridge. No map or report showed such a bridge there, but he could not get the sight out of his mind. Two years later he arranged with Bob Gilbreath, a helicopter pilot, to land in Nankoweap Canyon. The two then began an exhausting four-hour hike through unexplored country, and at last they arrived at the base of the natural bridge, a gorgeous stone monolith soaring two hundred feet into the air. Far above it a spectacular waterfall gushed a filmy torrent down the mountainside. Bone-weary though he was, Barry Goldwater at that moment enjoyed one of the most satisfying experiences of his life.

When he graduated from Stanford University with a Bachelor of Arts in business in 1931, Bob Goldwater worked at Goldwater's for a time and then decided to learn the mercantile business as a one-dollar-per-week trainee at Bullock's in Los Angeles.

In 1933, Walter Bimson, the new president of the Valley National Bank, offered Bob a job in the bank's bookkeeping department in Phoenix. At the same time, his mother designated him as the person she wished to represent the Goldwater stock holdings (third largest in the bank) in Valley National.

"So there I was," says Bob, "leaving my ledgers in the accounting department to put on my coat, go upstairs, and join the big wheels for a board meeting. As a twenty-three-year old entry-level employee, I felt just a little uncomfortable doing that. So Mr. Bimson and I decided that I should leave the board for the time being. But I came back later and served as a Valley Bank director for some forty years."

In 1937, Barry asked Bob to join him in the store management. Bob agreed, and brought with him a fellow Valley Bank employee, Bill Saufley, who stayed on to become one of the top executives at Goldwater's for many years. Ina Babbitt, the corporation's legendary office manager, had just died, and so Bob took over many of the administrative and financial areas of the store.

"I tried to be a merchandiser," Bob says, "but I really wasn't cut out for that role. I remember buying several thousand dollars worth of alabaster, which I thought would be a great seller. It sat around in drawers and boxes for years."

There has never been a show in Phoenix quite like "The Masque of the Yellow Moon." Phoenix Union High School staged the giant pageant each year in Montgomery Stadium, and half the town became involved in one way or another. The enormous cast worked for weeks to prepare a spectacular that would top all previous productions.

Every girl at Phoenix Union High—some three thousand of them—dreamed of being elected Queen of the Masque of the Yellow Moon. In 1930, her graduation year, Carolyn Goldwater had that dream come true.

It was the crowning achievement of a highly successful four years for Carolyn, who also had been president of the X Club for girls, vice-president of her class for four years, a leader in Girls League, and an excellent student. She teamed with Jeanette Judson to win the girls tennis doubles championship of Arizona, and came in second in the balloting for the Goldwater Cup.

"I was thinking of enrolling at the University of Arizona," Carolyn remembers, "but Barry and Bob said no, that I must go to UCLA, where they thought the academic standards were higher." She was graduated from UCLA with a BA degree in history in 1934 after writing a thesis on India's Gandhi.

Back home in Phoenix, she moved back into her family home with her mother and became active in charitable and civic work, especially for the Humane Society and Planned Parenthood. On August 28, 1936, she married Paul Sexson, son of a Phoenix hospital administrator. Paul had been secretary to former President Herbert Hoover, and later was active in Phoenix civic affairs. Married in Barry's Phoenix home, they departed amid a shower of rice for a Hawaii honeymoon.

Weddings were plentiful for the Goldwater family in those mid-Depression years.

Barry's came on September 22, 1934, at the Grace Episcopal Church of Muncie, Indiana. He had been pursuing pretty Margaret (Peggy) Johnson ever since she had come in to Goldwater's on a shopping trip with her mother some two years before. The daughter of Ray Prescott Johnson, president of Warner Gear Company, Peggy was a popular socialite, both in Muncie and in Phoenix, where the Johnsons wintered.

The young lady had exceptional talent as a fashion designer, as she demonstrated at Grand Central Art School and the David Crystal Company in New York City. It was a perfect combination: Peggy designing ladies' fashions, and Barry selling them—or so it seemed. Fate had other plans for the young couple. Soon, World War II took Barry away from his role as merchant, and then politics made that separation permanent.

Peggy Johnson Goldwater's ancestors on both sides of her family came from the British Isles. Her mother, Anna Davis Johnson, was of Welsh descent; her father had an English heritage. Anna Johnson grew up in Terre Haute, Indiana, where she was a talented pianist. Her uncle, Charles Davis, served for many years as president of the Borg-Warner Company after Warner Gear merged with that firm. After her husband's death, Anna Johnson moved to Phoenix and for years, resided next door to Barry and Peggy Goldwater in Country Club Manor.

Although she was a very private person, bordering on shyness, Peggy Goldwater was never afraid to express her opinions and take control when the situation warranted. One interviewer described her role in the boisterous Goldwater family as that of "a Junior League matron at an American Legion convention." Barry sought her advice about matters of importance for decades.

"We have different tastes about many things, including vacations," Peggy once explained. "He likes to rough it in the back country more than I do, so I sometimes insist on making the vacation choice. One year, for example, we took a Caribbean cruise, which he went on for my sake. But the next year I found myself going down an Idaho river in a rubber boat!"

Bob married a Pittsburgh, Pennsylvania, girl, Mary Johnston, at the Goldwater family home in 1936. Bob was working at the Valley Bank at the time and moved his bride into a home in the new Country Club Manor adjoining the Phoenix Country Club golf course.

"The bank had taken over a thirty-acre plot and couldn't sell it in those Depression times at one thousand dollars an acre," recalls Bob. "So I suggested to Walter Bimson that the bank keep it and develop the land as Country Club Manor. I bought the first lot and Barry bought the second, across the street."

Because of Bob's foresight, Valley Bank eventually realized twenty times as much revenue from the thirty acres as it had hoped to get. (A footnote to the story of the first Country Club Manor home was that Bob got struggling young contractor Del Webb—later one of America's richest men—to build his house for six thousand, seven hundred dollars.)

When the Goldwater brothers joined forces in the store management in 1937, the future of America and the world looked grim. Despite President Franklin D. Roosevelt's economic experimentation, the Depression appeared permanent, and many young people were deserting free-enterprise capitalism for such ideologies as socialism, technocracy, and even communism. In revitalized Germany, Adolf Hitler was building a Nazi war machine that would soon plunge the world into war.

Barry, who had sneaked away from home for early-morning flying lessons from Jack Thornburg in 1930, was incurably infected by the flying fever that has never left him. Flying was to be the Goldwater contribution in World War II—Barry as a pilot in the Air Corps and Bob as state commander of the Civil Air Patrol. But first, for Barry, were years of Army National Guard training. His love of the military had been nurtured at Staunton Military Academy, and he continued his army involvement through the 1930s.

One of his summer training bases was Camp Little, near Nogales. It was just across the Mexican border, in Nogales, Sonora, that he became involved in one of his wilder youthful escapades. It was 1930, in the Prohibition era, so Barry, Paul Morris, and A. J. Bayless (later an Arizona grocery magnate) went across the line to imbibe at a sidewalk cafe.

"We were fooling around, drinking beer out of coffee cans, when Morris sloshed some beer at me," Barry says. "A Mexican policeman was passing at the moment, and the beer flew by me and hit him in the face. Bayless and Morris ran for the border and made it, but I had a leg in a cast from a basketball injury, so I had to go with the policeman to jail."

Barry sat behind bars until evening, shooting craps with the jailer and losing all his money and most of his clothing in the game. Then he asked the right question: How much of a bribe would it take to spring him loose?

"The jailer said twenty-five dollars would do," relates Barry, "but I had no money left, so I had to write him a check."

Barry signed "A. J. Bayless" to the check and a moment later was free to limp back to the American side of the border. Bayless, who never tired of telling the story, kept the check framed in his office until his death.

During the spring of 1938, Barry succeeded in re-opening the Prescott Goldwater's store, which had been closed following Morris's retirement. Barry joined Prescott's famed Smoki People during that period, and helped put on their Indian ceremonial dances in August 1939. This group of non-Indian Prescott citizens had been simulating the ancient dances of Southwest Indians for many years.

"I'll never forget our Smoki initiation," remembers Barry's old friend, Lester (Budge) Ruffner of Prescott. "Barry and I were assigned to go pick up a load of bull snakes that had been collected by a nearby forest ranger for the snake dance that climaxes the show. We put them in a basket in the trunk of his Packard convertible, but when we got back to Prescott, we were amazed to find the trunk empty!

"Somehow those snakes had crawled through holes in the back of the trunk and were inside doors, in chassis openings, all over that car. We practically had to tear the Packard apart to recover all those snakes."

One of Barry's most important contributions to Arizona was the gift of land seven miles south of Prescott, which he made to the YMCA in 1938 for a permanent camping site. Grace Sparkes, secretary of the Yavapai Chamber of Commerce, suggested to Barry that the Lost Chance Mine property between Groom Creek and Wolf Creek was available for purchase. Moses Hazeltine, the pioneer Arizona banker, helped obtain clear title to the twenty and one-half acres of scenic pine-clad land. As he often did, Barry made the gift of the land to the YMCA anonymously. What he did not reveal until later was that he had to borrow money to pay for it. Today, half a century later, thousands of boys and girls enjoy camping at the YMCA Sky-Y Camp each year because somebody cared enough to make a sacrifice for them.

Life was ebbing slowly away from Morris Goldwater in the early months of 1939. Sallie had died seven years earlier, and he was again alone, his work done and his health failing. At eighty-seven, he was still as sharp, caustic, and funny as ever. (Barry remembers walking with him in Phoenix during this time when a man accosted Morris. "You don't know who I am, do you, Morris?" he asked. "No, and I don't give a damn, either," Morris shot back as he continued his walk.)

People recalled for his nephews many a story about Morris's wisdom and his humor. One of the favorites—corroborated by correspondence in his files—concerned the delegation of militant ladies who called on him in 1909 at the Prescott store to demand that he fire a female clerk who they claimed was a former prostitute.

Morris sat back in his chair and stared long and hard at the self-righteous delegation. "I've lived in Prescott for a long time," he said at last, "and I know a lot about your families in the early days. Some of you would be quite embarrassed if you knew how a few of the women made their living then."

The delegation retired in confusion and the matter was never brought up again.

On his eighty-fifth birthday, the thirteenth Arizona Legislature adopted a resolution that "there is probably no man living who has played a more interesting part in the history and development of Arizona, or more highly exemplified the life of a true pioneer and builder than has Morris Goldwater."

Then, on April 11, 1939, at age eighty-seven, Morris died quietly at his Prescott home. There was no place in Prescott big enough to hold the crowd at his funeral, but the local theatre was the largest available, so his family and friends held the service there.

Morris had left instructions for the kind of funeral he wanted, and he was the caustic comedian to the very last:

> The oftener I go to other people's funerals, the less I want to attend my own. . . . When I am laid out, do not go pussyfooting around as if you are afraid you would wake me up. If I wake or hear you, the chances are I will not talk back.
>
> I want to be buried as plainly and as cheaply as is consistent with decency and my station in life at the time I die. If you put notice of funeral in the papers, say "no flowers." Do not spend much money on a tombstone. I may want to get up some time and come back, and a heavy stone might hinder me. Do not wear any mourning for me. It will not do any good, and is a waste of money that can be better used
> . . .
>
> PS: I do not need any honorary (onery) pall bearers.

He asked that the "old" Masonic burial service be used, not the new one adopted in 1927. And he asked to be buried in the Masonic Cemetery in Prescott, not in the family plot in San Francisco. All his wishes were granted.

Newspapers across the state saluted Morris's contributions to the development of Arizona. One of the most touching editorials was that in the *Arizona Republic,* which said, in part:

> The citizens of the state will miss Morris Goldwater, but as the years roll on, they will know more and more how fortunate they were that his Creator allowed him so many long and useful years of service before He returned him to dust.
>
> Everywhere in Arizona are the monuments left by this noted pioneer, and no section of the state is without them.

Baron Goldwater had died on the eve of the Great Depression, and thus was spared the tribulations of that grim period. Now Morris was laid to rest as an apprehensive world teetered on the brink of global war.

There was not long to wait and worry, or to take last-minute measures to avoid the catastrophe. Adolf Hitler, claiming that the aggressive Poles had fired on peace-loving German soldiers, unleashed his overwhelming engines of war across the borders of Poland on September 1, 1939.

The world would never be the same again.

14

Into the Wild Blue Yonder

Barry Goldwater was not born at the controls of an airplane, but few can remember when aviation was not a vital and exciting part of his life.

Had he been a pioneer on the unmapped Arizona frontier, like Mike Goldwater, Barry undoubtedly would have guided massive freight wagons over the lonely deserts and mountain passes as his grandfather did, braving the unknown with the same adventuresome spirit. Facing danger with joyful enthusiasm and probing the mysteries of the unexplored always fascinated both Goldwaters.

For Barry, the blue vastness of the skies has had a mystic lure from the first time, when as a small boy, he watched barnstormers maneuver their fragile flying machines over Phoenix landing strips.

"Someday I'm going to be up there, too!" he promised himself. Few promises have been more faithfully kept.

For more than a half century, he has been putting the latest aircraft through their paces—from the trainers of the early 1930s to the fastest supersonic jet fighters the armed services have developed. It was a matter of pride to him that, until very recently, he had flown every aircraft in the American military inventory, and many foreign craft as well.

One of the best-known figures in the nation's aviation history, he has earned the two stars of an Air Force Reserve major general, headed the U.S. Air Force Academy Board of Visitors, achieved the elusive goal of chairing the Senate Armed Services Committee, and earned selection to aviation halls of fame around the nation.

Once, as a young man, he almost ended his flying career, and his life, when he crash-landed an airplane on the slopes of Arizona's Navajo Mountain. That mishap earned him "I told you so's" from

Navajo tribal leaders who had warned him that the gods would strike down any man who dared to fly over their sacred home. But he walked away from that near-tragedy, and he has never had a serious flying accident since.

Few men have been better suited for the air than he. His tempera-ment is an ideal mix of youthful daring, a love of the mechanical, and the cool competence that finds a way to overcome trouble and bring an aircraft home safely.

"He was a rare natural," declared one of his early flying instructors, Ruth Reinhold, who later piloted Barry all over the Southwest on campaign jaunts. "Barry is one of the finest pilots I have ever known, and he did everything right almost from the beginning—by instinct. If anyone was born to fly, it was Barry Goldwater."

Flying has played a major role in making Barry the national figure he has been for so long. It helped make him known to all Arizona in the 1930s and 1940s, and enabled him to upset a heavily favored incum-bent in his first major election campaign in 1952. His aerial missions as chairman of the Republican senatorial campaign committee gave him national visibility and put him on the road to winning the Repub-lican presidential nomination in 1964.

Aviation helped shape Barry Goldwater, and few men have done more to shape the course of American aviation.

PHOENIX, 1930

THE FIRST PRIMITIVE AIRPLANES FLEW INTO PHOENIX AND TUCSON FOR AIRSHOWS in 1910, to the amazement of the territorial populace. A half-dozen years later, Barry and Bob Goldwater joined their young friends to gape at the daredevils flying death-defying stunts at the Arizona State Fair.

The exploits of Arizona's great World War I ace, Frank Luke, whom the boys had known from afar when he was at Phoenix Union High School, were on everyone's lips. Luke was awarded the Congressional Medal of Honor after he heroically lost his life in the air over France. Today, his statue stands at the east entrance of the Arizona State Capitol in Phoenix.

One day in early 1930, Barry was walking down Central Avenue when he passed the R. D. Roper Company automobile salesroom. Inside was a Great Lakes trainer, as beautiful an airplane as he had ever seen. Enthralled, he went inside to get a closer look. A salesman at Roper's told him the price of the airplane—two thousand, five hundred dollars—and suggested that he see Jack Thornburg at the Phoenix airstrip on South 24th Street if he was interested in learning to fly one.

Barry was.

At the strip, located about where the north runway of Phoenix Sky Harbor International Airport is today, he found Thornburg and a pilot named Irving Kravitz, who teamed to teach the young aerial enthusiast how to fly.

"My first long cross-country was sometime in 1931," Barry recalls, "when I flew a Great Lakes plane to Los Angeles in six hours or so. We drive it that fast now. Then in 1932, I tried to enlist in the Army Air Corps aviation cadet program, but I couldn't pass the eye examination. But I never gave up hope of somehow becoming a military pilot."

When World War II erupted in Europe in 1939, Uncle Sam started training air corps pilots with a vengeance. But Barry was over thirty, had creaky knees from sports injuries, and his eyesight was no better than before. Besides, he was married and had children. So instead, he went for his commercial license in 1940.

For many months before the Japanese bombing of Pearl Harbor, Arizona was rapidly becoming an armed camp to meet the threat of German aggression. Gone now were the years of Depression belt-tightening, the years of grim despair and stagnation.

Suddenly, there was money moving again, and work for everyone, as military bases were built at a feverish pace all over the state. Arizona's warm, sunny climate was made to order for teaching young men how to fly, and the Army Air Corps took full advantage of it.

Four airfields were built in the Phoenix area: Luke Army Air Field on the west side of the Valley, Williams Army Air Field on the east side, and two private contract training bases—Thunderbird and Falcon Fields—in between.

Eager aviation cadets from all over the nation flooded into the valley with propellor insignia on their caps, fresh from pre-flight schools and ready to take to the air in Army trainers. With them came ruddy-cheeked British cadets and grim young Chinese airmen, eager to earn their wings and return to their troubled homelands.

The influx of military aviation trainees was one of the momentous events of the early 1940s that accelerated the development of southern and central Arizona in an unprecedented manner. It gave young men from all over America their first look at a state that many thousands chose to make their home after the shooting was over. Back they came in droves after 1945 to make new lives in a new land of opportunity.

As the Nazi legions swept across Europe in 1940, Barry Goldwater longed to get into uniform. His brother Bob, too, hoped that circumstances would enable him to be a combatant in the coming fight. But both were husbands and fathers, and both felt the heavy responsibilities of maintaining a business that provided the livelihood for more than two hundred employees and their families.

In mid-1941, Barry became chairman of the Military Affairs Committee of the Phoenix Chamber of Commerce. In that capacity he went to call on Lt. Col. Ennis Whitehead, commanding officer of the newly opened Luke Army Air Field near Litchfield Park. The sight of sleek fighter planes zooming overhead stirred up old longings.

"Colonel," Barry pleaded, "I have an Army Reserve commission as a first lieutenant, and I've been flying for more than ten years. Can't you find a place for me here?"

Whitehead, who later became one of Barry's best friends, took the opportunity. He sat Barry down with an application form, and two weeks later he was on active duty as a non-flying officer at Luke. Fate offered Barry one more chance to fly army airplanes: Desperate for pilots, the air corps created a new rating, Service Pilot, for veteran civilian fliers. He was accepted—an air corps pilot at last.

He instructed in air-to-air gunnery at Luke, and while doing so, took in-flight photographs of pilots to send home. In return, the grateful pilots agreed to give Barry some after-hours instruction in the army way to fly.

With Group Captain Teddy Donaldson of the Royal Air Force, Barry devised a "curve-of-pursuit" concept that was soon adopted as standard teaching technique for gunnery in the air corps.

"We were never given any recognition for developing that gunnery system, which was no small factor in improving our combat success," says Barry. "But it's like Uncle Morris used to say so often: There's no limit to what you can accomplish if you don't worry about who gets the credit for it."

Barry served for a time at Yuma (Arizona) Army Air Field and then was assigned to Ferry Command duty after qualifying for regular air corps pilot status. His aircraft delivery missions took him all over the world. For months, he was stationed in the China-Burma-India Theater, ferrying aircraft over the Hump in some of the most treacherous weather and terrain to be found anywhere.

One night in Calcutta, he was drinking with a friend, Major Hap Carswell, in the Officers Club. They were both well along toward euphoria when a radiogram was delivered to Barry, instructing him to return "by first available aircraft" to the United States. Certain that this was his long-awaited call to B-29 bomber duty, he sobered up, called in a crew, and took off on a three-day trip to New York.

"When I called my commanding officer to ask for a couple of days' leave, he was amazed to hear my voice and asked me what I was doing in the States," says Barry. "The radiogram had been intended for my friend Major

Carswell, so there was nothing for me to do but fly right back to India. It was a twenty-six thousand-mile ride for nothing, but I did get to come home for a couple of days."

The war's end found him stationed in southern California, training pilots for combat duty in P-51 and P-38 fighters. His long quest for combat duty in fighters had ended in frustration. So had his burning desire to fly B-29s against the Japanese in the South Pacific.

But he did have one satisfaction: He was the first Goldwater in ninety years of the family's American saga to wear a military uniform in wartime. Later he was to log more than twelve thousand flying hours in 165 different types of aircraft.

And still later, he was to wear the stars of an Air Force Reserve major general.

The years just before and during World War II were years of Goldwater births. Mike's great-grandchildren arrived in happy profusion.

Barry and Peggy's first child was Joanne, born in Phoenix. Barry Jr., next in line, arrived in Los Angeles. Mike was born in Phoenix. The last of the four was Peggy, usually called "Little Peggy" by the family, who was born in La Jolla, California, while her father was in the Ferry Command, flying an airplane en route to Cairo.

Bob and Mary had two children, Lynne and Robert Jr., both born in Phoenix. From Bob's 1951 marriage to Sally Harrington came two offspring, Sally and Don.

Carolyn and her husband, Paul Sexson, had two sons, Tim and Paul. Because Paul worked for Lockheed Aircraft Company in North Hollywood during much of the war, Carolyn was away from her family and Arizona friends during this period. Following a divorce from Sexson, Carolyn married Jack Thompson in 1948, and they had a son, John. When she married Bernard Erskine in 1958, Erskine adopted the boy.

Each new grandchild gave added meaning to Josephine Goldwater's life. As she had during World War I, she participated in wartime charitable and civilian support agencies during the early 1940s, but there was always time in her busy schedule for those new babies.

In 1940, Jo moved to Country Club Manor, where Bob and Barry had built homes four years earlier. It was not easy for her to leave the old house where so many memories of Baron and the children still hovered, though.

Just before they demolished the grand old house, the family hosted "one last big bash" there—a "come as you were" party. Bob, Barry, and Carolyn wore children's outfits, Jo was attired in flapper dress and beads, and guests were costumed out of their past. It was, by all accounts, a memorable evening.

Bob Goldwater took up flying later than his brother, but he had his share of wartime flight service.

"I learned to fly in 1941, in a single-engine Waco that I bought for three thousand, five hundred dollars," Bob recalls. "I'll swear that plane had a built-in ground loop, along with some other faults. Ruth Reinhold aged considerably while she was getting me ready to solo."

His decision to become a pilot was born of necessity. Bob sent his family to Colorado Springs when the mercury in Phoenix topped one hundred degrees, and he joined them there on weekends when he could get away. Because it took so long to reach Colorado Springs by commercial routes, he learned to fly to save time when making the trip.

A few weeks after the bombing of Pearl Harbor, Bob offered his services to the Arizona Civil Air Patrol. By that time he had a sleek Navion, which he flew on many a search and rescue mission for the CAP.

A vital adjunct to the war effort, the CAP performed countless missions in support of the military, and even flew the mail on occasion. Bob moved up the command chain, and at the end of the war, was appointed commander of the Arizona Civil Air Patrol, with rank of lieutenant colonel.

One of his prized mementos is a framed Certificate of Appreciation from the U.S. War Department, detailing his dedicated service during the period of 1942 through 1946.

The business journal *Retail Management,* in its issue of August 1943, featured an article devoted to one of Bob Goldwater's best wartime ideas. Entitled "Goldwater's Gift to Employees—Arizona Store Promotes Patriotic and Recreational Project," it told of the new Jack Thornton Farm at Broadway Road and South 30th St., southeast of Phoenix:

> A far-sighted development has been conceived and is in the process of formation by R. W. Goldwater, President of Goldwater's (Phoenix, Arizona). With the idea in mind that it would be both good business and a means of alleviating the national food shortage and supplying employees with recreation and essential food, the management purchased 21½ acres located about eight miles from the store as a cooperative undertaking for their employees. . . .

The farm was named for venerable Jack Thornton, dean of the two hundred Goldwater's employees. Thornton had long been a popular management figure, and naming the farm for him accentuated the employee involvement in all decisions regarding the property.

Barry had instituted many employee benefits—insurance, retirement, bonuses, profit-sharing, and others—and the company-owned airplane made possible the formation of the "Flying G" company flying club. Any employee who wished to learn to fly could join the club and take lessons.

Bob wisely continued and extended employee benefits after Barry went into active Army Air Corps service.

"The farm was a great morale builder in a time of wartime shortages and worries over families and friends stationed far away," Bob recalls.

In addition to the practical benefits—especially food production—the farm offered horseback riding, picnicking, playgrounds and other recreation. There were cows to be milked, eggs to be gathered, horses to be saddled, rabbits to be fed. There was work and fun for everybody. At the end of the war the management added a swimming pool and clubhouse, and the society pages of Phoenix newspapers printed many a picture of social events at the Jack Thornton Farm.

Larry Andrews, popular *Phoenix Gazette* columnist and radio personality, devoted one 1947 radio broadcast to the Goldwater enterprises during the war. He said, in part:

> I could spend an hour or more telling you about that farm and how much it means to the Goldwater employees. But if I did, that would be more than has ever been said by the Goldwaters, because it would never occur to them to try to capitalize on that project.
>
> Remember how we started the Red Cross canteen at the Union Station? The Phoenix Salvage Committee got the building erected, with all materials and labor donated. But limited funds delayed the opening. It was the Goldwaters who came to the rescue. They contributed all the proceeds of a Desert Fashions show at the Biltmore Hotel, about two thousand dollars. But the Goldwaters didn't want any publicity for that, and there was no publicity for the many other things they do of a civic nature. . . .

Many Phoenix businessmen gave generously of their time and money during the grim war years when others were giving their lives on far-flung battlefields. But few did it more effectively than Bob Goldwater. His support of charitable and war effort programs was never widely publicized, and that's the way he wanted it.

When Lieutenant Colonel Barry Goldwater returned home in November 1945, to become a civilian once more, he found it difficult to make the transition overnight. After more than four years of roaming the world and living the military life, his former routine seemed a little tame.

One thing was certain: his horizons had been broadened beyond measure, and his thinking would from now on be in global terms.

In his autobiography, *With No Apologies,* he wrote:

> When one sits at the controls of an aircraft on a long ferry flight or

cargo run, there is time to think. How did we blunder into the bloodshed and waste of war? How could it be avoided in the future?

I became convinced that the isolationist mood of the country after World War I, not the harsh terms of the Treaty of Versailles, had made World War II inevitable. If we had maintained our military superiority throughout the twenties and thirties, President Roosevelt could have warned Hitler not to invade any neutral countries and that warning would have been heeded.

Barry's devotion to maintaining peace through military strength has never faltered from that day to this.

He had been home only a few weeks when another military assignment beckoned alluringly. Governor Sidney P. Osborn, who had served as a fourteen-year-old page in the 1899 legislature when Morris Goldwater was Council president, was eager to establish the Arizona Air National Guard. After consulting his advisors, he came up with a name for the top commander—Barry Goldwater.

"Governor Osborn asked me if I would organize the Air National Guard, which I did," Barry relates. "I took a reduction in rank to captain, because that was the highest rank they had provided for the Air National Guard. Then I asked Larry Bell, who was a student of mine at Luke, to be my deputy. Larry had become an ace and a major in combat in Italy, and I was impressed by his abilities."

Arizona was full of young air corps veterans, most of them eager to continue their romance with flying, so recruiting for the new air guard was not difficult. Barry commanded the unit until he got into politics several years later, then Bell became the commander.

One of Barry's favorite stories about his service in the Arizona Air National Guard concerned a cross-country flight he took not long after the unit was organized. He had reverted to the rank of captain to accept the command of the guard, and he appeared much too old for that rank, especially since his hair had begun to go prematurely gray.

"I was standing at the Operations counter in St. Louis during this cross-country," he remembers, "wearing my flight suit with captain's bars. A young lieutenant took one look at my rank, and another at my hair, and sidled up to me with his face a question mark.

"'Tell me, captain,' he asked. 'Where did you foul up?'"

The demands of politics did not separate Barry Goldwater from the air corps, which became the United States Air Force in 1947. He took air reserve assignments, in the rank of colonel, with the Fourth Air Force and then the Air Defense Command. And when he went to the U.S. Senate in

1953 he organized the 9999th Air Reserve Squadron, composed of members of Congress and their staffs.

Bob Goldwater carried his wartime flying fervor over into a venture known as Arizona Airways, persuading Johnny Bulla and several other famous touring golf professionals to invest in the company in the late 1940s. Arizona Airways was a short-lived operation, and was soon absorbed into a larger regional air service which became Frontier Airlines.

Barry played an important role in the development of today's giant civilian aviation industry. First in Phoenix, as a civic leader and city councilman, and later in the U.S. Senate, he worked tirelessly for better and safer airport facilities and communications networks. For decades he has been a spokesman for aviation across America and around the world.

The intrepid aerial barnstormers who stirred the imagination of a seven-year-old boy in 1916, and the auto dealer whose display moved him to take flying lessons in 1930, never knew how important they were in shaping the career of Barry Goldwater, pilot and tireless spokesman for aviation progress.

15

The Merchant Tastes Politics

Pity the unfortunate man who never becomes passionately involved in anything—whose life is a bland progression from routine job to indifferent family evenings, to boring weekends, and then back to the job again.

But feel some compassion, too, for the restless seeker whose pulse is quickened by every siren call, who climbs first one mountain and then another, always searching for the ultimate experience and the one challenge worth giving one's life to.

Just such a seeker was Barry Goldwater, who by 1946 had reached more goals and garnered more laurels than most people aspire to in several lifetimes. Photographer, radio ham, athlete, writer, social lion, merchant, airman—he had played all those roles and more, and had starred in most of them.

Why, then, did he suffer this gnawing hunger for some indefinable something that he felt he still must achieve?

He had returned to civilian life in 1945 with a creditable military record, but it had not been quite up to Barry's high expectations. Stretching ahead was the dreary prospect of resuming his position as a department store executive, hardly a challenge to make a man's blood race. For an adventurer who had roamed the exotic outposts of the world and had braved death in the sky routinely, this future was not enough.

Mike Goldwater had experienced that same vague lack of fulfill-ment in 1852, and had deserted the good life with family and friends in London to search for his destiny in the wilds of western America. Mike's ambitious son, Baron, had forsaken the familiar certainties of the Prescott store to risk his reputation in a daring Phoenix mercantile venture.

Barry now stood at that same crossroads. With an unexplainable restlessness, he put aside his fifty-mission cap and his air corps uniform, and tried to resume the life that once had satisfied him so completely.

But it was not to be.

PHOENIX, 1941

B Y THE TIME THE DAPPER BARON HAD BREATHED HIS LAST IN MARCH 1929, GOLD-water's was unchallenged as Arizona's leading women's wear store. He had managed to corral exclusive rights to many of the most desired merchandise lines in America, and he knew how to present them to his customers with a special charm that no competitor could quite equal.

Rare is the Arizonan today who has never read a Goldwater's advertisement, or shopped in one of the fine Goldwater's stores, or thrilled at receiving a gift in the distinctive Goldwater's box.

"The Best, Always" was more than a company slogan. It was a promise of quality and a special excitement that brought customers, their children, and their grandchildren, back for more. Mike and Morris's Prescott store was serviceable and dependable enough, but it was not until Baron worked his merchandising magic in Phoenix that the Goldwater's mystique was born.

One of Baron's many innovations was the Goldwater's style shows—probably the first ever presented in Arizona. Later the company trademark, "Desert Fashions," one of Barry's ideas, became known far and wide. Barry coined a Spanish-language title, "El Desfile de las Modas del Desierto" (A Parade of Desert Fashions) to give later style shows a Southwestern flavor.

Barry proved to be a master merchandiser, and the store at 31 North First Street continued to be a magnet for fashion-conscious Arizona women during his years as president of Goldwater's. He had the flair for the spectacular, and the innovative mind of the born salesman.

Goldwater's thrived and prospered, both under his direction and under that of his brother, Bob. During the quarter century following Barry's departure for air corps duty in 1941, the boss at Goldwater's was Bob. While not the salesman Barry was, he had a much keener sense of financial opportunity, and a foresight that kept Goldwater's a step ahead of the competition.

True, others did the imaginative buying, the clever advertising, the effective selling, and the on-the-spot managing. Bob brought in many of those creative people, and was able to keep the best ones through progressive personnel policies.

Bob was able, too, to peer into the murky future and determine what kind of store Arizonans would want in five or ten years. The dawn of the shopping center had arrived, and merchandising was to be vastly different in the post-war years.

Phoenix was changing even more, as the thousands of ex-servicemen and sun seekers poured into the city to make their homes. The sleepy little town in the desert was beginning to have ambitions as a metropolis.

The old ways, the old locations, would not do for Goldwater's in this exciting era of skyrocketing growth.

Bob had seen it all coming, well before the end of World War II.

"We could see that Phoenix was about to boom, and that some formidable competition was about to come in—Bullock's of Los Angeles, perhaps, or other fine stores," he recalls. "When that happened, our monopoly of top lines, and thus our dominance, would come to an end. We had to move with the times."

Phoenix, most forecasters agreed, would be growing north. Goldwater's looked northward for a new location, and Bob recalls driving around the Phoenix area with architect Frank Lloyd Wright (who spent his winters at nearby Taliesen West), looking for a site where a Wright-designed building for Goldwater's might be placed. Del Webb, by then a millionaire building contractor, also made suggestions.

The eventual choice was a site two and a half miles north of the city center, which was at that time occupied by a dairy farm. It was far out in the boondocks, many feared, but it did have room for parking. Ralph Burgbacher, who proposed building a major shopping center to be known as Park Central, approached Bob about locating the new Goldwater's store there, and Bob said yes with little further discussion. Once Goldwater's had signed, other major stores followed, and Park Central was a success.

"I had plenty of misgivings and sleepless nights about moving so far from the only major business district Phoenix had ever had," Bob says. "Some people who knew Phoenix well told me the move would be the end of Goldwater's."

By that time, Barry had moved on to other things, and the decision rested squarely on Bob's shoulders. Hindsight tells us it was an obvious decision to make, but it was a risky move at the time. It was a decision Mike and Morris and Baron would have approved.

"I was nominally president of Goldwater's in the years just after World War II," explains Barry, "but the problems of merchandising no longer interested me as much as in earlier days. Bob and others were doing a good job managing the store, so I gave my attention to other matters."

He maintained office hours at the store, but his new-found fascination with public matters took him away with increasing frequency. He had been home only a few weeks when he was appointed by Democratic

Governor Sidney P. Osborn in 1945 to organize the Arizona Air National Guard. That was a mammoth task that captured his attention for more than a year. Before the job was done, he was given another—an assignment to the Colorado River Commission, with the ultimate goal of winning approval for the gigantic Central Arizona Project, a multi-billion-dollar plan to bring water for power and irrigation to central Arizona from the Colorado River.

That appointment brought him in close working relationship with venerable Senator Carl Hayden, Arizona's grand old man of politics and one of the nation's leaders in irrigation and reclamation projects. Hayden was a noted Democrat, but Barry labored effectively with him for many years.

Public service was soon crowding out most everything else in Barry Goldwater's life. In 1946, he accepted a position of leadership on behalf of Arizona's right-to-work legislation. A harbinger of political positions yet to come, it placed him in bitter conflict with the state's labor leaders. But he felt strongly that a person should have the right to hold a job without joining a labor union, and was vociferous in his views. That campaign was crowned with success in November 1946, when voters appoved the proposal and made Arizona the third right-to-work state in the nation. (Leaders of organized labor, in Arizona and around the United States, did not forget or forgive.)

Within the next two years, Barry accepted appointments to the Arizona Interstate Stream Commission and to the U.S. Interior Department's advisory commission on Indian affairs.

Little wonder, then, that the staff at Goldwater's store saw him less frequently than in the relaxed days before the war.

Old-timers who watched his rise to prominence in Phoenix nodded their heads and remembered how Mike had helped develop La Paz and Ehrenberg, and had given his time so freely to Prescott improvement projects. They recalled Joe's pioneering services to half a dozen raw Arizona towns, and Morris's unparalleled volunteering.

Baron and Jo Goldwater had carried on that tradition, and they had passed it along to their children.

Bob Goldwater had become active in Phoenix community work even before he joined Barry in the Goldwater's management in 1937. A member of the second group to be voted into the hard-working Phoenix Thunderbirds, special-events group of the Phoenix Chamber of Commerce, he became one of the early "Big Chiefs" of that organization. In 1935, he persuaded the Thunderbirds to take on sponsorship of the Phoenix Open Golf Tournament. The Thunderbirds still host that world-renowned event, and Bob has been honored ever since as "The Father of the Phoenix Open."

Carolyn plunged into community service immediately after her graduation from UCLA. Her devoted labors on behalf of countless Phoenix charities—Humane Society, Planned Parenthood, and St. Luke's Hospital, among others—have earned her a place of honor among Phoenix builders.

Barry had been a supporter of Phoenix youth organizations from the early 1930s, and his pre-war efforts on behalf of the Phoenix Chamber of Commerce, Thunderbirds, Masons, YMCA, and many other service groups had been widely recognized. But the restless energy he channeled into his community work in the late 1940s put his earlier efforts in the shade.

When the Phoenix Advertising Club inaugurated its "Phoenix Man of the Year" award in 1949, the easy winner of that coveted honor was Barry Goldwater.

His service to Goldwater's was nearing its end as 1950 approached, but Barry stayed around long enough to assist in planning store expansion. One of the projects was the establishment of a small branch store at suburban Scottsdale in 1950. Scottsdale was a little-known crossroads at that time, and few could have foreseen that it would soon become a world-famous resort and fashion center. With typical foresight, the Goldwater brothers entered that market early. (Today's grand Goldwater's store in Scottsdale Fashion Square evolved from the humble beginning of that 1950 shop.)

The planning of the Fashion Square store was one of Bob's last *tours de force* for the family-owned Goldwater's. In 1962, when the company staged its gala one hundredth anniversary celebration, Bob was already planning to sell the Goldwater stores to a national chain.

The Associated Dry Goods Company, with corporate headquarters in New York City, operated such prestigious stores as Lord and Taylor of New York and Robinson's in Los Angeles. Under terms of their generous offer for the Goldwater's properties and name, Associated Dry Goods retained Bob Goldwater as president of Goldwater's, and gave him a vice-presidency in the parent firm, as well.

Bob stayed on as Goldwater's president until 1966, when he moved up to chairman of the board as a first step toward relinquishing operational control. Not long thereafter, he retired from the store management.

For the first time in more than a century, there were no Goldwaters occupying leadership positions in Arizona's pioneer department store organization.

Phoenix had gained a notorious reputation during World War II as a hotbed of prostitution and gambling. Several times, the nearby military air base commanders had declared Phoenix "off limits" to their personnel until short-lived reform movements succeeded in cleaning things up.

At the end of the war, Phoenix city government still operated as it had in the days when Phoenix was a frontier village. The citizenry fretted over reports of graft, inefficiency, and cronyism. Many Phoenicians—Barry among them—believed it was time to revamp the Phoenix city government structure to accommodate the realities of its emerging metropolitan status.

By 1948, the Charter Government Committee had drawn up, over the protests of the old-time politicians, a new Phoenix city charter and had won enthusiastic approval of it by the electorate. Barry's efforts in that campaign were fresh in the minds of the "Man of the Year" selection committee in 1949.

Having helped with the reorganization Phoenix city government, and having played a leadership role in setting his city on an efficient course, Barry thought he had won at least a brief respite from his community labors. But there were other plans being made for him.

Not surprisingly, he was urged to enter the political arena for the first time as a candidate for city council on the Charter Government's 1949 slate. One by one, Phoenix's men of power and prestige approached him with their best arm-twisting techniques.

His answer at first was "no." Later, as the pressure became irritating, he responded with a more vociferous "hell, no." To his brother Bob, and to Goldwater's store manager Bill Saufley, he gave assurances that he was not about to leave the store management for the bruising battles of city politics.

As the deadline for candidate filing approached, one place remained open on the Charter Government council slate. Several prominent Phoenix business and professional leaders were approached, but all declined the dubious honor.

Finally, the other candidates for city council pleaded with Harry Rosenzweig (who had already agreed to run) to persuade his best friend to join the slate.

"You want Barry?" asked Rosenzweig. "I'll get him."

Then, as Harry recalls it, he invited Barry over for drinks and conversation one evening, and they had several pleasant hours of both. They were in a mellow mood as Barry prepared to depart.

"Barry was about to leave," recalls Rosenzweig, "when he suddenly asked me what it was I had called him to talk about. I said we all wanted him to join us in the city council race. After reminding me several times that he had already said 'no,' he finally agreed to run. And that was that."

Now Barry was faced with the unpleasant task of telling Bob and Saufley that he had changed his mind about running. Both were away at the moment, so he wrote them a letter which has become a classic in the saga of Goldwater's political career:

Dear Willie and Bob:

You both will probably think me seven kinds of a dirty bastard when you hear that I have decided to run for councilman with Harry. . . . I don't think a man can live with himself when he asks others to do his dirty work for him. I couldn't criticize the government of this city if I myself refused to help.

I don't know if we can win, but if we do, then I know Phoenix will have two years of damned good government that I hope will set a pattern for the coming years and the coming generations.

There has always been one, and sometimes two, Goldwaters damned fools enough to get into politics, and they always did it with service in their minds. . . . My unbounded confidence in the organization of this firm gives me assurance of its being well run no matter who is around, and that helps a lot. . . .

The city needs help more than any of our governments. Maybe we can give it to them. Maybe we will suffer in doing it, but in our minds we will be doing what Americans should always be doing: helping each other.

Don't cuss me too much. It ain't for life, and it may be fun.

Barry

His closing statement was only half correct. It certainly was for fun, as every campaign has been for Barry Goldwater, but, as things turned out, it was "for life."

He had tried the military, flying, business, radio, photography, and a dozen other ventures—and had given himself enthusiastically to each. But the call of politics was more compelling than any of the others.

The store had lost Barry Goldwater, and politics was about to claim his body and soul.

16

Vote for Goldwater

The drug called politics is one of the most addictive known to man. It begins with fooling around in a little local election—because all your friends are doing it—and you say to yourself "I can quit any time I feel like it."

Then someone you admire comes along and offers some of more potent stuff, and soon you are reaching highs you never knew existed. The excitement and euphoria are matched by few other human experiences, and only a disastrous defeat can make you quit cold turkey. Even after laying off a while, you're likely to find the temptation too great and you return.

Certainly, Barry Goldwater had no intentions of making politics a lifetime habit when he reluctantly gave in and agreed to run for a place on the Phoenix City Council. But once he started campaigning, he found it great fun. He discovered, too, that he was very good at it, and that people listened when he spoke. Nobody was better than he in a small group, mingling after a barbecue or morning coffee.

He loved the give-and-take of campaigning—answering an opponent's charge and throwing a bigger one right back at him. Moreover, he had an uncanny sense of what people were concerned about, and what they believed to be important.

It was immediately evident that this young Phoenix merchant was not a politician in the traditional mold. Like his sometimes-gruff old Uncle Morris, he spoke his mind—came right out and said unpopular things—answered the tough questions that campaign strategists had counseled him to avoid—and occasionally stubbed his toe in his efforts to be frank and aboveboard.

Arizona voters generally appreciate that kind of honesty and that willingness to take a stand. They admire a man who will express his opinion on almost any subject and let the chips fall where they may.

News people liked Goldwater, too, and they found him to be great copy. There was always a good quote to be garnered from an interview with him. They, too, were generally forgiving of minor errors and contradictions in his off-the-cuff remarks, and concentrated on the central meaning of the message.

Much later, in the big league of political competition, national reporters covering the 1964 presidential campaign were to find his unguarded frankness an irresistible target. To his enemies, he provided both cross and nails for a crucifixion. As a result, the vital message he wanted so earnestly to convey in his major speeches was too often obscured by the headline value of some incidental remark.

But in 1949, 1950, and 1952, the Goldwater style was pure magic. It brought him from relative obscurity to the peak of political achievement in Arizona, and did so in three short years.

Soon after he entered politics, it became evident to Barry Goldwater that his past was now only prologue. All those other occupations and avocations which had once seemed so important faded before this new light in his life.

He was not as prepared for a political career as some others. He did not own a degree in political science, had not argued law in a courtroom, had not read deeply in the philosophy of government, and had not worked his way up through the party hierarchy. But throughout his life, he had been formulating ideas about how people should be governed, and had tested those ideas in an array of life experiences.

Who cared that he was not a political savant? He was a refreshing new personality on the Arizona political scene, and he was able to express his beliefs convincingly.

Those who watched his performance in the city council race of 1949 and his management of Howard Pyle's gubernatorial campaign in 1950 became convinced that this fellow Goldwater was a man to watch.

PHOENIX–WASHINGTON, D.C., 1949

FOR MORE THAN TWO DECADES, THE GOLDWATER NAME HAD BEEN MISSING FROM the ballot in Arizona. It was the longest absence of that noted name since 1874, when Mike, Joe, and Morris had all entered the political arena. Of the three—all staunch Democrats—only Morris had become a politician of statewide stature. Seldom had he been out of office from 1874 until his final term as Prescott mayor in the late 1920s.

Now it was 1949, and voters of the City of Phoenix were being urged to

"Vote for Goldwater." This time it was Barry, embarking on his maiden voyage on the stormy political seas.

One of the many myths of the Goldwater saga is that Barry and Bob Goldwater were so apolitical that they flipped a coin to determine who would register as a Democrat and who as a Republican. Another is that Barry had harbored no thoughts of political office until Harry Rosenzweig twisted his arm and led him, protesting, into the Phoenix City Council campaign of 1949.

There is some slight truth in both stories. Bob had followed the family preference for the Democratic Party (only his Midwestern-born mother, of all the Goldwaters, had dared to be a Republican) and he was so registered. There was some feeling that it might be good business to have both parties represented in the Goldwater's store management. But Barry was destined early in life to be a Republican. His love of the underdog and his distaste for the arrogance of the ruling Democrats in Arizona led him to the Republican fold, and his dismay at Franklin D. Roosevelt's New Deal policies hardened his resolve.

Bob, like many other Arizonans with inborn sympathies for the Republican free-enterprise philosophy, did not change his registration for a good reason: until 1950, the significant Arizona political races were settled in the Democratic primaries. Unless one was registered Democratic, one simply did not have a voice in Arizona government.

As to Barry's political involvement: it had surfaced long before 1949. Uncle Morris had first whetted Barry's political appetite in the 1920s. Barry proved to be an effective campaigner in elections at both Phoenix Union High and the University of Arizona. A recently discovered column from a 1941 Phoenix newspaper provides the startling information that he was being touted even then as a Republican gubernatorial candidate while serving in the air corps at Luke Field.

So it was not surprising that Barry was given two key appointments by Governor Sidney P. Osborn. The first, in 1945, was non-political: the assignment to organize the Arizona Air National Guard. The other, in 1946, was of equal importance: a seat on Arizona's Colorado River Commission.

The Central Arizona Project, which will bring irrigation water from the Colorado River to central and southern Arizona in the late 1980s, has been high on Goldwater's agenda ever since.

Barry's involvement in Phoenix city politics can be traced to his 1947 appointment by Mayor Ray Busey to the forty-person committee charged with writing a new charter capable of serving a city in transition to metropolitan status.

Until 1947, the Phoenix city charter had vested complete control of city operations in the council. As a result, ever-shifting coalitions on the council hired and fired city officials with alarming frequency. City managers, for example, could expect a tenure of no more than twelve months.

Unless some stability could be achieved, and the opportunities for inefficiency and graft removed, Phoenix could look forward to nothing but chaos, it was felt.

Many of Phoenix's most able leaders labored to write a modern charter for a city destined to be among America's largest. It was approved by the voters in a special 1948 election, and a new council was elected. Like others on the charter committee, Barry thought they had achieved their goals.

But they were wrong. Several council members seemed to prefer the old system, and they ignored the new charter when it got in their way.

"I learned then that no written document is of much value unless the people elected to power are faithful to that document," declares Barry. "This conclusion has been reinforced many times by my experiences in the Congress."

Dismayed by the turn of events in Phoenix city government, but unwilling to admit defeat, members of the citizens' group reconvened, brought in new members, and adopted the name "Charter Government Committee." It sought out council candidates and became a potent force in Phoenix for years to come.

Barry, who had been talking loudly about improving Phoenix city government, was now being asked by his fellow citizens to start *doing* something about it. For the first time, he had to decide whether to forsake the comfortable role of the civic advisor and put his name before the voters as a candidate for public office.

His aforementioned letter to Bob and Bill Saufley revealed a landmark decision, and one that changed the young merchant's life for all time to come.

The Charter Government ticket won handily in the fall of 1949, and the reluctant Barry Goldwater—the last person who had agreed to run—led all the rest. It was heady stuff, and the kind of tonic which encourages a man to seek political office again.

On January 1, 1950, the *Arizona Republic* ushered in a new decade and a new half-century with a front page photograph of the new Phoenix government. Arrayed at a long table were Councilmen Hohen Foster, Frank Murphy, Margaret Kober, Charles Walters, Harry Rosenzweig, and Barry Goldwater. With them was Mayor Nicholas Udall and, whispering in the mayor's ear, the new city manager, Ray Wilson.

It was truly the beginning of a new era in Phoenix politics.

So rapidly did the Charter Government councilmen keep their promises that Phoenix was honored as an "All-American City" by the National

Municipal League and *Look* magazine at the end of 1950. Vice was drastically reduced, and city operations were run more economically.

Jack Williams, a Phoenix radio executive who later served on the Phoenix City Council with Barry and went on to become governor of Arizona, recalled Goldwater's hatred of wasting the taxpayer's money:

"He raised cain at budget hearings whenever he thought we were spending too much," said Williams. "He always disliked contingency funds, which he thought were a temptation for excessive spending. And he told local merchants that if they wanted downtown parking lots, they would have to build them themselves."

Barry stepped on a lot of toes in those hectic months, but he built a reputation as an economy advocate and was viewed as a plain-speaking reformer and a breath of fresh air on the Phoenix political scene.

In the period just after the end of World War II, Arizona politicians still devoted the bulk of their efforts to September of the even years—Democratic primary election time—as they had since statehood. That was when it all happened, and the November balloting was strictly anticlimactic.

But there were signs of change in the air. Democrats still outnumbered Republicans at least three-to-one across Arizona, but those thousands of post-war newcomers flooding into the state were largely from the Midwest and North, Republican country. Moreover, people in Arizona who had been registering as Democrats to have a voice in the primaries were considering a return to the GOP. A fiesty Republican publisher from Indiana, Eugene C. Pulliam, had come to Phoenix and bought the two daily newspapers from Wes Knorpp and Charlie Stauffer. The *Arizona Republic* and *Phoenix Gazette* were strong Republican voices and were beginning to influence elections in a more effective way.

Novelist Clarence Budington Kelland was now a prestigious Republican National Committeeman from Arizona, and energetic Charlie Garland was an effective chairman of the Arizona Republican Party. Other new Republican personalities were emerging.

Many Arizonans who didn't care much either way were starting to lean to the Republicans merely to stir up some competition in the political process. By 1950, for the first time in memory, there were indications that the two-party system was about to be born in Arizona.

So it was with some optimism that the Arizona Young Republicans met at the Adams Hotel in Phoenix one Saturday morning in the spring of 1950 to beat the drums and come up with a solid Republican candidate for governor. To help, convention leaders invited Howard Pyle of radio station KTAR to address the young activists of the Arizona GOP. Pyle was probably the state's best-known radio voice, and his efforts on behalf of the forlorn candidacy of Republican rancher Bruce Brockett for governor in recent years were appreciated by the party.

Pyle, who is now one of Arizona's most revered elder statesmen, remembers that Saturday as though it were last week:

> I made my best pulpit-pounding speech to the Young Republicans, exhorting them to get active in the community and political life. And I especially urged them to give their best efforts to the coming political campaign.
>
> When I was through, I returned to my office across the street and got on with other things. A couple of hours later, I received a telephone call from Harvey Mott of the *Arizona Republic.*
>
> "You'd better get back over here," he told me with excitement in his voice. "Those kids are about to endorse you as their candidate for governor! You may want to come right away and put out this fire."
>
> I rushed back to the convention and tried to get them to think things over before making such a rash move. I'd never run for any elective office in my life, and had not planned to do so. "Can you raise $50,000 to get a campaign going?" I asked them. "And how about the senior Republican leaders? They have other ideas about who should run."
>
> But they were fired up and wouldn't take "no" for an answer. After all I had said about sacrificing personal interests for the sake of better government, I could hardly make a flat refusal at that point. The next morning, the *Republic* headlined the news that "Young Republicans Endorse Pyle for Governor."

The exciting news started a firestorm of activity among previously lethargic Republicans. This was a sensational idea—fielding a candidate whose voice was known to almost every Arizonan who owned a radio, and a man who was regarded as a model of civic virtue. Besides, the Democrats were somewhat in disarray, with four or five candidates planning to seek the office currently held by Governor Dan Garvey. This year, the Republicans might have at least an outside chance to win!

The day after the announcement of Pyle's endorsement, Barry Goldwater showed up at the KTAR offices to congratulate him.

"He had just returned from one of his trips to the back country, and he needed a shave and a change of clothes," recalls Pyle, "but he was full of enthusiasm. 'So they caught you with your mouth open too wide!' he joked." (Years later, when Goldwater was nominated for President, Pyle sent him a telegram: "So they caught you with your mouth open too wide!")

Barry offered his support, his time, his airplane, anything. Gratefully,

Pyle accepted them all, and soon announced that Goldwater would be his campaign manager.

The *Arizona Republic* of May 28, 1950, said in an editorial:

The choice of Barry Goldwater as campaign manager for Howard Pyle, Republican candidate for Governor of Arizona, is a particularly fortunate one. He is a young man full of enthusiasm as well as sound ideas, and should add a great deal of strength to the already formidable movement to give new life to the party in Arizona . . .

One refreshing aspect is that neither is a saddle-galled politician who has spent his life at the public trough.

Optimism mounted in the Republican ranks until the Democratic primary nominated Anna Frohmiller for Governor. One of Arizona's best-known political figures, Mrs. Frohmiller had served as state auditor for as long as anybody could remember and was so unbeatable that she seldom had any opposition.

"Some of our people were devastated when they learned that Mrs. Frohmiller would be our opponent," says Pyle, "and a few thought we should pull out. But Barry scoffed at that. 'The worst thing they can do is beat us,' he said. 'Let's give it the best shot we can.'"

Barry's airplane proved to be a major weapon in the whirlwind campaign, which took Howard Pyle to every corner of Arizona.

Before it was over, his red, white, and blue Beechcraft had logged twenty-two thousand miles. Pyle, one of the most persuasive speakers of the era, impressed people wherever he appeared. Barry, renewing old friendships at every stop and having a ball doing it, swung many a vote to his candidate. And, as had been the case in the City Council campaign the year before, loyal Bob Goldwater and Harry Rosenzweig worked effectively behind the scenes, raising money and getting out the vote.

When the ballots were counted on the first Tuesday in November, the issue was in doubt until the early morning hours. But the final tally gave victory to the amazed Howard Pyle by just under three thousand votes.

Political historians still mark that night as the beginning of a new era: the night the two-party system took its first breath in Arizona.

"I'll admit that I thoroughly enjoyed running Howard Pyle's campaign, and that I thought more than once that it would be exciting to run for governor myself," Barry recalls. "But I could see after only a few months of Howard's administration that the governorship was a frustrating position. The legislature was heavily Democratic, and he found it very hard to get any of his programs enacted."

So Barry Goldwater, more than a little intoxicated by the wine of political success, started casting about for an office in which a dedicated Republican could have some real impact.

He soon realized that only an office of national scope would suffice, now that his horizons had been broadened by global military service and regional government participation. The United States Senate might have seemed an impossible goal for any other fledgling politician, but not for Barry. It was made even more difficult by the impressive credentials of the men occupying Arizona's two Senate seats in 1951: Carl Hayden, an Arizona idol and a national institution; and Ernest W. McFarland, Majority Leader of the Senate. Both, of course, were Democrats.

McFarland's second term was coming to an end in 1952, so he became the logical target for Barry's upset try. Pyle and others exhorted him to announce his candidacy.

Goldwater was so unhappy with the ruling Democrats at that point that he would have taken on almost any foe to gain a chance to get to Washington and try to change things. He was deeply troubled about the size, power, and cost of the federal government—about restrictions on individual freedoms—about President Truman's dismantling of the American military establishment—about Truman's dismissal of General Douglas MacArthur from command of American forces in Korea. The list went on.

After he had waged a successful campaign for re-election to the Phoenix City Council in the fall of 1951, he started laying the groundwork for his Senate bid. As always, the first person in whom he confided was Peggy.

"She was considerably less than thrilled about the idea," Barry recalls. "She pointed out that my political philosophy was out of step with the New Deal regime currently in power. She asked why I thought I could beat the overwhelming odds. And she expressed doubts that she could be happy as the wife of a public figure in Washington. She was a reserved, very private person, and the prospect dismayed her."

Having spoken her piece, however, she pledged that, if that's what Barry really wanted, she would help in any way she could.

Barry had felt sure that was what she would say. Although many of her personal likes and dislikes conflicted with Barry's, she always put aside her preferences and was the supportive wife.

Early in 1952, after winning the enthusiastic backing of state Republican leaders, he started building his organization. For his campaign manager, he went to Steve Shadegg, who had directed successful campaigns for Arizona Democrats, and who had been a leader in Senator Hayden's 1950 re-election campaign. Shadegg was a registered Democrat, but he shared many of Barry's ideas about what ailed America's government.

To the surprise of many, Shadegg agreed to run Goldwater's campaign, but only on one condition: that he would not make any off-the-cuff speeches or take any positions that had not been discussed and agreed upon.

Bob Creighton, publisher of a prestigious political journal and a long-time friend of Barry's, echoed Shadegg's concern that every action and statement should be weighed for potential political gain or loss. So Barry accepted Shadegg's dictum and agreed to let him run the campaign as he deemed best.

Although Barry had been a supporter of Senator Robert Taft—"Mr. Republican"—for years, he surprised delegates to the 1952 Arizona Republican convention by siding with Dwight Eisenhower's supporters, who favored sending uninstructed delegates to the national GOP convention.

It was a rash move, and it angered some state convention delegates, who were seen to publicly tear up their "Goldwater for Senate" nominating petitions. But Barry soon became enured to the fact that, whenever a public figure acts decisively, some people will cheer and others will jeer.

Before his campaign was ready for launching, Barry took Peggy to Mexico City for a week of intensive brushing up on his Spanish language fluency. One of his goals was to win a sizable piece of the normally Democratic Hispanic vote, so he wanted to address those voters in their native tongue.

"The only trouble with my Mexico City trip," he recalls, "was that everybody there seemed to want to use me to practice their English!"

With his large following on the Indian reservations and his growing Mexican-American support, Goldwater courted the underprivileged and built defenses against McFarland charges that he was a rich, pro-business, high society candidate who owned a beach home at La Jolla.

Barry chose Prescott as the launching pad for his national political career, and he returned to the "Mile-High City"for the opening speech of each succeeding campaign.

"We put the podium on the Yavapai County Courthouse steps," remembers Shadegg, "and we scheduled the speech for evening, when the crowd would be largest. Midway in Barry's speech, the podium light went out. So he made some good-natured remark about McFarland cutting off the power and finished with the help of a flashlight.

"Afterward, Barry made the rounds of the bars on Whiskey Row, greeting a lot of old friends, and he didn't get to bed until the wee hours. Next morning I confronted him at breakfast and told him that bar-hopping was not a good idea, and could cost him votes. He wasn't happy about my scolding, but he thought it over, and he didn't do it any more."

Early in the campaign, an editorial by powerful publisher William R. Mathews of the *Arizona Daily Star* in Tucson challenged the neophyte to reveal his true political colors. Mathews headed his challenge "What Kind of Republican Are You, Mr. Goldwater?" Barry was quick to respond, and his answer mapped out a political course that he has been following through most of his long career:

> I am not a "me too" Republican. I am not a Fair Deal Republican. I am a Republican who believes that all Republicans and all Democrats must practice in their personal and business lives those principles of honesty, integrity, devotion and thrift which all of us long to see re-established in our national government. I am a Republican opposed to the super-state, gigantic bureaucratic centralized authority, whether it be administered by Democrats or Republicans.
>
> I am a Republican who is opposed to appeasement, who is shocked and saddened at the failure of our "now do nothing—now do anything" State Department, whose vacillating policies have resulted in a deterioration of world affairs and the loss of prestige and respect for the flag I hold dear.
>
> I am a Republican who is opposed to Communism, and particularly to the Communist-inclined sympathizers and the Communist-inclined policy makers and their companion wishful thinkers. They have exercised far too much influence upon our stand in world concerns.
>
> I am a Republican who gives more than lip service to a balanced budget. I believe that individuals and local government, city councils, county supervisors, and state legislatures must reassert their independence and their responsibility, that we the free people of this nation must demand an end to government subsidies, deficit financing and living beyond our income.

It was a credo that won him thousands of friends and got him off to a running start.

Senator McFarland, who was so far ahead in the mid-summer opinion polls that he never really took Goldwater seriously, stayed in Washington and let his spokesman, attorney Frank Beer, represent him in Arizona. Beer hammered on the thesis that Goldwater was an elitist, a country club playboy who was totally unprepared for high office.

When a Goldwater pamphlet was circulated with the erroneous statement that he was a University of Arizona graduate, Beer tried to make capital of the slip-up. But Barry's candid explanation that he left the university after a year because of his father's death seemed to satisfy the electorate.

Capitalizing on his candidate's good looks and ready smile, Shadegg put him on the new medium of television as often as campaign funds would allow. One program that featured the Goldwater family was particularly effective.

Barry spoke eloquently about his conservative political principles and pounded on the themes of the bloated federal government, the threat of Communism, and the traditional values of American self-reliance.

One Goldwater campaign tool had everybody talking. Some two hundred sets of roadside signs, *a la* Burma Shave ads, were placed around the state. The most memorable one, tying McFarland to Harry Truman, read:

Mac is for Harry
But Harry is through.
You be for Barry
'Cause Barry's for *you.*

It was a small-scale, low-cost campaign, compared with modern Senate races that can cost millions of dollars. Fund-raising efforts of such stalwarts as Harry Rosenzweig in Phoenix, Alex Jacome in Tucson, and many others, brought in around eighty-five thousand dollars.

Howard Pyle ran for re-election as governor in 1952, and a newcomer, Mesa attorney John Rhodes, challenged veteran Democrat John Murdock for his seat in the U.S. House of Representatives. The Republican revival seemed to bring candidates out of the shadows all over the state.

Despite the Republican hoopla, Democratic incumbents never seemed to recognize the precarious nature of their positions. General Eisenhower was a national hero, and his popularity promised coat-tail bonanzas to Republican candidates throughout the nation. But McFarland and Murdock waited too long to come home and fight for their political lives.

"I had no business beating Mac," says Barry, "and I never would have done it without the help of Eisenhower's popularity and Mac's over-confidence."

When the votes were counted on election night, the major contests were close all the way. But the rising sun found all three Republicans—Pyle, Rhodes, and Goldwater—in the winners' column.

Barry's winning margin was hardly a landslide: seven thousand votes.

The Goldwater victory was destined to change the course of American political history for decades to come. President Ronald Reagan, in a 1984 interview for television, credited Barry's efforts with bringing about the American conservative revival.

"We helped elect Barry, and he changed the course of empire," declares Shadegg with pride. "How many people can say that?"

17

The Junior Senator
from Arizona

*Conflict! It's the spice that creates best-selling novels, Oscar-winning
movies—and national political reputations.*

*Almost from the moment he arrived in Washington in 1953, the
rookie senator from Arizona was embroiled in conflict. Barry Goldwater was involved in well-publicized battles with the "big spenders"
and the "appeasers" of both parties. He made war against the foes of
Senator Joe McCarthy, and even took on President Eisenhower.*

*But it was Goldwater's one-man crusade against the barons of Big
Labor that put his name in headlines across the nation and built for
him a formidable reputation almost overnight. Walter Reuther, the
United Auto Workers Union president, was his special target.*

*One of the minor conflicts of those early years in Washington was
with an ambitious young Massachusetts senator named John F.
Kennedy, who had entered the Senate in Goldwater's freshman class.
Goldwater differed with Kennedy on almost every philosophical point,
but the two became personal friends while they were serving together
on the famed McClellan Labor Rackets Committee. It was a strange
sort of friendship, but it endured until Kennedy's assassination in
1963.*

*Goldwater entered the national political arena breathing fire. His
courageous stands against the liberal establishment of the era infuriated those in power and gave fresh hope to downtrodden conservatives
everywhere.*

*Before he had completed his first term—and faced an uphill battle
to avoid making it his last—Barry Goldwater had become a man of
national stature.*

WASHINGTON, D.C., 1953

"THE LABOR COMMITTEE!" EXCLAIMED FRESHMAN SENATOR BARRY GOLDWATER in obvious disappointment. "What do I know about labor relations? Arizona doesn't have much industry, so we don't have a lot of dealings with the big labor unions. I was really hoping to be assigned to Armed Services."

Ohio Senator Robert Taft smiled. New senators can't be choosers, he reminded Goldwater. Besides, Taft pointed out, he wanted at least one good conservative on the Senate Labor and Public Welfare Committee "to help counter all those liberals."

Fate works in wondrous ways.

Disappointed as he was, Barry accepted the assignment (along with one on the Banking and Commerce Committee) and made the best of it. Amazingly, it was the Labor Committee assignment that was to make him a national figure and place him on the first rung of the ladder leading to nomination for the American Presidency.

He had arrived in Washington alone and had checked in at the Congressional Hotel near Capitol Hill, leaving Peggy in Phoenix for the time being because he expected to devote every waking moment for several months to his new job.

Having been born in Phoenix and spent most of his forty-four years of life there, it had been hard for him to say goodbye. He still felt the glow of the memorable farewell party a hundred friends had given him at the Phoenix Country Club. His long-time buddy, Vic Armstrong, had headed the planning committee for the party, which featured a series of hilarious skits poking good-natured fun at Barry's television commercials during the senatorial campaign. One pictured him using glasses of bourbon instead of water in his pitch for more Colorado River water allocations. Another portrayed him in a Roman toga and laurel wreath, inquiring about Senate jobs for his sons. When the kidding was over, Barry took the microphone and recalled personal experiences involving almost everyone present, a remarkable feat of memory.

His induction into the United States Senate came on January 3, 1953, when he was escorted to the front of the historic Senate chamber by his sponsor, seventy-five-year-old Carl Hayden of Arizona, to swear his allegiance to the Constitution of the United States.

Later, Hayden recalled that his father had brought his new bride to Ehrenberg in the fall of 1876, en route from Visalia, California, to Tempe, and that there the couple had been guests of Barry's grandfather, Mike Goldwater.

Barry always had the friendliest of relations with the venerable Hayden, and with a noted former Arizona senator, Henry Fountain Ashurst, who still made his home in Washington. It was during his first year in the Senate that Barry completed the editing and publication of selected Ashurst addresses.

Barry chose attorney Henry Zipf of Tucson as his chief administrative assistant. When Zipf left the staff in 1954, he was succeeded by Charles Farrington Jr. of Tucson. After a year, young Dean Burch, another Tucson attorney, took over the top staff position in the Goldwater office.

One of Goldwater's first appointments was that of motherly Edna Coerver as his receptionist and secretary. She was to stay a dozen years as his employee and friend. Judy Rooney Eisenhower, who joined the staff in 1955, still serves as Goldwater's administrative assistant and is a powerful presence in his office.

What people and forces shaped Barry Goldwater's conservative philosophy?

New York *Post* columnist Irwin Ross once suggested that he "started mouthing platitudes he overheard at the country club, and through a series of happy accidents found himself at the head of a marching throng." Liberal journalists have been making the mistake of under-rating Barry's philosophy during all of the quarter century since Ross first wrote that flippant observation.

Goldwater's convictions have much deeper roots. Certainly, growing up in a frontier state had its effect. Uncle Morris's political philosophy was another major influence. His experiences in the military and in business made their mark.

Although not a scholar, he has read widely, and his ability to read a book in a single evening and retain its substance is well-known by his family. His reading of Edmund Burke and John Locke excited him. One of the books that most influenced his thinking in the late 1940s was Professor H. A. Hayek's *The Road to Serfdom,* a devastating indictment of collectivism. Such conservative scholars as political scientist Russell Kirk and economist Milton Friedman have contributed to his philosophy.

The few embattled conservatives on the national scene welcomed him warmly in 1953. At the time of his election to the Senate, according to political commentator Lionel Trilling, "In the United States at this time, liberalism is not only the dominant but even the sole intellectual tradition."

Goldwater was eager to leap into the philosophical battle and do what he could to even the odds a bit.

Anyone interested in knowing what motivated him and guided his controversial career needed only to read the statement that he often called "the perfect campaign speech" for a conservative politician:

I have little interest in streamlining government or in making it more efficient, for I mean to reduce its size. I do not undertake to promote welfare, for I propose to extend freedom. My aim is not to pass laws, but to repeal them. It is not to inaugurate new programs, but to cancel old ones that do violence to the Constitution, or that have failed in their purpose, or that impose on the people an unwarranted financial burden.

I will not attempt to discover whether legislation is "needed" before I have first determined whether it is constitutionally permissible. And if I should later be attacked for neglecting any constituent's "interests," I shall reply that I was informed their main interest is liberty and in that cause I am doing the very best I can.

Most of his future stands in the Senate had their roots in that statement. Like every true conservative, he believes that individual Americans should be responsible for their own destiny insofar as that is possible; and when government action is necessary for the public good, such action should be taken, wherever practicable, at the local or state level, rather than by the federal government.

On May 12, 1953, only four months after he took his seat in the Senate, Goldwater made his first major speech from the floor: a ringing appeal to abolish federal price controls, which he considered an impediment to free enterprise and a federal intrusion on individual freedom.

The speech did not send reporters dashing to their telephones, but it did elicit a two-word comment from President Eisenhower: "Atta boy." Thus encouraged, Barry took the floor again two months later, this time making an impassioned plea against deficit spending—an evil he opposes just as vociferously today. This excerpt from his 1953 speech on federal deficits has a timeless quality about it:

The dangers involved in continuing deficit spending are so apparent to the people of this country that I am amazed they do not shine like a bright red light into the face of every member of Congress . . . The day of reckoning is going to be dreadful. . . .

Goldwater's determination to keep America strong during the post–World War II years, and to fight the spread of Communism throughout the world, brought him into immediate conflict with advocates of disarmament and into somewhat reluctant support of the anti-Communist campaign of Wisconsin Senator Joe McCarthy. Although he often winced at McCarthy's excesses and his indiscriminate charges of traitorous behavior, Barry believed McCarthy was serving his country by shining the spotlight of publicity on Communist sympathizers.

Goldwater was one of the last to remain loyal to the fiery Wisconsin senator, and was one of twenty-two Republicans who voted against the Senate resolution to censure McCarthy. While the motion was being debated on the floor, Senator Price McDaniel of Texas came to Barry and said that, if McCarthy would sign letters of apology to two senators he had insulted, the censure move would fail. Barry risked possible arrest to get that message to McCarthy, who was a patient at Bethesda Hospital, as he related in *With No Apologies:*

> I contacted McCarthy's attorney, Edward Bennett Williams. The two of us drove out to Bethesda Hospital, where McCarthy was undergoing treatment. Because our mission was a very sensitive one, we thought it best to attempt to avoid being seen. We walked up thirteen flights of stairs, slipped past the nurse's station, and entered McCarthy's room. . . .
>
> Williams urged him to sign [the letters], arguing that it really wasn't a retreat from principle and warning that his critics in the Senate probably had enough votes to pass the censure resolution. This upset McCarthy. He threw the pen across the room, started swearing at both of us, and pounded the table.

At that point the floor nurse came running, and a doctor called the admiral in charge of the hospital, who threatened to call the Shore Patrol and ordered Goldwater and Williams never to come back to see his patient without permission.

The censure motion passed, McCarthy was destroyed politically, and a tense period of American history came to an angry close.

When the news of Barry Goldwater's public statements blasting national labor union officials first reached the press, his friends in Phoenix recalled that as early as 1946 he had been a leader in the fight against compulsory unionism in Arizona.

Now, more than a decade later, he was serving on the Senate Labor Committee and making headlines with revelations of abuses in union leadership. When the evidence of wrongdoing became too clear to ignore, a Senate select committee was formed in January, 1957 to investigate these activities. Officially named the "Select Committee To Investigate Improper Activities in Labor/Management Relations," it was headed by John McClellan of Arkansas and popularly called the McClellan Rackets Committee.

Freshman Barry Goldwater was named to that committee, as was freshman John F. Kennedy of Massachusetts. Kennedy's younger brother, Robert, was chosen as chief counsel. It was a panel of well-known names, including Karl Mundt of South Dakota, Sam Ervin of North Carolina, Irving Ives of New York, Patrick McNamara of Michigan, and Joseph McCarthy of Wisconsin. Senator Carl Curtis of Nebraska soon replaced the ailing McCarthy.

Barry had learned a lot about union management abuses since being appointed to the labor committee. First, there had been the information provided by Mike Bernstein, Republican counsel to the committee and a man who had first-hand knowledge of union operations. There were the thousands of letters from union members, many of whom were too afraid to sign their names. Barry's own reading and probing had uncovered more facts and figures.

And then there was the case of Willie Bioff.

Bioff had been convicted of extortion and other crimes while working for a major union, but had long since taken a new name, Nelson, and lived quietly in Phoenix. It was as Willie Nelson that Goldwater first knew him. The former hood risked his cover to come to Barry, reveal his true identity, and give him a store of information about how union rackets really work.

Somehow the wrong people learned about Willie Bioff. One morning in the summer of 1955, he stepped on the starter of his pickup truck and detonated a charge of explosives that blew him to bits. For Barry, it was a sobering demonstration that this was a desperate game being played by men who would readily kill to silence their enemies.

The McClellan Rackets Committee took immediate aim at Jimmy Hoffa, president of the Teamsters Union, and Dave Beck, the Teamsters' West Coast boss. The evidence uncovered by the committee was overwhelming against both men, and in 1957, the AFL-CIO expelled the Teamsters.

Barry then demanded that the investigation turn the heat on Walter Reuther, president of the United Auto Workers. Convinced that Reuther was using union funds and influence illegally in a massive effort to elect public officials friendly to his union, Goldwater hounded him.

"I would rather have Hoffa stealing my money than Reuther stealing my freedom," Goldwater once declared.

As the feud boiled hotter, Reuther charged in the press that "Barry Goldwater is this country's number one political fanatic, labor baiter, and peddler of class hatred."

In a January 1958, speech in Detroit, Goldwater blistered Reuther again, and finished with the memorable declaration that "Reuther is more dangerous than the sputniks or anything Russia might do."

Throughout the Rackets committee hearings, Barry fumed at the Kennedy brothers' obvious reluctance to press Reuther too closely. Because Jack Kennedy was readying his bid for the presidency in 1960, Barry believed, he did not wish to antagonize the nation's top labor leader.

The junior senator from Arizona had no such restraint, and he pressed his case against Reuther until both men tired of the feud and went on to other things. But Big Labor did not forgive or forget, and the AFL-CIO's Committee on Political Education (COPE) marked Goldwater as a prime target for defeat in 1958.

The McClellan committee's findings resulted in several pieces of proposed legislation to remedy labor abuses. The one that President Eisenhower and most senators favored was the Kennedy-Ervin Labor Reform Bill of 1959. Barry considered the bill totally ineffective, however, and he was the only senator to oppose it in the ninety-five to one vote.

"I consider that vote the most important in my first Senate term," he has often declared.

His courageous, but politically dangerous, stand was later vindicated. The House of Representatives rejected Kennedy-Ervin and substituted the tougher Landrum-Griffin Bill, which Goldwater considered much more effective. It survived conference committees and passed the Senate with only two dissenting votes, neither of which was Goldwater's.

When the battle was over, Barry Goldwater emerged as a national figure—cursed by many, but admired by more—and was on his way to writing more headlines in the years to come.

It was Harry Truman's controversial firing of General Douglas MacArthur as commander of American and United Nations forces in the Korean conflict, and Truman's apparent reluctance to maintain America's world leadership, that had goaded Barry to run for the Senate in 1952. But he had been in Washington only a short time before he realized that Truman had often demonstrated courageous leadership during eight critical post-war years. Truman's ability to make difficult decisions quickly, and to stick to his guns under heavy criticism, earned Goldwater's admiration.

On the other hand, Dwight D. Eisenhower, who was inaugurated seventeen days after the new Senate class had been seated, disappointed Goldwater early and often. Much as he liked Ike personally, he despaired at what he felt was the new president's failure to move decisively and take a firm grasp on the reins of American government.

Under the Eisenhower administration, Barry had hoped, the federal budget would be substantially trimmed, and the scope of government activity diminished. So it was with angry disappointment that he rose on the Senate floor one day in 1957 and blasted the big-spending federal budget that Eisenhower had proposed.

"A $71.8 billion dollar budget not only shocks me," he declared, "but it weakens my faith in the constant assurances we have received from this administration that its aim was to cut spending. . . ."

It was Goldwater's first salvo against Ike's "Modern Republicanism," and the press trumpeted the news that the speech was his "bill of divorcement" from Eisenhower. The speech was regarded by many as an act of political suicide by a man who owed his Senate seat to Eisenhower's ample coat tails.

It was an act of rash courage, since Goldwater had only that morning been invited to the White House for lunch to discuss his 1958 re-election campaign. Knowing that he was preparing to criticize the President in a few hours, Goldwater refused the invitation.

It was the first of many jabs Goldwater was to take at Eisenhower's concession to liberal pressures, and they cost him Ike's favor.

"Dwight D. Eisenhower never really grasped the political complexities of his office," Barry was later to say in his autobiography. "His courage, his quality, his wholesomeness helped greatly to restore our faith in the institution of government. It was within his power to undo some of the mischief resulting from errors in national judgment under Roosevelt and Truman. He was ambitious to bring about reform—his political talent was unequal to the task."

The junior senator from Arizona faced much more formidable opposition in 1958 than in his 1952 election campaign. Eisenhower's coat tails—even his enthusiastic support—were missing this time. The giants of organized labor had mobilized a national effort to unseat their most infuriating enemy.

Arizona Democrats had Ernest W. McFarland, who had been a popular governor since 1954, to throw against him. This time McFarland would not repeat the mistake of taking Goldwater lightly, and this time he was aching to avenge the humiliation of his 1952 defeat. All the experts figured the odds favored McFarland, and the polls throughout the summer of 1958 made Barry the underdog.

But the Goldwater forces held some trump cards, too. Barry had won many friends in Arizona during his first six Senate years, and he had a canny campaign manager in Steve Shadegg. Barry made a better impression on television than did McFarland. His style of campaigning—flying around the state with his old friend and flight instructor, Ruth Reinhold, at the controls of his airplane, and making rousing speeches at every stop—was effective.

Still, the polls favored the folksy McFarland as the campaign entered its final days. Had it not been for the "Stalin handbill" incident, the political career of Barry Goldwater might well have ended abruptly and ignominiously.

It's an oft-told story, the details of which grace many pages of Goldwater biographies. Suffice it to say that a scurrilous handbill was placed on parked cars around Phoenix four days before the 1958 election, proclaiming that Josef Stalin would be pleased if Goldwater were re-elected. Contrary to law, there was no sponsor identified on the handbill.

Shadegg rushed several of the offending flyers to the major Arizona newspapers, and the story made front pages all over the nation. Many voters were quick to assume that here was another smear attempt on the part of the AFL-CIO's Committee on Political Education.

Although McFarland supporters frantically protested that this was a Shadegg trick to win sympathy for Goldwater, the incident apparently swung many a vote to the Goldwater column the following Tuesday.

Enough voters came over to the Goldwater side to bring him home a winner by a comfortable thirty-five thousand-vote margin. Thus it was that the Goldwater political phenomenon, so nearly snuffed out before it really got started, was kept alive to continue fueling America's conservative revival.

Being chairman of the Republican Senatorial Campaign Committee does not automatically make a senator a celebrity. Barry had served a two-year term in that position in 1955-56 without becoming a household word, but he had won the gratitude of the party by raising campaign funds, speaking, and getting Republicans elected.

The job normally goes to a senator who is not up for re-election during that two-year period. So it was not surprising that, after his upset victory in 1958, he was asked to chair the campaign committee again.

"It's a time-consuming, demanding job, and I'd about decided not to accept," he recalls, "but then I heard that Jacob Javits of New York was opposing me, and spreading the word that my selection would alienate liberal Republicans. That irritated me enough to change my mind and accept the chairmanship."

Barry's battles with the liberal Senator Javits filled many a newspaper column of the period, and Goldwater sometimes suggested that Javits should "go straight" and register Democratic, since he usually voted that way.

His decision to head the campaign committee again did much to propel Goldwater still more prominently onto the national scene and to move him a step closer to the party's presidential nomination in 1964.

"What I liked about the assignment was the chance to study the face of the Republican Party, to engage in thoughtful discussion about the future of the Republic," he wrote in his autobiography. "What I found encouraged me. Despite the failures of the Eisenhower administration to make any significant changes, government spending had been checked, U.S. foreign policy was strong and determined, and we had made some progress in our efforts to drag racketeers out of organized labor. The economy had prospered.

"My appearances before local Republican groups convinced me that they longed for a return to prudent fiscal policies and reduction in the size of the federal government."

What Barry sensed was that the Republican Party, at least, was ready for a conservative renewal. And each passing month made it more obvious that Senator Goldwater was the man whom conservatives wanted to carry their banner.

An important milestone in the Goldwater march to the presidential nomination was the 1959 Western Republican Conference in the Los Angeles Biltmore Hotel. New York Governor Nelson Rockefeller, at that moment the only announced candidate for the Republican nomination, was a principal speaker. His address reiterated the liberal Republican philosophy, which was hardly distinguishable from that of the New Deal and Fair Deal. The assembled Republicans responded with polite applause.

Goldwater was the next speaker, and his stemwinding speech both shocked and delighted the big crowd. He ripped into the liberal record unmercifully, declaring that liberals had transferred Uncle Sam into a wet nurse, "dispensing a cockeyed kind of patent medicine labeled 'something for nothing,' passing out the soothing syrup and rattles and pacifiers in return for votes."

He concluded with the declaration that "My kind of Republican Party is committed to a free state, limited central power, a reduction in bureaucracy, and a balanced budget."

And then he sat down.

The throng erupted in thunderous applause and cheering, and the standing ovation continued for several minutes. Everyone present, and especially Nelson Rockefeller, got the message. Barry Goldwater had thrown down the gauntlet and conservatives were ready to battle for their beliefs.

Goldwater's Los Angeles speech produced immediate political dividends. First, there was the Los Angeles *Times* invitation to write a thrice-weekly column on the conservative viewpoint. Shadegg did much of the composition of these columns, but the ideas came from Barry's tape-recorded observations. Within three months, the column had become so popular that one hundred forty newspapers across the nation were buying it from the Times-Mirror Syndicate.

So overwhelming was the reader response that the Goldwater secretarial staff was inundated by mail. Letters came in from blue collar workers and professional people, from local politicians and college professors. (Judy Eisenhower and those in the secretarial corps will attest that the mail volume has not subsided appreciably to this day.)

Another major impetus of the Goldwater thrust to national prominence came when his political philosophies were captured between the covers of a small book called *The Conscience of a Conservative.*

"Dean Clarence Manion of the Notre Dame law school is responsible for the writing of that book," says Barry. "He suggested there was a need for a simple, straightforward delineation of conservative principles."

Manion helped make arrangements with the Victor Publishing Company of Shepherdsville, Kentucky, to print the book, which was put together with the help of L. Brent Bozell, an editor of *National Review* and William Buckley's brother-in-law.

The tiny publishing house felt sure the initial printing of ten thousand copies would be sufficient. No one could have anticipated the amazing national response. A second printing was ordered almost immediately, and succeeding editions followed as fast as presses could turn them out.

The Conscience of a Conservative, in hardcover and paperback, became one of the great best-sellers of the period. It still sells today, and sales are approaching a total of four million.

Barry Goldwater for president?

How ridiculous the idea would have seemed in 1958, less than two years before, when the little-known westerner was struggling against big odds just to hang onto his Senate seat.

Now here he was in South Carolina, addressing the state Republican convention at the invitation of Chairman Greg Shorey. He had come to motivate South Carolina Republicans in 1960 to wrest their state from decades of Democratic domination.

South Carolina conservatives saw in Goldwater the knight in shining armor they had awaited so long. When Barry had finished his address, to a long and noisy ovation, the convention plunged ahead over his objections to pledge its delegates to him for president in 1960.

"I didn't expect that, and I didn't want it," he recalls in all sincerity. "I had no plans for a presidential bid, no organization, no money, nothing. It put me in an embarrassing position with party leaders, and especially with my friends in Arizona—Representative John Rhodes and Dick Kleindienst, the party's state chairman, among others—because they were supporting Richard Nixon and wanted to keep the Arizona delegation united."

With President Eisenhower's eight-year administration nearing an end, the scramble for power in both parties was unbelievably intense. Already it seemed that popular young Jack Kennedy of Massachusetts would win out over Texan Lyndon Johnson in the battle for the Democratic nomination. Vice-President Nixon, by now the seemingly sure Republican choice, did not need a "Goldwater for President" grassfire before going into the big campaign.

America's conservatives would not be silent or bow to the party leadership. They had found their champion, and the Goldwater fever mounted as the Nixon-controlled Republican National Convention in Chicago approached.

At the Chicago convention, Goldwater supporters ("my amateur band of eager beavers," Barry called them) assured him they could count two hundred eighty-seven delegate votes and pleaded with Barry to let them place his name in nomination. But he could see that such an uprising would fall short, and could only hurt the conservative cause and damage his future relations with the Nixon people.

It was a temptation for Barry to permit his "eager beavers" to plunge ahead, particularly after Nixon lied to him and made a secret deal with Rockefeller and his eastern liberals on the platform wording ("the American Munich," Goldwater angrily termed the Nixon-Rockefeller meeting). The temptation and his own irritation grew more intense when convention managers gave a band of Goldwater supporters tickets to the wrong convention session, and when ushers guided Goldwater demonstrators out of the hall instead of onto the floor.

But he held his temper, resisted temptation, and agreed to support Nixon's nomination. As a gesture of gratitude to his conservative loyalists, however, he agreed to let Arizona Governor Paul Fannin, his friend since boyhood, place his name in nomination—on the condition that Barry would immediately step forward and withdraw himself from consideration.

Fannin's brief nominating speech for Goldwater set off a riotous eleven-minute demonstration that had Nixon managers glancing at their watches and wondering if this might be 1940 and Wendell Willkie all over again.

Barry Goldwater was unwilling to play the Willkie role in 1960. He stepped before the cheering convention mob, and after trying unsuccessfully to quiet the crowd, at last managed to be heard:

Thank you, Mr. Chairman, delegates to the convention, and fellow Republicans. I respectfully ask the chairman to withdraw my name from nomination. [thunderous "no"s]

Please. I release my delegation from their pledge to me, and while I am not a delegate, I would suggest that they give these votes to Richard Nixon.

Then he made a powerful plea for conservatives to forget their disappointments and work hard for Nixon in the coming campaign. In conclusion, he said:

I am a conservative. I am going to devote all my time from now to November to electing Republicans from the top of the ticket to the bottom, and I call upon my fellow conservatives to do the same.

Had he been given the gift of prophecy and had been able to foresee the behavior of defeated party liberals after his 1964 nomination, he might have found it harder to be so gracious a team player.

But, chances are he would have swallowed his anger and supported the party's ticket just the same.

18

Goldwater for President

Averill Harriman, who understood politics as well as anybody, once declared that the one essential, indispensable quality of a presidential candidate was an overpowering lust for the job.

Barry Goldwater did not have that "overpowering lust" for the presidency. He was, in fact, one of history's few reluctant presidential candidates.

Jack Kennedy had a joyful zest for presidential campaigning, and he stirred in Barry a responsive competitive urge. Goldwater would have enjoyed a spirited battle, based on philosophical issues, against his friend from Massachusetts.

But when Kennedy was assassinated, Barry's eagerness for the Republican presidential nomination cooled. Lyndon Johnson now had the political deck stacked formidably in his favor, and only a miracle could beat him. Moreover, Johnson had that lust for the presidency, and his was an all-consuming passion that few others had ever matched.

Goldwater examined his options, searching for some way to avoid the hopeless campaign without destroying the conservative renaissance he had been leading for so long.

There was no honorable way.

Too many people had given everything to the conservative cause, and untold millions of Americans were counting on him to carry their banner into battle in 1964. Dark as his prospects appeared in December 1963, he could not turn back.

He did his best, taxed his energies to their limits, and endangered his health in the brutal and disheartening campaign. But even his closest friends admit that he should have made it a closer race.

Theodore White—not one of Barry's particular friends—summed it up well in his book, The Making of the President, 1964:

*Of Barry Goldwater's campaign it may be fairly said that no man ever
began a Presidential effort more deeply wounded by his own nomination, suffering more insurmountable handicaps.*
  And then it must be added that he made the worst of them.

*So it was that the man from Arizona, who had succeeded brilliantly
in virtually everything he had ever attempted, failed in this one great
bid for historical immortality.*
  But did he really fail?
  *Barry Goldwater's burning passion was not to be president, but to
lead America back to the conservative path toward national salvation.
That, he fervently believed, was a goal a man could give his life for.*

THE NATION, 1964

DESPITE THEIR OBVIOUS PHILOSOPHICAL DIFFERENCES, BARRY GOLDWATER AND
John F. Kennedy maintained a cordial friendship during their decade
of service together in Washington. The two had much in common: ambition, winning personalities, family position, and fierce competitive spirit,
as well as an ingrained certainty of being in the right.

They had come to the Senate as freshmen in 1953, and within a few
months, both had impressed their colleagues as stars of the future.

Kennedy's potential was recognized and trumpeted from the outset, but
Goldwater's took a little longer. President Eisenhower soon recognized
Barry's ability, as evidenced by Bob Goldwater's recollection about a 1953
golf game with Ike at Cherry Hills Country Club in Denver.

"Eisenhower said to me, 'that brother of yours is special. He stands out
in that group of freshman senators like a thoroughbred horse in a herd of
balderpate,'" Bob recalls.

There was one important difference in the ambitions of the two senators. Kennedy early had his eye on the presidency and looked forward with
anticipation to making a run for the nation's choicest political prize.
Goldwater was more interested in spreading the conservative gospel than
in seeking the presidency, and he actually viewed with apprehension the
prospect of life in the White House.

"Jack Kennedy was always more thrilled about *running* for president
than about *being* president," Barry said later. "To him, the presidency was a
trophy to be won, and he gloried in the trappings of the office. But my first
priority always has been to bring this country of ours back to responsible
conservative principles. I had no burning ambition to seek the presidency."

The two achievers had a healthy respect for each other's talents, and
they had frequent discussions about national problems over the years.

One of the most dramatic of those discussions came during the third month of Kennedy's presidency. Barry described it in his autobiography, *With No Apologies:*

On Saturday, April 15, 1961, I was strapping myself into the cockpit of an F-86 fighter plane at Andrews Air Force Base, preparing to fly to Luke Air Force Base in Arizona. As a member of the active Reserve, I was expected to fly a certain number of hours each month to maintain my proficiency rating.

I was in the middle of my pre-flight checklist when a sergeant climbed up on the wing . . . and told me the President of the United States wanted to see me at the White House.

Changing back into street clothes, he drove to 1600 Pennsylvania Avenue and was ushered immediately into the Oval Office, where President Kennedy was waiting alone. Grimly, and with some bitterness, the president told Goldwater that the invasion of the Bay of Pigs by Cuban insurgents was going badly.

This operation, designed to overthrow Communist dictator Fidel Castro, had been planned during the Eisenhower administration but was postponed when Kennedy scored his narrow victory over Richard Nixon in November 1960. Kennedy had harbored doubts about the advisability of the plan, and at this moment he was heartily sorry he had permitted United States participation in it.

"You know, Barry," Kennedy said, "I made a statement at my press conference on Wednesday that no American forces would be used to invade Cuba."

So far, only Cubans had been involved, he said, but the gamble appeared doomed to failure unless the United States gave the freedom fighters some air cover immediately. What would Barry suggest?

"I'd do whatever is necessary to make this invasion a success," he told Kennedy. "Our friends around the world will applaud you, and the American people will back you if it will rid our hemisphere of Fidel Castro."

Kennedy appeared relieved.

"I knew what you'd say, and I think you're right," he declared.

Goldwater left the Oval Office convinced that he had won. But Kennedy talked to other advisers that day, and American military support for the beleaguered Bay of Pigs invaders never materialized. The bloody fiasco ended in total failure, and Castro's hand was immeasureably strengthened by it. The problem of Castro's exportation of Communist revolution to other Latin American countries remains a thorny one to this day.

In 1963, when Goldwater began to emerge as the leading Republican contender for the presidency, Barry and Jack met privately on several occasions to discuss what sort of 1964 campaign it might be.

"We talked of appearing in public together," says Goldwater. "We hoped that we could debate the issues and call the voters' attention to the major problems facing the nation."

Barry thought he might have some chance of winning if the contest were one of liberal vs. conservative philosophies. At least, he reasoned, he could make a good enough showing to accelerate the conservative revival.

But the rifle shots that ended the life of John F. Kennedy that fateful November 22, 1963, in Dallas also killed what little hope Barry Goldwater had to win the presidency. Now there could be no duel between liberal and conservative ideas, no debate between two mutually respectful friends. The new president, Lyndon Baines Johnson, would undoubtedly be the Democratic standard bearer in 1964. He and Goldwater had never liked each other, and no campaign based on issues would be likely.

Much more important, to Goldwater's way of thinking, was the near certainty that the American people, so recently bereaved, would refuse to change presidents again in so short a time.

As the nation mourned the tragedy of the Kennedy assassination, Barry Goldwater faced up to a bitter truth: fate decreed that Lyndon Johnson would be the occupant of the White House for yet another term.

Life in the fast lane of high-pressure national politics can be a breathtaking experience, one that sometimes forces a political figure into decisions not entirely of his own making.

Such was the situation in December 1963, when Barry Goldwater was forced into the Republican presidential race by events that had been set in motion many months before.

As early as October 1961, a group of men bound together by conservative principles and political opportunism had met in Chicago to organize a national "Draft Goldwater" campaign. It was headed by talented New Yorker F. Clifton White, a former professor of political science who left the classroom to pursue practical politics. The group included William Rusher, a colleague of publisher William Buckley, and Congressman John Ashford of Ohio. The cabal gradually expanded to include Peter O'Donnell, the youthful Texas Republican chairman; John Grenier, the Alabama Republican chairman; Wirt Yerger, the Mississippi Republican chairman; and a number of conservatives in the Congress and in state government.

They became increasingly certain that Barry Goldwater was the best Republican hope to carry the conservative banner against the popular President Kennedy. But they labored with one troublesome disadvantage:

the senator from Arizona refused to give them any encouragement at all. Because of Goldwater's unwillingness to accept a draft, the group met and planned for months without an identifying name.

But Clif White would not be discouraged. If Goldwater would not consent to be a candidate, the "no name" group would draft him anyway. By April of 1963, the fast-expanding group opened an office in Washington, D.C., and proclaimed that the "National Draft Goldwater Committee" was in business. By that time, the committee had chairmen in thirty-three states and important backing from the precinct level all the way up to the National Committee.

Even then, however, Barry Goldwater resisted the presidential bid. He surprised the political pros by announcing that he had chosen an old Phoenix friend, attorney Denison Kitchel, to manage his 1964 campaign for the Senate, much to the chagrin of Steve Shadegg, who had successfully directed Goldwater's first two efforts.

Kitchel had been legal counsel for Phelps Dodge Mining Corporation in Washington and had worked closely with Goldwater on labor legislation. He was to be a key figure in the Goldwater drama during the next stormy eighteen months.

In mid-summer of 1963, Kitchel moved his campaign office from Phoenix to the Carroll Arms, across the street from the Old Senate Office Building in Washington. In October, he was joined there by Dean Burch, a brilliant young Tucson attorney who had served as Goldwater's chief aide in 1959. Political observers viewed that move as evidence that the Arizona senator would soon bow to the mounting pressure and become a candidate—willing or not—for the Republican presidential nomination.

Kennedy's assassination in November convinced Barry that his chances of winning the presidency had gone from doubtful to impossible. He searched for some way to avoid making the run, yet he knew that too many people had joined his conservative crusade, and too many eager volunteers had put their trust in him as the prophet who would lead America back to its former greatness. He had gone too far to turn back.

Kitchel recalls the early December meeting of Goldwater confidantes, held late one Sunday afternoon in Barry's Washington apartment. Senator Norris Cotton's impassioned plea for Goldwater to accept the call was especially memorable.

"Barry and I sat there in the gathering gloom, after everyone else had left," says Kitchel, "We reviewed the situation once more, and then he said, with a sigh, 'All right—I'll go.'"

Kitchel, Burch, strategist Bill Baroody, and other Goldwater team members had envisioned a Goldwater announcement event staged in

Washington, which would be attended by all the giants of the national press.

But Goldwater, in love with Arizona and mystically attuned to his native state, insisted that the press conference be held there. So it was that on January 3, 1964, with the candidate on crutches from foot surgery, the grand entry of Barry Goldwater into the presidential sweepstakes was announced from his hilltop home in Phoenix.

He told assembled reporters that he had decided to seek the Republican nomination for president in response to the pleas of millions of Americans who longed for a choice in political philosophies. He had entered the race, he declared, to represent the cause of freedom and individual responsibility against the entrenched advocates of the welfare state.

At the close of his brief address, he announced that Denison Kitchel would be "the general director of this campaign—the head honcho," and that Dean Burch would be Kitchel's assistant. Mrs. Emory Johnson of Tucson would head the women's campaign, and attorney Richard Kleindienst would be field director.

Political pros gasped when they heard the news. Kleindienst had been Arizona Republican chairman, but the others were regarded as amateurs in the intricate science of practical campaign planning. They were all Arizonans (promptly dubbed "The Arizona Mafia" by the press) and trusted friends of the candidate, but there was little political experience in the group.

The "Draft Goldwater" people, who had long been laboring in the vineyard, were conspicuously absent from the team. Not until later, and largely through Kleindienst's efforts, were they brought back into the campaign.

The story of Barry Goldwater's uphill battle to the Republican nomination, and of his devastating loss to Lyndon Johnson in the 1964 election, has been told and retold in several books and countless articles. Students of the Goldwater candidacy will find it instructive to read Theodore White's *The Making of the President: 1964* for the view of a liberal who was at least trying to be fair; Steve Shadegg's *What Happened to Goldwater?* for the account of a conservative insider who was disappointed in the conduct of the campaign; and the opinions expressed in Goldwater's own *With No Apologies,* written fifteen years after battle emotions had cooled.

Although they differ in some details, all three books agree on some salient points: that Goldwater was the lonely champion of a cause which had not yet gained popular acceptance; that he had little chance to win; that his own reluctance to run, and a resulting lack of solid planning, added to his difficulties; and that a hostile press fanned the public's fears of

Goldwater as a warmonger, a racist, and a foe of federal handouts to the aged, farmers, the poor, and others.

"If I had been the kind of guy the press made me out to be," declared Barry after the campaign, "I wouldn't have voted for Goldwater myself—and neither would Peggy."

The times and the circumstances made it virtually impossible for Barry Goldwater to win in 1964, just as the prevailing national mood in 1984 made it impossible for Democrat Walter Mondale to make a good showing against popular Ronald Reagan. But political historians still marvel that a candidate with Goldwater's personal appeal and devoted following could have suffered such a devastating defeat.

Much of the blame for that defeat must go to Goldwater's fellow Republicans—presidential aspirants Nelson Rockefeller, William Scranton, Henry Cabot Lodge, George Romney, and their supporters—who feared that a Goldwater candidacy would doom party candidates at all levels. So fanatically did they oppose Goldwater that they made their fear a self-fulfilling prophecy.

Their "Stop Goldwater" campaign started with the New Hampshire primary in March, and its fury did not subside even with Goldwater's nomination in July. The reckless charges they made against the Arizonan provided an awesome arsenal for the grateful Democrats in the presidential campaign.

Barry's remark at a New Hampshire rally that the commander of NATO should have some discretion in the use of tactical nuclear weapons made national headlines, which proclaimed that he advocated use of nuclear bombs. His later comments about defoliation of Vietnam jungles (an option that he never proposed) reinforced his image as the irresponsible war candidate.

His discussion of needed changes in Social Security to keep it from bankruptcy was headlined "Goldwater To Destroy Social Security." Rockefeller had thousands of copies of that newspaper story and headline circulated within hours.

Barry's lifelong habit of speaking frankly about controversial issues gave the press a never-failing stockpile of material for negative articles and television commentary. Later Dwight Eisenhower was to berate him: "Barry, you speak too quick and too loud!"

Grotesquely overscheduled in New Hampshire (eighteen hours on many days), Barry appeared tired and irritable as the pace of the campaign and the pain of his recent surgery wore him down. The result was a primary victory for write-in candidate Lodge, and an embarrassing defeat for the favorite from Arizona.

But the Goldwater brain trust learned from their New Hampshire mistakes and won victory after victory in state conventions and primaries across the nation. Rockefeller won a much-publicized triumph in the Oregon primary, but in the all-important California primary on June 2, superior organization and an amazing last-minute effort on the precinct level brought Goldwater from behind to a fifty-eight thousand-vote victory margin. Rockefeller reportedly spent more than three million dollars in his last-ditch California effort.

The delegates he collected in California all but assured that Barry Goldwater—barring some unforeseen revolt at the convention—would be the Republican candidate for president.

"The record says I was defeated by Lyndon Baines Johnson in the 1964 presidential election," Goldwater declares. "The truth is that I lost whatever slim chance I had to be president in the Republican National Convention at San Francisco."

It was in San Francisco's cavernous Cow Palace and in the venerable Mark Hopkins Hotel—ironically, the headquarters for both the Goldwater and "Stop Goldwater" factions—that the last skirmishes of the battle were fought in mid-July. Scranton, the governor of Pennsylvania, had somewhat reluctantly accepted the role of giant killer, and the eastern wing of the Republican Party closed ranks behind him after the California primary, in one last desperate attempt to derail the Goldwater express.

Words were spoken and deeds done in that convention that catastrophically split the Republican Party and made the forthcoming campaign an exercise in futility. After San Francisco, huge segments of the party sat out the campaign and refused to acknowledge that they had even heard of Barry Goldwater.

Scranton and Goldwater were long-time friends, and Barry had hoped the Pennsylvanian might fill the number two spot on the ticket to bring the eastern wing of the party behind the campaign. But the tactics of Scranton and the other "Stop Goldwater" warriors in San Francisco so angered Barry that he crossed Scranton from his vice-presidential list and instead chose a lesser-known congressman, William Miller of New York.

One fateful letter, incredibly intemperate and divisive, did the most damage. Written by some young firebrands on Scranton's team, with his knowledge but not read or signed by him, it so infuriated Goldwater supporters and undecided delegates that it ensured Goldwater's first-ballot victory.

Addressed to "Senator Goldwater," it read, in part:

Dear Senator:
As we move rapidly towards the climax of this convention, the

Republican Party faces a continuing struggle on two counts. The first involves, of course, selection of a candidate.

Here the issue is extremely clear. It is simply this: Will the convention choose a candidate overwhelmingly favored by the Republican voters, or will it choose you?

Your organization does not even argue the merits of the question. They admit that you are a minority candidate, but they feel they have bought, beaten, and compromised enough delegate support to make the result a foregone conclusion. . . .

Barry read the letter with mounting anger and disbelief:

You have too often casually prescribed nuclear war as a solution to a troubled world.

You have too often allowed the radical extremists to use you.

You have too often stood for irresponsibility in the serious question of racial holocaust.

[This statement mirrored a general apprehension about Goldwater's vote a month before against the 1964 Civil Rights Bill. Although he proclaimed his support for the bill's aims, he opposed it on constitutional grounds. "If my vote is misconstrued," he declared, "let it be."]

You have too often read Taft and Eisenhower and Lincoln out of the Republican Party. . . .

Goldwaterism has come to stand for being afraid to condemn right-wing extremists.

Goldwaterism has come to stand for refusing to stand for law and order and maintaining racial peace.

In short, Goldwaterism has come to stand for a whole crazy-quilt collection of absurd and dangerous positions that would be soundly repudiated by the American people in November.

The letter, which concluded with a challenge to a debate on the convention floor, had Scranton's typewritten name, but no signature, at the bottom.

Barely containing his rage, Barry told the press he "couldn't believe my old friend Bill Scranton had written such a letter." Its intemperate language embarrassed the urbane Pennsylvania governor; later Scranton was one of the few eastern Republican leaders to campaign with some vigor for the Goldwater-Miller ticket.

But the poisonous contents of the Scranton letter were exposed for all to see, underlining the disarray of the Republicans, and providing a neatly packaged indictment of Goldwater for later use by the Democrats.

Despite the rancor, the business of the convention went on. On the evening of nominations, Senator Everett Dirksen of Illinois nominated Barry Goldwater for president in a stirring speech that proudly called him "the peddler's grandson" (Big Mike would have been beaming) and signaled a cascade of gold foil from the rafters.

Goldwater delegates held fast through some incredible arm-twisting by the opposition. When the first-ballot roll call was called for, the votes fell in line as expected, and Goldwater was put over the top by South Carolina, the state that had given birth to his candidacy four years before.

Bob Goldwater, who was in Barry's suite at the Mark Hopkins when the winning total was achieved, vividly remembers the scene of celebration. With Barry and Bob at the moment of victory were Kitchel, Bill Baroody, Ed McCabe, and press aide Tony Smith.

The Goldwater acceptance speech was already written, and Barry had gone over every word with great care. It was designed to point a new conservative direction for the nation, and it offered no olive branches to the losers.

His foes had embittered Goldwater beyond forgiveness. They had called him untrustworthy, stupid, bloodthirsty, and a racist. There would be no compromise. Barry Goldwater had decided to go it alone.

The content of the address has been largely forgotten, except for one declaration inserted by speechwriter Harry Jaffa that will long live in political lore:

"Extremism in the defense of liberty is no vice, and . . . moderation in the pursuit of justice is no virtue."

Barry and many of those close to him during the convention still defend the use of the statement, which seemed far more explosive that night than it does two decades later. Barry repeated it, in fact, at the 1984 Republican convention, and there was little criticism of it. But at the time, it was a dagger thrust into still-painful wounds. The traditional demonstrations on behalf of party unity were glaringly missing and many a Republican left the Cow Palace that night with a premonition of disaster ahead.

Yet all was not grim doomsaying. There were many who exulted in the triumph of a brash westerner who had defied the select circle of Republican nobility, and there was some good-natured levity. Harry Golden, publisher of the *Carolina Israelite* and one of the great wits of the period, wrote:

"Wouldn't you know it! The first Jew to be nominated for president of the United States turns out to be an Episcopalian!"

Remembering his talks with President Kennedy about the conduct of the 1964 presidential campaign, Barry decided to attempt the same kinds of agreements with President Johnson. The two met in confidence shortly after Johnson had been nominated at the August Democratic Convention.

"I did not want the campaign to interfere with our conduct of the war in Vietnam," Goldwater recalls, "so I suggested to Johnson that we should agree not to make Vietnam an issue. I promised I would not do so, and he thanked me, with apparent relief, for my offer. I also told him I felt the same way about the civil rights question—that heated campaign debate about it would only inflame the nation further. Again he agreed."

The two shook hands, and both kept their word.

"I'm sure our strategists could have made political capital out of both these emotional issues," Barry now says, "and perhaps made the election considerably closer. But I have no regrets. I'm glad we put national welfare ahead of partisan considerations."

By the time of the Goldwater-Johnson meeting in late August, the contest appeared all but over. Every poll placed the president ahead by margins approximating seventy to thirty percent.

No appeal in the Goldwater arsenal succeeded in narrowing the gap appreciably. He crisscrossed the nation time and again in his specially equipped Boeing 727—nicknamed Yai-Bi-Kin, Navajo for "House in the Sky"—visiting forty-five states in one of the most strenuous efforts ever put forth by a presidential candidate.

From his opening address in Prescott to his campaign wrap up at tiny Fredonia, Arizona, on the Utah border, he hammered on his major issues—Big Government's infringement on private citizens, deterioration of the quality of life, growing tax burdens, the erosion of basic freedoms.

The great debate he had once envisioned—the conservative philosophy versus the liberal—never materialized. The Johnson forces, secure in their poll ratings, would never join the battle.

Journalists who accompanied Goldwater on his tortuous travels were, by general estimation, ninety percent opposed to his candidacy, and their reporting showed it. But most of them grew to like Barry personally and to admire his courageous efforts against overwhelming odds. On occasion, they whiled away the hours by composing such ditties as the following, according to Theodore White, sung to the tune of "The Sweetheart of Sigma Chi."

The man of our dreams has lost his hair,
His glasses are blank and black.
He hates to mess with the Eastern press,
His knife is in Lyndon's back.
The man of our dreams is free from care,
He's certain he's going to win.
The polls say he's not, but he's sure that's a plot,
He's the sweetheart of Yai-Bi-Kin.

As Barry had feared, he came to detest the never-ending glare of public exposure and the wearisome hounding by the media. On one of his rare half-days at home, he pulled off a trick that permitted him to have a few restful hours alone with Peggy. He persuaded his brother Bob to dress in an Air Force general's uniform, wrap his wife Sally in one of Peggy's fur capes, and drive Barry's car out of his driveway. The ever-watchful journalists grabbed the bait and drove off in pursuit, leaving Barry and Peggy free to make their own getaway.

"Dad made us kids hide out of sight on the floor of the back seat until he had decoyed the reporters a mile or so away from the house," recalls Bob's son Don. "It was great fun."

Goldwater had chosen Dean Burch for the chairmanship of the National Republican Committee, with John Grenier as his executive director. Barry appointed Clif White chairman of "Citizens for Goldwater and Miller," an organization that operated separately from the Burch group; General James A. Doolittle and Clare Booth Luce accepted posts as co-chairmen. Denison Kitchel continued in his role as "general director" of the campaign.

This somewhat loosely structured organization suffered more than once from lack of coordination. But there were strengths: a memorable slogan, "In Your Heart You Know He's Right," . . . innovative sub-groups such as "Pilots for Goldwater" and "Mothers for a Moral America" . . . an excellent communications system masterminded by telephone executive Nick Volcheff of Phoenix . . . hosts of volunteers.

But the desertion of many important Republicans damaged the cause tremendously. In New England, New York, and the Northeast generally, most political candidates disassociated themselves completely from the Goldwater effort. President Eisenhower was cool, particularly early in the campaign.

Even the dyed-in-the-wool conservatives were less than effective. One campaign leader unburdened himself to Theodore White: "Where were they when we charged up San Juan Hill? They blew the trumpets, but when we charged, nobody followed. Where was Buckley? Kirk? Bozell?"

Fear was Barry Goldwater's worst enemy: the unreasoning fear that he would involve the world in nuclear holocaust; the fears of old folks and the needy that he would cut off their checks; fears of Midwest farmers that he would end their subsidies; and a general, unspoken fear that he would cut back a protective governmental blanket on which too many had come to depend.

The Democrats took nothing for granted, however. They pounded away on the list of perceived Goldwater deficiencies bequeathed to them at the Republican convention. Two television commercials were especially devasting to the Goldwater cause: one depicted a little girl picking daisies as the mushroom cloud of a nuclear explosion enveloped her; the other showed fingers tearing up a Social Security card.

"Barry and I did not spend much time discussing what we would do in the unlikely event of a Republican victory," recalls Kitchel. "But there was a tentative agreement about some key figures in a Goldwater cabinet. The Secretary of State was to be Richard Nixon, the Secretary of the Treasury, Ralph Cordiner, and I was to be the Attorney General."

In the final week of the campaign, an ex-New Deal Democrat who had been converted to Goldwater conservatism came forward to make one of the most notable addresses of the Goldwater effort. Ronald Reagan, the former movie actor who was at that time touring on behalf of the General Electric Company, was chosen to deliver an address called "A Time for Choosing," which was filmed and shown on television across the nation. It so skillfully articulated the Goldwater case that Republicans everywhere started asking "why didn't we have that fellow speaking for us earlier?"

The address gave Reagan national political stature almost overnight, and his rapid climb to national office can be traced back to it.

As he always had before, Barry Goldwater wound up his campaign in Fredonia, Arizona, population three hundred. It was obvious that he was glad to be back home, among friends, in the land that had become a mystical part of him.

"I am proud and happy to be back amongst the people who I am sure understand every word that I have been saying," he told the small gathering. "I have been speaking about man, the whole man, about man's rights and man's freedom. I've been speaking about man's obligations to himself and to his family, to do things himself . . . and only to take help when everything else has failed."

When he had finished, it was after sundown, and he flew home on that election eve, stopping briefly at a party for him at Camelback Inn and then gratefully escaping to his home overlooking the spectacular vista of Phoenix at night.

The next evening, when the election night watch began, the issue had already been decided. There were few surprises. Goldwater's pollsters told him he would carry five states: Alabama, Arizona, Louisiana, Mississippi, and South Carolina. All five came through, and with them came Georgia.

Under the circumstances, the only real surprise was that so many millions of American voters—27,174,898 in all—supported him on election day. Johnson's 43,126,218 votes gave him one of the most lopsided victories in American political history, and there were those who were ready to declare that the Republican Party and the conservative philosophy were wounded beyond recovery.

Losers of presidential campaigns usually are tossed unceremoniously into the trash bin of history, rarely to be heard from again. How many people can remember whatever became of Al Smith? Alf Landon? Tom Dewey? How many can even recall who lost to Harding or Coolidge?

Oblivion was not to be Barry Goldwater's fate, however. A new generation has come from birth to adulthood since his defeat in 1964, and Goldwater continues to be a national celebrity. What seemed to be the end of his career has proved to be a beginning, not only for the man but for the conservative philosophy he so vigorously champions.

Richard Cohen of the liberal *Washington Post* lamented in an April 10, 1985, column that "America is smack-dab in what may be called one day 'the Golden Age of Conservatism.'"

Although he meant the comment as a disparaging observation on the present political climate, which he regards as selfish and materialistic, his observation reveals how far the idealogical pendulum has swung since 1964.

Denison Kitchel, who had driven himself to the limits of endurance during the long campaign, could find no trace of a silver lining in the dark cloud that enveloped him after the election. The American voter had heard the Goldwater philosophy articulated for many months, and had apparently rejected it.

But two years later came an incident that made Kitchel understand that the efforts of the Goldwater team had not been in vain.

"Ronald Reagan had decided to run for the Republican nomination for governor of California in 1966," Kitchel relates, "and of course we were following his conservative candidacy with great interest. The day after he won that election, he and Nancy came to Phoenix to visit her parents, and he found time to telephone me.

"'Denny,' he said, 'I never could have won this election if it hadn't been for the work you guys did two years ago.'"

Barry Goldwater took some solace in Reagan's nomination and eventual election to the governorship. Because he had rejected the option of running for his safe Senate seat while he was seeking the presidency (which he could legally have done), he was for the moment unemployed. Many doubted that Goldwater would ever return to the political wars.

But a strange thing was happening. Within a year after his 1964 defeat, his mail volume started to build rapidly, speaking invitations piled up, and writers were seeking interviews again. Much of the mail had a single message: "I'm sorry now that I voted against you. You were right all along."

Barry Goldwater and conservatism were very much alive.

19

Bouncing Off the Ropes

Recovering from personal calamity has become routine procedure in the Goldwater family.

Mike and Joe had struggled back from bankruptcies and humiliations so many times they had lost count. Morris had suffered major defeats, and both Baron and Jo had demonstrated their ability to recover from fate's capricious poundings.

Rare, indeed, are the achieving people who have not suffered calamitous setbacks. It is the way they battle back from those setbacks that determines their real worth.

Certainly, 1965 was a testing time for Barry Goldwater. For a while it seemed that everything he had worked for in his political career was lost. It appeared that both Goldwater and the conservative revival had been soundly repudiated by the American electorate.

For the first time in his life, he was temporarily cast adrift, occupying no power base, leading no cause, even without gainful employment. He found the relative peace and the absence of pressures healing for a few months, but he was never completely out of the public spotlight. Soon, he was moving back into the busy schedule of speaking engagements and public obligations.

The defeat of 1964 had hurt—it still does—but he reached back for strength to a family tradition of comebacks, and he pressed on to new beginnings.

PHOENIX–WASHINGTON, D.C., 1965

JO GOLDWATER REACHED HER NINETIETH BIRTHDAY IN 1965, STILL MAKING LIARS OF all those doctors who had repeatedly predicted her early demise. To her son Barry in that gloomy year, she was a symbol of strength, standing firm against all the disasters fate could throw at her.

"I remember how Mun marched through the bad times with her head held high," Barry says. "I could still hear her telling us to get up after we'd been decked in some game, to shake it off and get back in the contest. I did a lot of boxing, and her example helped me many times to bounce off the ropes after taking a punch to the jaw."

Among the poems Barry's mother had taught him as a youngster was Rudyard Kipling's *If*, and the words came back to him in those weeks after his defeat in the presidential election:

If you can bear to hear the truth you've spoken
Twisted by knaves to make a trap for fools
And watch the things you gave your life to, broken . . .

The election defeat had been a severe blow, but Barry Goldwater was already bouncing off the ropes. After several months of getting reacquainted with his family, working traffic in his ham radio room, and photographing the Arizona back country, he began to get restless for another fling at political combat.

One of his major concerns was the conflict in Southeast Asia. As he had feared, the Vietnam war was escalating out of control, and he longed to help bring a halt to that endless tragedy.

Earl Eisenhower, a Goldwater aide who had been one of the full-time workers in the presidential campaign, remembers with clarity the 1964 Goldwater message about Vietnam: "At all costs, we must avoid a large-scale land war in Southeast Asia."

"The Senator believed we could deny the North Vietnamese the resources for making war," Eisenhower says, "and that we could do it with air and naval forces. But instead we kept pouring ground troops into the jungles."

Few experts knew as much about the Vietnam military problem as Goldwater. He went to Southeast Asia, conferred with commanders, and listened to the combat pilots. Invited to air his views at the White House in the spring of 1965, he told President Johnson, "Mr. President, I've been to Vietnam five times, and I understand our problems there. Until you take the hobbles off our commanders, there's no way we can win."

Barry was referring to the policies of Defense Secretary Robert McNamara, which prevented pilots from attacking Communist rocket-launching sites, supply trains, and many other targets without prior approval from distant headquarters. By the time the approval was obtained, the targets usually had been moved. He was referring, too, to a host of restrictions that continued to frustrate American efforts and cost American lives.

"I told the President with as much fervor as I could muster that either victory or defeat would be much better than the no-win policies being pursued," he said.

The first priority of a Goldwater presidency would have been ending the war, either by winning or by withdrawing American forces. Like many others, Goldwater could see that the endless continuation of the conflict was likely to inflict more harm on the American people than any other event of the century. Win it, lose it, withdraw with whatever dignity was possible—anything—but end it. That, he believed with all his heart, was the only solution.

It was not to be. For four more years of the Johnson administration, and into the second Nixon presidency, the cancer of Vietnam ate away at the American spirit. Its poisons still afflict our nation today.

The mountain of mail that piled up in Goldwater's office after 1965 was unmistakable evidence that the American public had heard his 1964 messages more clearly than he had imagined. Vietnam . . . the failure of Lyndon Johnson's costly anti-poverty programs . . . economic worries . . . loss of American prestige abroad . . . these and many other failures of the unhappy Texan wheeler-dealer in the White House made it increasingly apparent that Johnson would not dare to seek the re-election that traditionally rewards successful presidents.

Goldwater conservatism sprouted anew across the nation, with young and old joining to spread the philosophy and to elect conservative candidates.

A new group emerged, which some journalists erroneously viewed as the core of a third party: the Free Society Association. Denison Kitchel was elected its president, and such prestigious conservatives as Clare Booth Luce, George Humphrey, Robert Galvin, and William Baroody combined their resources and their talents to propose conservative solutions to the nation's problems.

"We had seven hundred members," says Kitchel. "We planned to publish 'The New Federalist Papers,' and other monographs on conservative philosophy. William Rehnquist (later appointed to the Supreme Court) was an enthusiastic member of the group. But after four years, our financing ran out and we had to cease operation."

Barry himself was soon back in the spotlight. In 1965, former President Eisenhower formed the Republican Policy Group to offer alternatives to Johnson policies. Senator Everett Dirksen of Illinois was a key member, as were Representative Charles Halleck of Indiana, national GOP chairman Len Hall, and Tom Dewey. Eisenhower gave Goldwater a warm personal invitation to join the group, and he gladly accepted.

Doughty Jo Goldwater, still battling to be as independent as possible, fell and broke her hip in August 1966. As always, she refused to give in to this latest disaster, and demanded to be sent home from the hospital as soon as she was able.

Jo had already survived three physical crises, and didn't anticipate that this one would be any different. First, the Chicago medical specialists gave her six months to live and sent her to Arizona as a last forlorn hope in 1903. Then, in 1921, she was on the edge of death when she was crushed in an automobile accident. Finally, in 1936, Phoenix physicians told her she had inoperable cancer of the colon, and that there was nothing more they could do for her.

Jo would not accept this judgment, but went to the Mayo Clinic at Rochester, Minnesota, for another opinion. There a new surgical procedure successfully removed all the cancerous growth, but left her with an ostomy; refusing to accept the indignity of wearing an external bag for the rest of her life, she adjusted her schedule to accommodate her affliction. Thus, she was able to enjoy almost-normal activity, and even to make trips to Alaska and Europe.

This was a lady who simply would not acknowledge defeat. But even her magnificent spirit could not hold back time forever. She clung to life until the Christmas gathering of her children and grandchildren in 1966. Then, two days later, at age ninety-one, she died.

By 1966, Goldwater had made up his mind to seek the Senate seat that had been occupied with distinction by Carl Hayden since 1926. Hayden, who would mark his ninety-first birthday in 1968, was so venerated in Arizona that Barry held his plans in abeyance until the dean of the Senate made his retirement definite.

Hayden gave his luke-warm endorsement to his thirty-eight-year old Senate aide, Roy Elson. There had been mutual respect between the Goldwater and Hayden families in Arizona for more than a century, so it was not surprising that the aged Hayden chose not to mount any strenuous opposition to Goldwater's candidacy in 1968.

Dean Burch, chairman of the Republican National Committee during the 1964 presidential campaign, was Goldwater's choice to manage his crucial campaign to regain his Senate seat. This time around, the slogan was "Senator Barry Goldwater: Doesn't That Sound Great?" As always, Barry's airplane—with the faithful Ruth Reinhold at the controls—was an important factor in bringing the campaign to people all over the state.

It soon became evident that a majority of Arizona's voters agreed, and the polls placed Goldwater far ahead through most of the contest.

Fearing overconfidence among Goldwater financial supporters, Burch did his best to picture the battle as a close one. In a letter to William Buckley, published in the August 27, 1968, issue of *National Review,* Burch exhorted conservatives everywhere to contribute to the campaign, which he said was short on money and long on smugness. There was little cause for alarm, as it turned out. Elson had much more serious financial problems, and Goldwater won by a comfortable margin of sixty-one thousand votes.

Newsweek, in its summary of the 1968 Senate elections, said Barry won "by inveighing against judicial permissiveness and for the bombing of Haiphong [in North Vietnam]." Although the Democrats remained firmly in control of the Senate, Goldwater was one of the winners who gave the GOP a gain of five seats in the election.

Richard Nixon, who became the only man in the twentieth century to win the presidency after a previous defeat, owed a great debt to Goldwater, who helped secure his nomination in Miami and campaigned for him untiringly across the country in 1968. Nixon's paper-thin victory over Hubert Humphrey brought him into office with less than half of the popular votes cast, an embarrassment that haunted Nixon through his first four years in the White House and fueled his fanatical determination to win by a landslide in 1972.

It was that fanaticism that led to such unnecessary 1972 tactics as the "dirty tricks" and the fateful break-in at the Democratic National Headquarters in Washington.

One of the most memorable meetings in Barry Goldwater's long career came on January 9, 1969, just eleven days before Lyndon Johnson left the White House.

The two old warriors had a drink together at Lyndon's invitation and reviewed the political situation in an atmosphere of unaccustomed friendship.

"Lyndon was more bewildered than bitter," Barry recalls. "He had tried his best, but he had failed. At the end of his long public career he was weary and more than a little sad. All those billions of dollars spent on social programs had alleviated [inequities] not at all. Defiant, bearded young men demonstrated outside the White House and called him a murderer for his conduct of the Vietnam War. His real friends were few."

As he prepared to say goodbye to Barry for the last time as president, LBJ rose and suggested that his 1964 rival might give Dick Nixon a call and offer his best wishes. "This job's a killer, Barry," he declared.

"At that moment I got a little clearer concept of the tremendous weight the presidency puts on a man's shoulders," Goldwater recalls.

Barry could have been pardoned for wondering, after that poignant farewell, which man had really won in 1964 and which had been the loser.

Sixteen years earlier, when Harry Truman had just turned the presidency over to Dwight Eisenhower, Barry Goldwater had enjoyed the privilege of a private talk with Truman. One startling piece of advice the battle-wise Missourian offered on that occasion was this: "Tell the General he should fire Democrats, replace them with his own people, and take control of the government fast. If he doesn't do it by May, he won't do it at all."

The memory of that conversation was still fresh in Barry's mind when he held his first face-to-face meeting with Richard Nixon a few weeks after he had taken the oath of office in January 1969.

"I urged Nixon to get rid of the holdover advisors who had been responsible for our disastrous no-win policies in Vietnam," says Goldwater. "I reminded him that he had a great opportunity to set a new course for America, and that he should take firm control as soon as possible."

Unfortunately, in Goldwater's view, Nixon did not do so. He postponed hard decisions, kept appointees in office who did not agree with his policies, and lost the fleeting opportunity to take charge at the beginning of his administration.

There was another, more sinister, facet of Nixon's presidential style. Mistrustful of the press and irritated by criticism, he soon retreated inside a wall of his close advisors and lost touch with the American people. His choices for key White House aides, especially John Erlichman and Robert Haldeman, exacerbated the situation. Steely, arrogant, and overly protective, they shielded Nixon from dissent and good advice while building their own empires in the presidential entourage.

The appointments of such men, and the new president's increasing isolation, worried Barry and many other Republican leaders who were doing their best to support Nixon programs.

But the newly elected junior senator from Arizona (his old friend Paul Fannin had won Goldwater's vacated seat in 1964 and was now the senior senator) put aside his misgivings about this strangely secretive president and happily engrossed himself in the work of the nation's most prestigious legislative body.

Goldwater was welcomed back to the Senate by old friends and new, and was treated with a respect accorded to few others. His personal legislative agenda was a busy one, and one that surprised critics who still scorned him as a progress-resisting mossback. Summarizing his third term legislative efforts, the *Reader's Digest* later reported:

Among the notable pieces of legislation he has fathered or helped to father . . . are those (1) giving the vote to 18-year olds, (2) abolishing state residency restrictions so as to enable citizens on the move (some ten million) to vote for President, (3) ending the draft and bringing forward the Volunteer Army; (4) saving Radio Free Europe and Radio Liberty from extinction for lack of funds; and (5) making it a crime to print and send smut through the mails. All the while his breadth of influence in the Senate has expanded steadily.

The Vietnam conflict escalated during the last tense years of the 1960s, and so did the alienation of the young against their government. Torn between loyalty toward Nixon and his mounting repugnance at the conduct of the war, Goldwater fumed at his inability to help achieve a solution to the problem that threatened to destroy America.

When Nixon shocked the world with his July 1971 announcement that he was going to Peking to try to patch up relations with Red China, Goldwater viewed the move as a signal that America was abandoning friendly Taiwan. So concerned was Henry Kissinger over Barry's probable reaction that he radioed Goldwater during the latter's flight in an Air Force fighter to the West Coast. Kissinger told him, over the noisy radio connection, that he hoped Goldwater would not blast the Nixon decision in the media, at least until he had been briefed on all the facts.

Goldwater reluctantly agreed, and kept his word. But his worst fears were realized after Nixon returned from China. The official communiqué issued after the visit declared that the United States intended "the withdrawal of all United States forces and military installations from Taiwan" and recognized that Taiwan was "a part of China."

Said Goldwater later: "The China communiqué became the basis for President Carter's recognition of the Red Chinese government. Its existence provided Carter with an excuse to withdraw recognition of Nationalist China and abrogate our mutual defense treaty."

At the time, he added with some sadness, "both Nixon and Kissinger assured me this would never happen."

Nixon's China trip put one more strain on Barry Goldwater's already-weakening confidence in the man he had worked so hard to elect.

Richard Nixon started his campaign for re-election almost as soon as he succeeded Lyndon Johnson in the White House. A man of ego, he fretted over the slim margin that he had achieved over Hubert Humphrey in 1968, and devoted much of his energy during the next four years to winning big in 1972.

He had little cause for worry. Although loved by few American voters, he was generally respected for his ability to get things done. Nixon could have conceivably relaxed in the Oval Office through all of 1972, and still won in November.

To oppose him, the Democrats nominated South Dakota Senator George McGovern, a little-known liberal who never was able to get his campaign off the ground. But Nixon was fanatical in his determination to be absolutely certain that the 1972 election would erase the fearful memory of his narrow escape in 1968.

It was from the secrecy and the excesses of Nixon's Committee to Re-Elect the President that most of the mischief of 1972 had its origin. So quietly did the president's men operate, however, that little was discovered about the campaign crimes of 1972 until the whole operation was placed under the media microscope a year later.

Thus, the bizarre burglary of the Democratic National Headquarters offices in the Watergate residence hotel on June 17, 1972, merited only a few inches of space in newspapers across the nation.

John Mitchell, the former U.S. attorney general who had resigned to head the Nixon re-election effort, heatedly denied that there was any connection between the burglary and the Committee to Re-elect the President. But when Watergate burglar James McCord was identified as an employee of the CRP, the "minor story" started building slowly to the status of a national scandal.

"I couldn't believe that Mitchell, or anybody else in his right mind, would authorize any caper so stupidly risky and unnecessary as the Watergate break-in," Goldwater recalled later. "So I accepted the White House denial as truth. Obviously, I should have been less trusting."

With the evidence of overwhelming victory piling ever higher on election night, 1972, Richard Nixon exulted in his mandate and went to work setting the course for his second term. Among Republican leaders whom he called in for consultation during that November was Barry Goldwater, who was invited to a private conference at Camp David.

"We discussed the still-festering Vietnam conflict, cabinet appointments, legislative strategy—many things," recalls Barry. "I confided that I was considering retirement from the Senate when my term ended in 1974. When he heard that, Nixon suggested that I accept a diplomatic post after 1974, and offered me the ambassadorship to Mexico when I left the Senate."

The Camp David meeting did much to convince Barry that Nixon sincerely planned to take firmer command of the Executive Office during his second term and correct many of the mistakes that had been worrying Nixon's friends.

But throughout that winter, ominous hints of impending scandal over the nagging Watergate problem made Goldwater even more worried than before. He made it a point to quiz colleagues close to the White House. What they said, and sometimes how they said it, convinced him that Nixon himself may not have been telling the whole truth about the incident and the frantic efforts to cover it up.

In an interview with Godfrey Sperling Jr. of the *Christian Science Monitor,* published April 11, 1973, he made a characteristically quotable Goldwater comment: "There's a smell to it," he said. "Let's get rid of the smell."

After giving Nixon ample time to clear away the smell, Goldwater went public again. This time he blasted the president for hiding behind executive privilege and withholding tapes of presidential conversations.

"The American people aren't going to be satisfied with that kind of quibbling," he declared. "They want and deserve the truth."

A small army of American investigative reporters, many of them ravening for Nixon's blood, were already hard at work digging up evidence to connect the president with the Watergate mess. Their sensational revelations during early 1974, and Nixon's indignant denials of personal knowledge, pushed every other story off the front pages for many months.

On June 20, 1974, Goldwater sent Nixon a long letter with his personal distress evident in every word, urging that the president "come out of his shell," end the national paralysis of Watergate doubts, and get on with the reforms they had discussed at Camp David.

Then, on the afternoon of August 5, his old friend Dean Burch—at that time a presidential advisor—called Goldwater with an anguished request for an immediate meeting. Showing Barry a long statement from Nixon, Burch summarized it in a brief, sad statement:

"He says he hasn't been telling the truth."

When Vice President Spiro Agnew resigned in disgrace on October 10, 1973, after pleading "no contest" to income tax evasion charges, the scramble for consideration as Agnew's replacement was the talk of Washington. It would have been even more spirited a scramble had all concerned been able to look into a crystal ball and predict that the selectee would soon be President of the United States.

"I recommended to President Nixon that he choose George Bush, then the Republican Party chairman," says Goldwater. "Bush was bright, articulate and well-regarded nationally. I thought he would make an excellent successor to Nixon. The president, however, chose Representative Jerry Ford of Michigan to be vice president, and on December 6, Ford was sworn. I considered his choice a good one."

So it was Gerald Ford, the former University of Michigan football player and "Mr. Nice Guy," who was waiting in the wings with some reluctance to receive the mantle of the presidency during the traumatic first week of August 1974.

When the "smoking gun" evidence of President Nixon's complicity in the Watergate cover-up hit the headlines, there was little doubt in anyone's mind that an American president was about to leave office in mid-term, by impeachment or by resignation, for the first time in history.

The wildest kinds of rumors raced around Washington: Nixon was about to call out the army to avoid removal from the White House; he would commit suicide or start a nuclear war in one final, insane act of retaliation.

How the tortured president would react to the bitter fact of impending impeachment and disgrace was critical to the very existence of the American nation.

To make certain that Richard Nixon understood the hopelessness of his political situation, and to ease him toward a resignation with some shred of dignity, it was decided that Barry Goldwater and Pennsylvania's Hugh Scott, the minority leader, must tell President Nixon on August 7 that he had to resign.

At the same time, House Republicans designated their minority leader, Barry's old friend John Rhodes of Arizona, to bear the bad news to Nixon.

"As we waited together in the White House to deliver our message of doom," recalls Goldwater, "I couldn't help noting that two of the three men selected for this task were from one small western state. It was a remarkable tribute to Arizona's influence in our federal government."

During that brief wait, two decades of memories came flooding back to Barry Goldwater, years of campaigning for Dick Nixon, believing in him, defending his programs.

When Goldwater, Scott, and Rhodes were ushered into the president's office, they met a Nixon who was surprisingly well-composed and cheerful. There was a bit of small talk, some reminiscences, and then Nixon asked Goldwater how things looked for him in the Senate. Barry replied with his usual frankness that he could count on no more than twelve sure votes against the impeachment charges in the Senate. Rhodes and Scott concurred that many of the usually loyal Republican stalwarts in both houses were now aligned against the president. There was no hope.

The devastating news did not seem to shake Nixon's calm. Goldwater later admitted that he had to fight back tears during the dramatic confrontation, but that the president seemed perfectly serene.

"It was one of the most remarkable performances I have ever seen" Barry says. "Here was a man facing one of the most calamitous situations in history, knowing he now must step down in disgrace from the most powerful office in the world and see the dreams of a lifetime destroyed.

"Despite my anger, I had to admit he displayed a brand of courage I had never seen matched anywhere."

Richard Nixon resigned as President of the United States the following day. Gerald Ford succeeded him in office and immediately granted Nixon a full pardon. Ford's action raised an indignant outcry from coast to coast, and probably caused his defeat in the 1976 presidential election.

Barry Goldwater considers Ford's decision "one of the most courageous ever taken by an American leader, and one which should have earned him the gratitude of all Americans."

Knowing full well the political explosiveness of the pardon, Ford nevertheless took that controversial step without hesitation.

"The lynch mob had put the noose around the neck of the man they hated," declared Goldwater in *With No Apologies*. "Ford stopped the hanging."

There were cries of collusion, and charges of a Nixon-Ford deal. It was not until much later, when emotions had cooled a bit, that many came to realize how well Ford had served his country by preventing a divisive Nixon trial and more devastating polarization of the nation.

Ford invited Barry to the White House three days after assuming the presidency. There he asked the Arizonan whether he was willing to be considered for the vice presidency. Goldwater thanked him for the honor, but suggested that the nation and the party would be better served by the selection of a man—or woman—who was younger and who would strengthen the Republican ticket in 1976.

Ford's eventual choice—Barry's old antagonist, Nelson Rockefeller—was a bitter disappointment to Goldwater. Although he did not oppose Rockefeller's confirmation as vice president, he made a promise at that moment that he would do all he could to keep the New Yorker off the Republican ticket in the next election.

Almost forgotten in the drama of the Nixon resignation was the nagging reality of Barry's upcoming campaign for re-election to the Senate. Arizona's Democrats, despite their Watergate ammunition, were again in disarray. Their candidate was Jonathan Marshall, the liberal publisher of the *Scottsdale Progress,* who was struggling to build name recognition in his uneven contest with an Arizona legend.

With Steve Shadegg back as campaign manager, and with the wave of personal popularity bolstered by his stabilizing role in the Nixon tragedy, Goldwater swept to the mightiest landslide of his political career. His total of more than three hundred seventeen thousand votes gave him a victory margin of ninety thousand.

Political observers around the nation marveled at the miraculous turn-around in Goldwater's career in the space of a decade. The man who in 1964 had been branded "the closest thing in American politics to Russian Stalinism" by Senator William Fulbright of Arkansas; "a raving, ranting demagogue" by President Johnson; and a dangerous, trigger-happy primitive by leaders of his own party, had climbed out of his political grave and was once again a potent force in national affairs.

In his widely reprinted 1974 *Reader's Digest* article, "Barry Goldwater's Second Wind," Charles J. V. Murphy noted that the *New York Times* now called Goldwater "one of the few political heroes left in the United States." He declared that the nation's turnaround on Goldwater was unique in political history. Said Murphy, "A politician who once seemed headed for the dustbin of history, he has now emerged, for many, as the conscience of Congress—a man who can be counted upon to stand up and speak the truth."

20

Hail to the Elder Statesman!

The final decade of Barry Goldwater's political career has produced noticeable changes in the senior senator from Arizona, and in the way America perceives him.

As he entered the final year of his long Senate tenure, he was almost as much in demand by the insatiable news media as he was when he was seeking the presidency. His picture appeared on Sunday newspaper supplement covers, and his comments on current issues graced the pages of national news magazines. He is a popular guest on radio and television talk shows, answering questions about American public policy as forthrightly as ever.

This is not quite the same Barry Goldwater that America has learned to love—or hate—for more than three decades. He is more mellow; he does not denigrate his enemies; his voice is more modulated, and his opinions more carefully expressed.

The interviewers have changed, too. Where once they tried to bully him, and goad him into making intemperate remarks, they now question him with a measure of veneration.

During Goldwater's late-1985 appearance on television's "Crossfire," for example, liberal inquisitor Tom Braden treated him with a deference he seldom bestows on any other guest.

The magazines are kinder, too. A recent Time *article called him "A Curmudgeon with a Conscience."*

Perhaps it is his grey hair, or the other subtle evidences that Barry is on the downhill side of seventy-five. More likely, it is the legend that has grown up around this one-of-a-kind public figure.

Not that The New Republic *will ever grant him sainthood, or the* Washington Post *adopt his philosophy in its editorial columns. His opponents will always be his opponents, but the man is at last being accorded respect.*

Barry Goldwater has achieved the coveted status of elder statesman.

WASHINGTON, 1976

THE PRESIDENTIAL SWEEPSTAKES OF 1976 PRESENTED SENATOR GOLDWATER WITH one of the more difficult decisions of his career: should he throw his support to Ronald Reagan, who had been a loyal Goldwater advocate in the 1964 campaign, or to President Gerald Ford, whose personal decency and courage had done so much to erase the stain of Watergate from the Republican Party?

Staunch party conservatives confidently predicted that he would back Reagan; more moderate Republicans were afraid he would do so.

Barry later explained his reasoning in reaching a decision:

"I was very grateful for Ron's help in 1964, and I offered to support him if he decided to go for the presidency in 1968," says Barry. "But the situation was different in 1976, when Reagan announced his intention to oppose President Ford.

"I decided, after much struggle, that President Ford deserved a chance to be elected on his own. More importantly, as the incumbent, he stood a better chance of winning."

Barry worked for Ford's nomination, and in so doing he alienated many of his conservative friends. "The Senator is dead wrong," roared Bill Buckley in *National Review.* Although he has been an enthusiastic Reagan supporter in every election and confrontation since that time, Barry feels that the President and Mrs. Reagan never have completely forgiven him for his defection in 1976.

Jimmy Carter came out of nowhere to capture the Democratic presidential nomination in 1976 and defeat President Ford in November. The Georgian's presidency, in Barry Goldwater's view, was one of the most disastrous in the nation's history.

"Strength through weakness," Barry derisively termed the Carter foreign policy. Carter methodically trimmed American military capability, withdrew support from friends, and encouraged enemies, Barry believes. At home, inflation rates soared and economic woes mounted. The American people yearned for a stronger, more capable presence in the White House and a more conservative philosophy in the conduct of their government.

Arizona's senior senator was enthusiastically optimistic about Republican prospects in 1980 and devoted much of his time in that summer and fall to working for the election of Ronald Reagan and bringing to Washington the conservative principles he had advocated in 1964. History records the Reagan victory over Carter as a major political landslide.

Goldwater's efforts on Reagan's behalf, and a long hospitalization for hip surgery, took precious time from his own 1980 campaign for re-election, and almost cost him the Senate seat.

When Arizona's Democrats selected little-known Bill Schulz, a million-aire real-estate developer, as their Senate candidate, many Republican leaders predicted another sweeping Goldwater victory in November. Over-confidence and a lackluster campaign effort hobbled the Goldwater forces all summer, however, and Schulz steadily closed the gap.

Television's awesome impact on modern elections was never more evident than in the 1980 Arizona Senate campaign. Schulz avoided per-sonal attacks on Goldwater, but instead, subtly drove home the point to television viewers that Goldwater, "an Arizona institution," had served well, but was really too old and infirm to continue in the Senate.

Barry managed to give the Schulz campaign a big boost when he insisted on leaving his hospital bed after surgery to appear on national television during the Republican Convention. Weak, perspiring, and in considerable pain, he gave the appearance of a man physically incapable of serving six more strenuous years.

Schulz's well-financed campaign continued to narrow the gap in the polls, but Goldwater was still rated the favorite as election day dawned. So it came as a tremendous shock, as the returns rolled in that evening, that Schulz was not only leading but increasing that lead with every passing hour.

Jack Kirwin, writing in the November 28, 1980 *National Review*, de-scribed the wrenching trauma of watching Reagan build his overwhelming margin over Carter while Goldwater was apparently going down to defeat. In an editorial headlined "What (Almost) Happened to Goldwater," he asked:

> How could "Mr. Conservative," who had held the fort so gallantly during all those dark years, almost get beaten while the rest of the country was practicing what he preached for so long?

Kirwin explained the close shave in three ways: (1) Schulz came out as a right-of-center candidate and mounted an intelligent and energetic cam-paign; (2) he was willing to spend $1.3 million of his own money; and (3) he used television more effectively than did Barry.

At the Barry Goldwater home that night, with his family assembled, tensions mounted as the gloomy news flooded in. At midnight, with some eighty percent of the vote in, jubilant Schulz supporters urged their candi-date to make a victory statement. But he wisely held off until the last GOP strongholds had been heard from, and until the sizable absentee vote had been counted.

As it turned out, those absentee ballots, assiduously courted by Republican workers, turned disaster into narrow victory. When the final tally was made the following day, Barry Goldwater had won with a margin of nine thousand votes in a total of eight hundred sixty thousand.

Frank as ever in times of crisis, Barry answered the inevitable questions about his feelings in these words:

"I was scared to death!"

The election of 1980 gave Republicans control of the U.S Senate for the first time in more than two decades. Barry Goldwater's seniority had, however, been interrupted by his four-year absence (1965-69), so he did not immediately become chairman of a Senate committee.

That particular honor was delayed until the organization of the Senate in January 1985, when he achieved his long-held ambition to serve as chairman of the Armed Services Committee. That position, together with his former chairmanship of the Senate Select Committee on Intelligence, has given him a high level of expertise concerning America's military capability and its role in world affairs.

He also chairs the Tactical Warfare Subcommittee in Armed Services and the Communications Subcommittee of Commerce, Science, and Transportation.

Over the years, Goldwater has worked hard to win funding for the Central Arizona Project and other Arizona water developments; to solve the problems of Arizona's huge Indian population; and to help his state accommodate the waves of newcomers who arrive each year.

More than three hundred pieces of legislation authored or co-authored by Goldwater have become law. Among his notable bills have been those banning unwanted smut mail; the Grand Canyon National Park Enlargement Act; funding for the Smithsonian Institution National Air and Space Museum; the amendment repealing the Social Security earnings test for persons seventy and older; and the Cable Television Act of 1984.

He has been a godfather of the Air Force Academy, having served three terms as chairman of its Board of Visitors, and has long been a member of the Board of Regents of the Smithsonian Institution.

Goldwater's friends across the nation have contributed well over a million dollars to the establishment of the Barry Goldwater Chair of American Institutions at Arizona State University. Three of the leading fund raisers in that effort were Barry's lifelong friend, Harry Rosenzweig; Washington attorney Ron Crawford, who has been raising money for Goldwater's political campaigns and his favorite charities for years; and his brother Bob.

Earnings from the Goldwater chair corpus were responsible for bringing futurist Herman Kahn to the ASU campus to teach, research, and write. Noted political scientists, historians, economists, and other scholars and public figures will occupy this academic post in years to come. Goldwater himself has been invited to serve in the Goldwater Chair sometime after he completes his tenure in the Senate.

As he nears the end of what he vows will be his final term in the Senate, Goldwater is an alluring subject for the news media. Writers and broadcasters seem to find the oft-told story irresistible: how the once-despised ogre of 1964 has regained popular favor throughout America.

Marvin Stone, in a 1983 *U.S. News and World Report* article, highlighted Goldwater's concern for the human rights of Indians in America, during Barry's push to settle the festering land dispute between the Hopi and Navajo tribes.

"We pay far more attention to human rights of people in South Africa and Central America than to the rights of Indians in our own states," he quoted Goldwater. "In over two hundred seven years, we have never, repeat never, lived up to the moral obligations we owe these people."

A year later, *Time* expressed surprise at the Arizona senator's concern over the huge sums being requested by the Reagan administration for national defense.

"Slash the Administration's defense budget . . . crack down on the [offending] defense contractors!" he was quoted as saying in a spirited denunciation of waste and overstaffing in the Pentagon.

Of this and other Goldwater statements, his Arizona colleague, Rep. John McCain, had this observation: "The sentiment on the Hill is 'Thank God Barry said what I didn't dare to say.'"

Members of Congress have been grateful to Barry Goldwater for saying what they dared not say for many a year.

In this world of political huckstering, of office holders striving desperately to be all things to all people, the forthright senator from Arizona shines like a jewel. He is one of a kind: a politician who calls them as he sees them. One may heartily agree with his positions, or may be infuriated by them. But even though he has mellowed a bit, there is seldom any doubt about where the man stands.

There was once a twenty-two-year period (1927-49) during which no member of the Goldwater family held elective office. Are we about to enter another?

Barry's departure from the U.S. Senate in January 1987, creates a gap in the family political narrative, but it is possible that others will come along to fill it.

Barry Jr., who served seven terms as a Congressman from California (1969-1983), made an unsuccessful run for the U.S. Senate in 1982. He may enter the political wars again. His brother Mike, who managed many of Barry Jr.'s campaigns, has not ruled out a possible political venture. Other members of the fourth generation of Goldwaters in Arizona have the ability, and perhaps the desire, to seek public office.

Soon, the fifth generation will be reaching maturity. It will be interesting to see whether any of these recipients of Michel Goldwater's genes will follow the trail he blazed to prominence in business, politics, and community service.

Big Mike was willing to become a peddler, or a freighter, or a mining speculator when those opportunities promised some chance of success. Joe and Morris and Baron loved to gamble on new stores in raw new towns.

Today's opportunities are vastly different, but the rewards are just as alluring and the competition just as formidable. The younger Goldwaters are making their way in industrial development, new product marketing, investment counseling, real estate sales, retailing, banking, and several other fields.

Are there future senators or governors among these descendants of Michel Goldwater? Bank presidents? Literary lights? Public benefactors?

The answers lie somewhere over the horizon.

Barry Goldwater sees no rocking chair in his post-Senate plans. The demands on his time promise to be enormous: speaking, writing, giving political counsel, submitting to interviews; perhaps occupying the Barry Goldwater Chair at Arizona State University for a term; he plans to spend much more time with his family. There is much to read, and many hobbies to be enjoyed.

There will be more offers of honorary degrees, positions on major boards, opportunities for political service. Answering his voluminous mail will be a full-time occupation in itself.

Through it all, we can be sure, Barry will continue his love affair with history, and will search for new insights into the lives of his illustrious forebears.

21

Enduring Monuments

THE PIONEER FAMILY THAT PRODUCED BARRY GOLDWATER HAD EARNED A SECURE place in Arizona history long before he came along. They braved incredible hardship and danger to carve a habitable territory out of the wilderness, and labored selflessly to build the foundations of today's prosperous state.

The *Arizona Republic* editorial writer was commenting on Morris Goldwater after his death in 1939, but his words apply equally well to the rest of the family during the past one hundred thirty years:

Everywhere in Arizona are the monuments left by this noted pioneer, and no section of the state is without them.

Few families have left their mark on a state more indelibly than the Goldwaters have on Arizona. Like most great families, they were not at all aware of their monument-building as they went about the daily chores of making a living and doing their share in solving community problems.

They did not sit self-consciously for their portraits in history. Had they been aware that later generations would be watching, the Goldwaters might have been more circumspect—and less interesting.

You will find few, if any, members of this family who qualify for sainthood. While they have not actually broken all the Ten Commandments (no Goldwater, for example, has been known to worship a graven image), they have severely dented several of them. They have sampled the pleasures of this earth with admirable diligence, and enjoyed them to the full. They have succeeded mightily—and failed spectacularly—in an impressive variety of business, political, and personal ventures.

As a result of their strivings, however, Arizona and America are the better for their living here.

Only a few of the enduring Goldwater monuments are made of marble, bronze, or stone. One such is the famed equestrian statue fronting the

247

Yavapai County courthouse in Prescott, which Morris helped to erect in honor of his old rival, Buckey O'Neill. There are hospital facilities, a library, shopping centers, military installations, and federal buildings that owe their existence in whole or part to Goldwaters.

Some of the monuments are towns, a few still thriving and others only historic ruins, that restless Goldwater pioneers helped to build: Prescott, Phoenix, La Paz, Ehrenberg, Seymour, Bisbee, Gillett, Parker, Fairbank . . . the list goes on.

Still other monuments serve humanity's craving for nature's beauty: Goldwater Lake, the statehood tree, the YMCA Sky-Y Camp, among them. Many are utilitarian, such as the wagon roads that Mike and his partner, Dr. Jones, pioneered for freighting supplies to army posts and mining camps from the Colorado River to New Mexico. Others followed these roads, bringing civilization in their wake. Goldwaters helped develop railroads and highway networks, air and space travel.

Mike and Joe performed the vital function of financing the early settlers, and for decades, the Goldwaters played major roles in Arizona banking. Morris brought the telegraph to Phoenix, and Baron pioneered the first improvements in store buildings. Henry's dreams of an irrigated Yuma County agricultural empire brought that miracle a little closer.

Goldwaters helped create some of the first Arizona militia units, formed to provide protection from Indian raids. They established one of the first fire-fighting companies in the young territory, and secured dependable sources of water for the people.

They were tireless workers for community good, through organizations as diverse as the Masonic Lodge, the Smoki People, the Phoenix Boys Club, and Planned Parenthood.

On the political front, Mike and Joe accepted the call to public service not long after their arrival in the territory. Morris's amazing record of unpaid— or minimally paid—service to his city, county, territory, and state will never be forgotten. When Morris was ready to lay down his burden of political service, he passed it on to his nephew, Barry.

The Goldwater women have left their legacy of good works to those who came after them. Josephine's monuments are numerous: leadership in community service, fostering early Phoenix social life, promoting golf, working for better health care. Her daughter, Carolyn, has been a leader in charitable work for decades, as was Peggy and other Goldwater wives.

Bob Goldwater's quiet contributions to his native state and city have rarely been given sufficient note. As a merchant, banker, developer, civic leader, and organizer, he has earned a place among the major builders of Arizona.

Barry has been building monuments in Arizona and across the nation all his life. Few Arizonans can match him for either the scope or magnitude of his achievements. In photography, radio, aviation, historic preservation, writing, the military, and many other fields, he has been a respected leader. America knows him best, of course, for his leadership of the conservative revival and for his prominence as a United States Senator and presidential candidate.

Big Mike Goldwater, who never knew he had founded a great family, would be delighted if he knew.

Delighted—and amazed.

Appendix A

Morris and Henry Goldwater were among the original volunteers of Prescott's Hook and Ladder Company, founded a few days after the 1880 fire. So it was logical that they, along with Sam, would be members of the new hose companies, established by Mayor I. L. Hall and the Common Council in 1884. The ordinance called for the creation of four companies of about twenty-five men each, with a city appropriation of sixty dollars for social activities. Fire houses and basic fire-fighting equipment were also provided, but each company had to raise money for its own distinctive uniforms and fraternal paraphernalia.

In his official history of the Prescott Volunteer Fireman's Association, former fire chief Robert Connell Jr. told of the first organizational plan in 1885:

Hose Company No. 1 was drawn from Whiskey Row—saloon keepers, bartenders, gamblers, and others on the block just west of the plaza. This hard-drinking, fun-loving company almost immediately called itself "The Toughs." They had a small firehouse in the middle of Whiskey Row, which gave them a slight advantage in speed of assembly for fire fighting.

The Toughs had one slight problem, however. The signal to assemble was three pistol shots fired in quick succession—but somebody was frequently shooting a pistol on Whiskey Row, and many a false alarm resulted. The trouble was removed when all the companies agreed to respond to the ringing of the courthouse bell.

Hose Company No. 2, says Connell, were "the elite of Prescott"—bank clerks, merchants, professional men—from the east and north sides of the plaza. Their firehouse was on the north side of the Gurley Street hill. This company soon was known as "The Dudes." There were other companies in the early years, but the emotional rivalry between the Toughs and Dudes outshone all their competitors.

As might be expected, Morris and his brothers cast their lot with the Dudes, and Morris served as secretary of the famed hose company for forty-five years. Next to his Masonic loyalty, his love of the Dudes was uppermost in his long life.

In April 1885, the Dudes issued a challenge to the Toughs for the great competition in racing the hose cart some two hundred yards to the hydrant, attaching the coupling, unreeling one hundred fifty feet of hose, and spraying water on a fire.

Fire Chief Al Whitney and others collected money for a silver trumpet to be awarded to the winning company in the race of April twenty.

The Toughs were more than willing to accept the challenge, and all

Prescott buzzed with anticipation of the great clash of firemen's skills and masculine egos. It was to be the first of a series of competitions that would continue for thirty years, fade for a while, and then be revived in contemporary times.

Among great fanfare, the Dudes won the first contest, but the Toughs demanded a November rematch.

The Toughs were resplendent in blue tights, white trunks, and white stripes running through the blue for the runners and red stripes for the couplers. The initial "T" was woven on the breasts of their shirts, and they topped it all off with black skull caps.

The Dudes showed up in white tights with red trunks, and were hatless.

The Prescott *Courier* reporter was caught up in the excitement of the high drama:

> On raced [the Dudes], straight as a regiment of soldiers on parade, in spite of their tremendous speed. The hydrant is reached, still the truck flies on, but the end of the hose remains in the hands of the fleet runners who rush with it to the hydrant, make the connection and turn on the water.
>
> Ah! Fatal delay! . . . the water comes not out. Yes, there she spouts, but a second of time has been lost at the hydrant, and the Dudes despond.

The Toughs rejoiced, but in their run they experienced the same trouble with slow water flow. As the *Courier* told it,

> Great Caesar! What's the matter with the hydrant? The water—two seconds pass. Here it comes, but too late, too late. The Dudes have won, the Toughs have lost.

Appendix B

A good measure of Henry Goldwater's self-assurance came from the fame he had won in 1881 for his role in uncovering the infamous "Star Route Scandal."

Anyone who thinks the Postal Service has delivery problems today should consider the impossible task faced by the U.S. Post Office in the pioneer West. Mining camps and isolated ranches were strewn all over the map, often with nearly impassable roads. Postmasters served part-time, for a pittance, and postal customers moved as often and as erratically as crickets on a hot stove.

The post office made heroic efforts to give the nomadic pioneers some kind of dependable mail service. A major portion of its budget went to pay Star Route mail contractors, who bid for their routes and hoped to make some profit from them.

With millions of dollars being spent for such contract routes, it was inevitable that fast-buck opportunists should move in to skim off some of the gravy. As government charges later revealed, Albert E. Boone, a Washington bureaucrat who had been discharged from the post office auditor's office for "cause," was one of these. Boone was part of a combine that operated under the firm name of James H. Ketner and Co., an oddity in itself, since Ketner was Boone's sixteen-year old stepson.

The firm mailed questionnaires to postmasters across the country, seeking information about contract mail routes, and then bid on them. During a four-year period in the 1870s, Boone bid on no less than 4,694 mail contracts, and won 102 of them in his own name. He had little intention of carrying out the delivery of mail on these routes, however.

Henry Goldwater, then only nineteen, was postmaster at Ehrenberg in 1878. It was his duty to supervise performance of the Star Route contractors in his area, one of whom was J. M. Peck. Peck was not only failing to deliver the mail to Mineral Park, but he gave no indication that he planned to do so. The undelivered mail started piling up, and nearly a ton of it accumulated before the sordid matter was settled. Meanwhile, irate Mineral Park residents complained in impotent rage.

All through this battle, contractor Peck was nowhere to be seen. Nearly five months after his service was to begin, he still had not delivered one piece of mail, but subterfuges were invented by his cohorts in Washington, continuing payments to him as long as possible.

Henry, who had copies of a dozen frantic messages sent to Washington warning them of trouble on this route, was fit to be tied. At last, a few months before he was to leave Ehrenberg for his duties in the store at

Prescott, Henry accumulated all his documentation and sent a long and accusatory letter to several federal officials describing the outrageous situation on this route, which he suspected might be occurring on many others.

Henry was right. Investigation showed rampant fraud in the Star Route contracts, much of it perpetrated by people in places of trust. The Star Route Scandal hit the national headlines in mid-1881, and was the biggest graft story to make the news since the malodorous revelations of dishonesty in the Grant administration.

When the conspirators were brought to trial June 1, 1882, the case had involved many of the top officials in Washington. Senator Stephen W. Dorsey of Arkansas was the chief target of newspaper indignation, although top postal officials and even the famed Senator Roscoe Conkling of New York were dragged into the mess.

Boone, whose company was one of the original contractors, was not brought to trial. He turned state's evidence and saved himself by telling what he knew about the others' wrongdoings. The first trial ended in a hung jury, so another trial was held, running from December 1882 to June 1883. This time the jury brought in "not guilty" verdicts on all the accused. According to the press, political pressures and strong evidence of jury bribery had come to the defendant's rescue.

Teen-aged Henry Goldwater was the person originally responsible for blowing the whistle on the Star Route contracts scheme. When the federal government was preparing its case in the Star Route trials, prosecutors contacted Henry in Prescott, escorted him in secret to Washington, and put him up for several weeks in the plush Willard Hotel. There, he was available for continual questioning by the many lawyers who tried to build a case strong enough to send some very powerful men to prison for long stretches. They failed to jail anybody in two years of trying, but reputations crumbled and the Post Office Department was at least temporarily purged of fraud.

Little wonder that students of Goldwater family history regard his role in the Star Route scandal as the greatest achievement in the life of Henry Goldwater.

Chapter Notes

All references to the Arizona Historical Foundation are abbreviated as AHF. All interviews conducted by the author are in the AHF archives, Hayden Library, Arizona State University, Tempe.

Chapter One, The New World Adventure Begins

Descriptions of San Francisco and its business practices are from Hubert H. Bancroft, *History of California,* vol. 6; from written recollections of Michel Goldwater to his daughters (Goldwater Collection, AHF); and the Morris Goldwater Collection (AHF).

The details of the Michel and Sarah Goldwater courtship and wedding are from correspondence from Evie Aronson Margolis (Margolis to Fireman, 1955); Jewish wedding customs, from the *Universal Jewish Encyclopedia* (London: n.p., n.d.); and the notice of their golden wedding celebration, from the *San Francisco Chronicle,* March 10, 1900, issue.

Information on the Michel Goldwater children came from the *Prescott Miner,* August 14, 1985, issue; on the Goldwaters in Poland, letters from Richard Goldwater to Fireman, especially the letter of May 15, 1957 (Goldwater collection, AHF); on the Drachman family association with the Goldwaters, from a letter to Barry Goldwater from Harry Arizona Drachman dated May 26, 1939; on Jewish merchants in San Francisco, from Harriet and Fred Rochlin, *Pioneer Jews* (Boston: Houghton-Mifflin, 1984); and on the Goldwater family's personal descriptions and physical characteristics, from Evie Aronson Margolis interview with Bert Fireman, 1955.

Chapter Two, M. Goldwater of Sonora

Much of the background information of this chapter, and some legal records, were researched at Senator Goldwater's request by Alice Fisher Simpson of Sacramento, California, in 1956. Her correspondence is in the Goldwater Collection, AHF.

Descriptions of Sonora, California, in 1854 are from William M. Kramer and Norton B. Stern, "Early California Associations of Michel Goldwater and His Family," *Western States Jewish Historical Quarterly* (July 1972, pp. 173-196); Bert Fireman letter to Norton B. Stern, dated November 20, 1968; and family recollections recorded in oral interviews. Business transactions at Sonora are described in Irena Narell's study, *Our City: The Jews of San Francisco* (San Diego: Howell-North Books, 1981).

Information on licensing and taxes paid by the Goldwater saloon at Sonora are detailed in Tuolumne county records, which also contain information on Michel's wife's separate property.

The story of "Big Anne," a Sonora prostitute, is from Edna Buckbee's unpublished account, *The Saga of Old Tuolumne,* in the holdings of the Tuolumne County Historical Museum, Sonora, California.

The arrival of the "Sierra Nevada," which carried Sarah Goldwater and her children, is reported in the July 2, 1854, issue of the *San Francisco Herald.* A copy of this newspaper is in the Goldwater Collection, AHF. Sarah's difficulties in Sonora were later recalled by Evie Aronson Margolis during an interview in 1955 with Bert Fireman.

The organization of the Hebrew Benevolent society, Michel Goldwater, vice president, is described in Robert E. Levinson, *The Jews in the California Gold Rush* (New York: KTAV Publishing House, 1978). Levinson also describes Sarah's business ventures in Sonora.

Bankruptcy actions involving the J. Goldwater and Company business at Sonora are described in the Tuolumne County records of February 1857.

The files of the *Sonora Union-Democrat* of 1856-1858 describe Michel Goldwater's mishap at Columbia, California, and his last months in business at Sonora.

Chapter Three, **The Peddler of Gila City**

Information on Michel and Joseph's business enterprises at the Bella Union Hotel, Los Angeles, is in the tax records of the city of Los Angeles, October through December 1858. The Bella Union Hotel is amply chronicled in Mamie R. Krythe, "The First Hotel in Old Los Angeles," *Historical Society of Southern California Quarterly* (March 1851), and in Harris Newmark, *Sixty Years in Southern California: 1853-1913* (Los Angeles: n.p., 1970).

Michel Goldwater's bankruptcy hearing was in the Los Angeles District Court, which declared him insolvent on March 19, 1860. The 1860 United States Census lists his total net worth at one hundred dollars, and lists the Goldwater family, consisting of Michel, Sarah, and five children, as residing in Los Angeles.

Bert Fireman's research (AHF) shows that Michel Goldwater first entered Arizona as a peddler in the fall of 1860.

J. Ross Browne, *A Tour Through Arizona—1864,* and other reports from the territory in that era, provide a rich background for the study of Arizona in its first territorial year.

Advertisements in the Los Angeles newspapers for the J. Goldwater store in the Bella Union Hotel are reproduced in Harris Newmark, *Sixty Years in Southern California: 1853-1913.* Masonic records in Los Angeles, as in Sonora, show Michel to be a member of the late 1850s.

Los Angeles newspapers, particularly the *News* and the *Herald* of the summer of 1862, tell of the La Paz gold strike. The San Francisco *Alta*

California carried several stories about La Paz in its October 1862 issues, as did the *San Francisco Bulletin.*

Chapter Four, **New Start at La Paz**

One of the best descriptions of the new town of La Paz is in the July 19, 1862, issue of the *San Francisco Bulletin;* another is in an 1895 address to the Arizona Pioneers Historical Society by Isaac Goldberg, contained in the files of the Arizona Historical Society, Tucson. The *Prescott Miner,* founded when the Arizona territorial government began operations in the new capital in 1864, has many interesting accounts of La Paz life in the mid-1860s. La Paz's bid to have the territorial capital moved there is described by George Kelly in *Legislative History of Arizona* (Phoenix: Arizona State Archives, 1926).

The shooting at the Cohn-Goldwater store at La Paz in May 1863 is reported in the July 1928 issue of the *Arizona Historical Review.* Lt. E. B. Tuttle of Fort Yuma recalled the incident in his memoirs. Morris Goldwater related the story of discovering Herman Ehrenberg's death, first to contemporary reporters and later to his family. Major General E. O. C. Ord reported on the Indian dangers in Arizona Territory in the 1869 *Report of the Secretary of War to Congress;* he stated that "Almost the only paying business the white inhabitants have in that Territory is supplying the troops . . . and most inhabitants are supported by the hostilities."

Several records of mining claims filed by Michel Goldwater at La Paz in the spring of 1863 are in AHF records. The Goldwater takeover of the Vulture Mine in 1867 is widely documented in the *San Bernardino Guardian* of July 27, 1867, and in other accounts in the B. Sacks Collection.

The 1864 United States Census records show Michel Goldwater's net worth at $15,000, and that of his partner, Bernard Cohn, at $5,000.

Steamboating on the Colorado River during the 1860s is colorfully described in the Dr. B. Sacks collection at AHF and in many accounts held by the Arizona Historical Society in Tucson.

The Bert Fireman files (AHF) on the Goldwaters in the 1860s have detailed records of Michel and Joseph and their La Paz businesses. Ledgers of the Goldwater stores in La Paz and Ehrenberg have been preserved in the Goldwater Collection (AHF). Michel was interviewed about La Paz and the Colorado River settlements by the San Francisco *Alta California* in its February 8, 1867, edition.

Chapter Five, **Ambush!**

The *Arizona Miner* of Prescott described the gathering of bidders for the army grain contracts in its issue of May 18, 1872. Stories of the awards, and of protests from unsuccessful bidders, appeared in the May and June issues. James M. Barney's research on the Salt River Valley's infant grain industry (1872) is in the AHF collections.

The Indian attack on Michel and Joseph Goldwater and Dr. W. W. Jones was reported in the June 15, 1872 issue of the *Arizona Miner* and the June 22, 1872, *Yuma Sentinel*, as well as in other territorial newspapers. There is a sizeable file on the incident in the Dr. B. Sacks Collection (AHF). The 1874 Annual Report of the Secretary of War lists the major freighting stations on the roads connecting California and Arizona communities.

Mrs. Caroline Cedarholm's lengthy missionary stay in Arizona Territory is chronicled in the Dr. B. Sacks files (AHF); in the Tucson *Arizona Citizen* of June 29, 1871; and in the Prescott *Arizona Miner* in almost every issue between September and December 1870.

The activities of Michel and Joseph Goldwater in San Francisco during the fall of 1872 are noted in family correspondence and recollections in the Goldwater Collection (AHF). Michel Goldwater's interest in a Phoenix store in 1872 is reported in the *Arizona Miner's* "Letter from Bob," on July 20, 1872. In its July 27 issue, the *Miner* said, "J. Goldwater and Bros. of Ehrenberg have bought a hall in the course of erection . . . from C. H. Gray, with the intention of starting a business here." Phoenix and the Salt River Valley settlements of the early 1870s are described by Rufus K. Wyllys, *Arizona: The History of a Frontier State* (Phoenix: Hobson and Herr, 1950). Maricopa County records show that the M. Goldwater & Co. took out its first retail sales license in Phoenix in December 1872, paying twenty dollars for a three-month permit.

Michel hired Barber and Pearson, contractors, to complete his Phoenix store building. The *Miner* of December 7, 1872, said that the building had "just been completed in the [northwest] corner of Montezuma [now 1st Street] and Jefferson Sts. facing on the southwest corner of the plaza." Business was started there on December 11. Sale of the first Goldwater store in Phoenix was reported in the June 2, 1875, *Miner:* "Goldwater and Co. have disposed of their mercantile business to Smith and Stearns. The new firm [has] a large and well-selected stock of goods."

Arizona historian James McClintock tells of Morris starting Phoenix's first telegraph service in *Arizona, The Youngest State* (Chicago: Clarke Publishing Co., 1916). Family records have much more detail about this achievement.

Chapter Six, **Success at Last**

The brief story of the Arizona and New Mexico Express, in which the Goldwater brothers were active, is told in detail in Dr. B. Sacks file (AHF), and in the Tucson *Arizona Star* in many issues through the summer of

1876. The final demise is reported in the *Star* of July 15, 1876.

At the short-lived Parker store, Joseph and Henry kept ledgers that are now part of the Goldwater Collection (AHF); the final entry was made on November 14, 1877. United States Government Indian Service records also tell the story of this store.

Martha Summerhayes, in her classic *Vanished Arizona* (Chicago: Lakeside Press, 1939), tells of life at Ehrenberg in the mid-1870s. She tells of her friends, the Goldwaters, on pages 197 and 198. The Yuma *Arizona Sentinel* of April 17, 1880, reported the robbery of the Ehrenberg store; Michel was tied up and the loss was three thousand dollars. The notice of partnership dissolution between Michel and Joseph Goldwater was printed in the May 18, 1880, edition of the *Miner* and several other newspapers.

The town of Prescott is described in detail in Richard Hinton, *Handbook to Arizona* (San Francisco: Payot, Upham Co., 1878). The *Arizona Miner* of February 13, 1874, first reported Michel Goldwater's interest in a Prescott store. The *Miner* of 1876 chronicled the building of the store and the progress in its receipt of merchandise; the January 1877 issues have detailed descriptions. Bert Fireman's research on Michel Goldwater's early years in Prescott shows the pattern of his interest in lots at Union and Cortez. He paid Levi Bashford $3,250 for this property in December 1878. The *Original Assessment Roll for Yavapai County, 1878,* showed the Goldwater resources in Prescott at $28,650 for merchandise and store building and $600 for an adjoining warehouse.

Yavapai County records show Goldwater purchases of county warrants on July 5, 1877, and deposits of county money with the Goldwaters. General August Kautz of Fort Whipple kept a diary, excerpts from which are in the Dr. B. Sacks Collection; Kautz tells of depositing army money with Goldwaters.

Michel's letter to Sarah about the birth of Evie Aronson Margolis is dated January 22, 1878; the original is in the Goldwater Collection.

Prescott Masonic records show that both Michel and Morris became official members of the Prescott lodge on May 26, 1877. Morris's first election to the position of mayor of Prescott is noted in the Minutes of the Common Council (Book 1:202, January 7, 1879). His carefully kept scrapbooks, now in the Goldwater Collection, contain clippings of most of the major activities of his several terms as mayor.

The disastrous Prescott fire of July 29, 1880, was reported in most Arizona newspapers, especially the *Miner* and the Prescott *Democrat,* during the week after the fire.

Organization of the Arizona Development Company, conductors of the first Arizona Lottery, is noted in the Prescott *Miner* of January 3, 1879, and George Kelly records the legislation creating the Arizona Lottery in *Legisla-*

tive History of Arizona (Phoenix: n.p., 1926). The "Inquirer" column of the Tucson *Arizona Citizen* of March 7, 1879, asked: Since gross lottery proceeds will be $60,000, prizes will be $32,000, and school/capitol funds will be $3,200, "now a legitimate inquiry arises as to what becomes of the balance of $28,000?" "Get Your Money Back" was the headline of the June 6, 1879, lottery story in the *Miner;* it included Michel's offer to refund all ticket money. Michel's open letter to the Postmaster General, published in several Arizona newspapers, protested that Arizona's lottery should not be barred from the mails. It was printed in the July 19, 1879, edition of the Prescott *Weekly Arizonan.*

Chapter Eight, **Wild and Woolly Politics**

The information on Buckey O'Neill comes from Ralph Keithley, *Buckey O'Neill: He Stayed With 'Em While He Lasted* (Caldwell, Idaho: Caxton Press, 1949); Jeanette Eaton, *Buckey O'Neill of Arizona* (New York: n.p., 1943); and the B. Sacks Index (AHF).

The "thieving thirteenth" legislature is chronicled in Kelly's *Legislative History;* in Ernest Hopkins and Alfred Thomas, *The ASU Story* (Phoenix: Southwest, 1960); and in many journal articles in the AHF collection.

Michel Goldwater's stormy seven months as mayor of Prescott are described in the Prescott council minutes and in the *Miner* of January through August 1885. His sale of all Arizona mercantile interests to his son, Morris, for $11,858 is recorded in a document in the Goldwater Collection (AHF).

The chronicle of Morris's achievements is found in Ray Vyne's nomination of Morris for Prescott's "Man of the Century" (1964), a copy of which is in the Goldwater Collection. Information on his political offices, on his relationship with Fiorello LaGuardia, and on his efforts to promote Arizona statehood can be found in Morris's scrapbooks.

Chapter Nine, **Chasing Rainbows**

Henry Goldwater told his brother, Morris, of his job at the railroad depot in Guanajuato, Mexico, in a letter dated November 23, 1884, found in the Goldwater Collection (AHF). Disturnell's *Arizona Business Directory, 1881,* lists Henry Goldwater as a cigar merchant in Prescott and also as a postmaster at Ehrenberg.

Evie Aaronson Margolis's correspondence with family members shows that Henry's role in the Star Route Scandal of 1882 was the most important event of his life. Dr. Ben Sacks later found documents in the National Archives that describe Henry's secret testimony to the postal inspectors regarding the scandal.

John and Lillian Theobald, *Arizona Territory Post Offices and Postmas-*

ters (Phoenix: Arizona Historical Foundation, 1961), show Henry assuming the position of Yuma postmaster on August 17, 1885.

Henry was the secretary of the new Mohawk Valley Canal Company in March 1885, according to reports in the Yuma *Sentinel* of that month; the *Sentinel* of May 16, 1885, reported on an allied enterprise, the Antelope Valley Canal Company.

Goldwater family recollections and correspondence tell of the crisis caused by Henry's decision to marry a gentile, Julia Kellogg, in 1893. The Prescott *Journal-Miner* of November 18, 1899, compliments Julia Goldwater for her work in bringing the Carnegie library to Prescott; correspondence between Julia and Andrew Carnegie is in the Goldwater Collection (AHF).

Documentation on the Henry Goldwater home in Prescott (1894) was provided by Bette Ruffner of the Prescott Historic Buildings Survey.

Henry's letter to Morris of April 25, 1918, from Los Angeles, tells of his job with a film laboratory and of his opportunity to stay and grow with the film industry. Henry often wrote to his brothers in his later years, and in a 1925 letter to Morris, expressed his regrets that he could not help him with his banking reverses.

Chapter Ten, **Baron and the Phoenix Store**

The agreement that launched the Phoenix Goldwater's partnership (1894) is in the archives of Goldwater's Fashion Square store, Scottsdale, Arizona, as are early billheads and logotypes with the slogans "The Best Always" and "Since 1862." Chet Goldberg, a lifelong friend and Phoenix retailer, spoke at length with Bert Fireman in 1959 about Baron and Phoenix retailing. Photographs and data on Phoenix in 1896 are found in Dorothy and Herb McLaughlin, *Phoenix, 1870-1970* (Phoenix: Arizona Photographic Associates, 1970); in Phoenix city directories of the late 1890s; and in the Goldwater Collection (AHF).

E. J. Bennitt, a long-time family friend and business associate, was Barry's godfather; an extensive file on Bennitt is in the Goldwater Collection. Baron's report cards and other school records are also in the Goldwater Collection; he attended Los Angeles schools before moving to San Francisco with his mother. Harry Rosenzwieg, Barry and Bob's life-long friend, provided many recollections about Baron and his family in the years just before and just after World War I. Records of Baron's involvement in financing early Phoenix hospitals can be found in Steven Shadegg, *Miss Lulu's Legacy* (Tempe: Arizona State University, 1984).

Chapter Eleven, **Families**

An extensive file on Sarah Shivers Fisher Goldwater, who married Morris

Goldwater in 1906, is in the Goldwater Collection (AHF). She was long honored as one of the earliest Prescott pioneers, and her reminiscences were recorded by Mrs. George Kitt on April 22, 1936; the transcript is also in the Goldwater Collection.

Josephine Williams Goldwater was the subject of a tape-recorded interview with her children, Barry, Bob, and Carolyn; the transcript is in the Goldwater Collection, as is Bert Fireman's unpublished article, "The Most Unforgettable Character I've Met." Josephine's family tree, dating back to colonial times, in on file at AHF. The automobile accident that killed Dr. Robert Brownfield is fully described in the May 1 and 2, 1921, issues of *The Arizona Republican.*

The new Goldwater's store at 33 North 1st Street, Phoenix, was opened on December 31, 1909; leases and other records of occupancy are in the Goldwater's Fashion Square archives, Scottsdale.

Morris Goldwater's scrapbooks and Barry Goldwater's recorded recollections of early Phoenix (recorded reminiscences, Arizona Pioneers Historical Society, 1940, Goldwater Collection, AHF) contain a great deal of information on E. J. Bennitt, while E. J. Hopkins, *Financing the Frontier* (Phoenix: Arizona Printers, 1950) tells the first complete story of Valley National Bank. Much of the detail about the 1914 panic is in this excellent narrative. During the week of November 10 through 16, 1914, the *Arizona Republican* carried major stories each day about the Valley Bank of Phoenix's battle for survival. Information on the remarkable career of engineer-banker Louis D. Ricketts may be found in monographs and related documents at the Arizona Historical Society, Tucson, and in the AHF archives.

Barry's childhood pranks are described graphically in Rob Wood and Dean Smith, *Barry Goldwater: The Biography of a Conservative* (New York: Avon, 1961). Phoenix Union High School yearbooks for 1926 and 1927 record Bob Goldwater's student achievements. A letter from Baron to Morris dated April 1, 1926, and sent from a Livermore, California, rest home, verifies Baron's health difficulties; "This enforced idleness is appalling," Baron wrote. Baron's obituary, will, and other final documents are in the Goldwater Collection.

Harry Rosenzweig's recollections of the "Center Street Gang" and its activities were recorded by the author. Phoenix Country Club historical information is available in the club's files.

Chapter Twelve, **A State is Born**
The Cincinnati newspaper, *The American Israelite,* of October 28, 1909, reported on President Taft's visit to Prescott and of his gift of a White House pass to Morris Goldwater; Morris's welcoming address to Taft is in the Goldwater Collection (AHF).

The Masonic Lodge was one of Morris's primary interests, and he kept meticulous records of his participation, from initiation to the final Masonic ceremonies, as well as a complete record of Arizona Masonry for six decades. Many who knew Morris thought that he had received his Scottish Rite 33rd degree during his 1919 London trip, but his own records show that he received it in San Francisco in 1903.

The Arizona State Library and Archives has the minutes and other documents of the 1910 Arizona Constitutional Convention. (Dr. John Goff, Phoenix College, has conducted intensive research on the convention and has a book on the subject in preparation.) Many of the letters and telegrams Morris received from lobbyists on the eve of the convention are in the Goldwater Collection. Rufus Kay Wyllys, *Arizona: The History of a Frontier State,* has an excellent discussion of the creation of the Arizona constitution, as does George Kelly, *Legislative History of Arizona.* The "statehood tree," a white oak growing on the north side of the Prescott city square, was planted on February 14, 1912.

Chapter Thirteen, **Fighting the Tide of Depression**

The author's interviews with Barry and Bob Goldwater and Carolyn Goldwater Erskine, with Mary Johnston Pratt, and with Peggy Goldwater provided most of the information for this chapter. A file of Morris Goldwater's personal recollection was collected by Bert Fireman and others (AHF); especially interesting are the reminiscences of Prescott's Perry Bones and Grace Sparkes.

The founding of the Prescott National Bank was reported in the *New York Times* of April 22, 1893. The Arizona State Banking Department verified repayment percentages (Commercial Trust, 83.25% and Prescott State Bank, 58.05%) in a September 2, 1959, letter from D. O. Saunders to Bert Fireman (AHF). R. E. Moore, president of Valley Bank, wrote an especially friendly letter to Morris, expressing faith in his character, on December 16, 1925; a similar letter came from Governor G. W. P. Hunt on May 13, 1926.

Lester (Budge) Ruffner provided the author with valuable information on the Smoki initiation. The Phoenix Metropolitan YMCA has records on the land gift for the Sky-Y Camp near Prescott. An undated column in the *Arizona Republic,* written by Henry Fuller, also summarizes the circumstances of this gift; this column is in the Goldwater Collection (AHF).

Chapter Fourteen, **Into the Wild Blue Yonder**

Ruth Reinhold, the Phoenix flight instructor who taught both Barry and Bob and was Barry's pilot during several political campaigns, was most helpful in providing information on the Goldwater flying era. Her book, *Sky*

Pioneering (Tucson: University of Arizona Press, 1982) has many references to the Goldwaters.

Barry's recorded recollections of his aviation experiences are in the Goldwater Collection; the author's interviews with Bob Goldwater also added valuable insight into the period. Edwin McDowell, *Barry Goldwater* (Chicago: Regnery, 1964) tells of Barry's early wartime flying.

The "last big bash," at the Goldwater home at 710 North Central Avenue before it was destroyed, is fondly remembered by Robert Creighton and other participants; photos of the 1940 event are in Bob Goldwater's possession.

Larry Andrews' 1947 radio script, which described Bob's civic service, is part of the Goldwater Collection (AHF).

Chapter Fifteen, **The Merchant Tastes Politics**

The author's interviews with Hoyt Pinaire, president of Goldwater's in 1984, and with Bob Goldwater form the basis of much of this chapter. The correspondence of Ina Babbitt, long-time secretary in the Goldwater's organization, also provided helpful information; this file is in the Goldwater Collection (AHF). The archives of the Goldwater's stores in Scottsdale Fashion Square contain detailed information on each store in the organization, and on personnel associated with each. *Women's Wear Daily,* October 15, 1964, carried a detailed analysis of Associated Dry Goods management of Goldwater's, and the stores' direction of growth.

Harry Rosenzweig, who persuaded Barry Goldwater to run for the Phoenix City Council in 1949, provided much helpful information about that period.

Chapter Sixteen, **Vote for Goldwater**

Information on Barry's early political involvement came from interviews with the Senator and from his recorded recollections; from his several biographies, especially Edwin McDowell, *Barry Goldwater: Portrait of an Arizonan* (Chicago: Regnery, 1964) and Steven Shadegg, *Barry Goldwater: Freedom is His Flight Plan* (New York: McFadden-Bartell, 1963). Former Arizona governor Jack Williams provided information about Barry's tenure on the council.

The author's many discussions with former Arizona governor Howard Pyle provided much of the information on Pyle's entrance into politics in 1950 and his choice of Barry to manage his campaign. The author is indebted to Steven Shadegg for his recollections of the first Goldwater-McFarland Senate race of 1952, and to Robert Creighton, a veteran Arizona political observer, for his account of the state's politics in the early 1950s.

Chapter Seventeen, **The Junior Senator from Arizona**
The friendship between Charles Trumbull Hayden and Michel Goldwater is documented in correspondence in both the Carl Hayden and Goldwater collections in the Hayden Library, Arizona State University. The author's 1961 interview with Edna Coerver, Barry's Washington, D.C., secretary, provided information for the section of the early Senate years, while later interviews with Judy Eisenhower and Doris Berry, key Goldwater staffers, were also helpful.

Barry's "Perfect Campaign Speech" is quoted in Wood and Smith, *Barry Goldwater: The Biography of a Conservative.* The relationship between Barry and President Eisenhower is discussed in the author's article "Goldwater Assesses His Eight Presidents," *Platte Valley Review,* Spring 1982. Former governor Howard Pyle, a member of Eisenhower's staff for several years, provided other information.

Barry's description of his visit to Senator Joseph McCarthy in a Washington, D.C., hospital appears in his book, *With No Apologies,* and his comment on the Republican Campaign Committee is in the same book.

Chapter Eighteen, **Goldwater for President**
The author's interview with Denison Kitchel, who managed the Goldwater-for-President campaign, provided much of the information for this chapter, as did the Senator's memoranda, which were an invaluable.

Barry Goldwater's relationship with presidents Kennedy and Johnson are discussed in his 1981 interview with the author. Discussions with Steven Shadegg about the 1964 presidential campaign gave the author valuable insights for this chapter; Shadegg's book, *What Happened to Goldwater?* (New York: Holt, Rinehart & Winston, 1965) and Lionel Lokos, *Hysteria 1964* (New York: Arlington House, 1967) are excellent references.

Other interviews that provided information for this chapter were with Earl Eisenhower, Mike Goldwater, Don Goldwater, Carolyn Goldwater Erskine, Peggy Goldwater, Dean Burch, Harry Rosenzweig, and Robert Creighton.

Quotes from Theodore White, *The Making of the President, 1964,* are noted in the text. The nominating speeches made by Everett Dirksen and Clare Booth Luce at the 1964 Republican Convention are in the Goldwater Collection (AHF). Harry Jaffa, in an August 1984 letter to Barry Goldwater, explained the sources and thought processes that led him to include the famous "extremism" statement in Goldwater's acceptance speech.

Chapter Nineteen, **Bouncing Off the Ropes**
The author's interviews with Barry Goldwater, the Senator's own memoranda on the period, and his statements in *With No Apologies* (New York:

William Morrow, 1979) were useful references for this chapter. Denison Kitchel provided information about the Free Society Association, and Barry Goldwater's recollection of his 1953 meeting with President Truman and his meetings with President Nixon are from an 1981 interview with the author. The Senator's quotes on Watergate are from *With No Apologies.* Charles J.V. Murphy's article, "Barry Goldwater's Second Wind," was originally published in the October 1974 issue of *Reader's Digest.*

Chapter Twenty, **Hail to the Elder Statesman**

Senator Goldwater's observations about his relationships with presidents Carter and Ford are from a 1981 interview with the author. Interviews with the Senator's sons, Barry Jr. and Mike, and his nephews, Robert Goldwater Jr. and Don Goldwater, provided insights from the younger generation.

Senator Goldwater's May 30, 1985, memorandum to the author gives his views on the surprising result of the 1980 United States Senate election. Jack Kerwin, "What (Almost) Happened to Goldwater," *National Review* (November 28, 1980) includes interesting information on this election, as well.

Staff members in the senator's Washington, D.C., office provided information on Goldwater-sponsored legislation and committee assignments in 1985. Marvin Stone's comments on Goldwater's concern for Native American rights were published in "Goldwater Tees Off," *U.S. News and World Report* (May 23, 1983). "Curmudgeon with a Conscience," *Time* (December 17, 1984) chronicles Goldwater's advocacy of defense budget reductions.

Chapter Twenty-One, **The Enduring Monuments**

The *Arizona Republic* editorial and obituaries on Morris Goldwater appeared on April 12, 1939. Regarding Joseph Goldwater's stormy and sometimes tragic career in Arizona, it should be mentioned that his son, Lemuel (who was with his father in Cochise County stores briefly in the late 1880s) became a great success as a manufacturer of work clothing in California and was a much-honored civic leader in his community. Plans for a future Goldwater High School west of Phoenix that will honor Barry and his family were announced in 1985.

Acknowledgments

In any undertaking of this scope, the author is beneficiary of the work and assistance of many individuals. Following are just a few of the people and institutions who have helped me in ways too numerous to mention.

Senator Barry Goldwater started work on the Goldwater family history nearly a half-century ago. He has been collecting documents and information ever since that time and will probably continue to do so.

Bert Fireman, one of Arizona's most distinguished historians, did a magnificent job of assembling nineteenth-century Goldwater materials, and worked with his colleague, Dr. Ben Sacks, to fill in gaps left in the research by earlier investigators (both Fireman, co-founder of the Arizona Historical Foundation, and Dr. Sacks are now deceased).

Susie Sato, senior member of the Arizona Historical Foundation staff, has been invaluable in assisting with research, interviews, photographs, and in many other ways.

Others have helped with the research, as well, especially Virginia Counts and Jan Dalrymple (general); Alice Simpson (early California period); and Linda Watts (Phoenix, turn of the century).

The Goldwater family has been immensely cooperative in providing materials and submitting to interviews. Particularly helpful were Barry, Bob, and Carolyn (Erskine); Don, Robert Jr., Mike, Joanne, Barry Jr.; and Peggy (Mrs. Barry) Goldwater. The author was fortunate to be able to interview Barry's mother, Mrs. Josephine Williams Goldwater, in 1961, five years before her death.

Arizona historians Dr. John Goff, Lester (Budge) Ruffner, Dr. Robert Trennert, and Marshall Trimble, all members of the board of directors of the Arizona Historical Foundation, gave counsel and assistance in many ways. Another board member, Esther Fireman, was an invaluable assistant to her late husband Bert in his research and writing on the Goldwater family.

The author is indebted to staff members at the following libraries for their help and patience: Arizona Historical Society, Arizona State Library and Archives, Arizona State University, Bisbee Historical Society, Blythe (California) Public Library, Northern Arizona University, Phoenix Public Library, Prescott Public Library, Sharlot Hall Museum (Prescott), and University of Arizona.

Susan McDonald, editor, and Bruce Andresen, publisher, of Northland Press were most helpful in polishing the manuscript and providing needed encouragement.

The Arizona Historical Foundation, the Goldwater family, and Herb and Dorothy McLaughlin provided photographs.

The author is grateful to Morris Goldwater, whose sense of history prompted him to keep scrapbooks, records, and correspondence.

Finally, I would like to recognize the many individuals who sat still for lengthy interviews. (I hope that I have not inadvertently omitted some; if so, I apologize.) The interviewees included: Maria Castaneda Baca (information on the Castaneda family); Doris Berry (Goldwater Senate staff); Dean Burch (politics); Robert Creighton (politics); Earl and Judy Eisenhower (Goldwater Senate staff); Henry Fuller (YMCA and other subjects); Gail Gardner (early Prescott); Sherman Hazeltine (banking history); Denison Kitchel (politics); Orme Lewis (politics); Willie Low (golf); Reg Manning (various topics); Joe Melczer Jr. (early Phoenix days); Hoyt Pinaire (Goldwater's store); Howard Pyle (politics); Joseph E. Refsnes (early Arizona); Ruth Reinhold (aviation); Representative John Rhodes (politics); Harry Rosenzweig (various topics); Steve Shadegg (politics); Joe Stocker (early family history); Morris Udall (politics); James Walton (Williams family genealogy); former Arizona governor Jack Williams (politics); and the late Rob Wood (early Goldwater manuscripts).

Index

THIS BOOK WAS DESIGNED BY LAURA BREMNER
AND COMPOSED IN USHERWOOD MEDIUM,
BY S & S COMPUTYPE OF OREGON, ILLINOIS.
THE PAPER IS 70 POUND WARREN'S OLD STYLE.
IT WAS PRINTED BY NORTHLAND PRESS, FLAGSTAFF,
AND BOUND BY ROSWELL BOOKBINDING,
PHOENIX, ARIZONA.